Dallas P. Elkheart

"BRONZE"

BLOODLINE OF THE PHOENIX

Only strong wings can fly. Nevertheless, they must be groomed to make it to the top of the mountain, but the infant must first pay a vigorous price for the grooming.

By

Dallas P. Elkheart

"Bronze" Bloodline of the Phoenix

"Bronze" Bloodline of the Phoenix

Copyright © 2019 by Dallas P. Elkheart (PGD) Europe and America

All rights are reserved by the Author and Publisher.

For Worldwide Distribution, Printed in the USA and Europe

First Edition, 2019.

No portion of this book may be duplicated, reproduced, stored in a retrieval system, conveyed, photocopied nor, recorded without the prior permission of the copyright owner. Any of these forms are strictly prohibited, and it is illegal.

DallasPElkheart@gmail.com

Book Formats Available:
ISBN: 978-1-7331998-0-3 Paperback
ISBN: 978-1-7331998-2-7 Hard Cover
ISBN: 978-1-7331998-1-0 eBook/ePub

Creator and Publisher: Dallas P. Elkheart & Associates, 2019.
Book Cover Design by Dallas P. Elkheart

Dallas P. Elkheart

This book is dedicated to:

Three extraordinary individuals, close to my heart that have supported me in the writing of this book and/or in my life. I have been asked so many times before if I would share my stories with the world, but I can justly say these three people made the difference in my decision to do so.

My husband Irvin, my love, my soul mate and, my best friend. This world had shown it could be so cold and so cruel, and you have spent all these years trying to undo what others have done. You have stood by me for twenty-eight plus years during my adventures and, endeavors. You have taken my soul to new heights. You taught me how to evolve, grow, groom, and spread my wings and soar. You gave me the courage to love again, reinvent myself, and recognize my self-worth. I love you with every beat of my heart; you will have my heart forever, and beyond. Without you, my soul shall no longer thrive.

I would also like to thank an extraordinary friend that walked into my life at a later point. You gave me the courage to find my author's voice while writing this book. Leonilda is known affectionately as "NiNi." You have been a good friend, and you've shared much knowledge with me. My world is a better place because of you: hugs and Kisses, my friend.

Daniel O., I would like to take this chance to also thank you for your friendship during such a difficult time with the

"Bronze" Bloodline of the Phoenix

transition from one country to another. You stood fast with us when others fled. You came into our lives for one primary purpose yet, found your way into our heart for another… your friendship beyond the sell is what sets you apart from others in your field.

It is now my pleasure to share with the world a story and the journey of an individual that learns with trepidation, fighting for life, love, and sheer survival that one can create the reanimation of a spirit and the regeneration of a bloodline.

Dallas P. Elkheart

Contents

"Bronze" Bloodline of the Phoenix ii

Contents v

PART I: Four Branches But, Only One Leaf 12

    Episode I: A Boundary with no Barriers 13

    Episode II: Midnight Encounter 17

    Episode III: Knocking on Heaven's Door 22

PART II: Shhh, No One Will Know 26

    Episode IV: Baby Talk 27

    Episode V: Tainted Goods 34

    Episode VI: Tattletale Delight 40

PART III: The Gift Bearing A Curse 47

    Episode VII: Family Secrets 48

    Episode VIII: The Chapel's Revenge 53

    Episode IX: That Lady in Red 58

    Episode X: Rollicking Raven, Hush 64

PART IV: Changing of the Guards 78

    Episode XI: Revelation & Prophecies 79

    Episode XII: That Old Devil 88

    Episode XIII: Pre-Cognitive Nightmare 97

    Episode XIV: Somebody, Stop Him 107

PART V: Fight or Flight 115

"Bronze" Bloodline of the Phoenix

Episode XV: She's No Baby!!! 116

Episode XVI: Loud and Clear 132

Episode XVII: A Million Pieces 137

Episode XVIII: Sister Margaret 161

PART VI: Love You up, Love You Down 174

Episode XIX: Look Ma, No Hands 175

Episode XX: Right, Out of The Skillet 189

Episode XXI: Hell's Gate 194

Episode XXII: Under Your Nose 207

PART VII: Now, Which Way Do I Go 214

Episode XXIII: Lord Hear My Cries 215

Episode XXIV: Dream in Color 220

Episode XXV: Blue Angel's Prayer 227

Episode XXVI: Ouija? What? I'm Not Alone 247

PART VIII: Treading New Ground 261

Episode XXVII: Two Little Devils 262

Episode XXVIII: Friends to The End 270

Episode XXIX: Double Shadows 283

Episode XXX: Christine's Legacy 288

PART VII: The Sparrow Watches Me 303

Episode XXXI: Haunting Memories 304

Episode XXXII: Teardrops Frozen in Time 317

Episode XXXIII: Nobody Listened 330

PART X: Each One, Teach One 341

Episode XXXIV: That Light 342

Episode XXXV: Taking A Higher Road 350

PART XI: Blurred Bloodline, Sure Destiny 358

Episode XXXVI: No Classroom is Required 359

Episode XXXVII: Who Do You Think You Are? ... 363

Episode XXXVIII: Letting Go 373

Episode XXXIX: Reanimation of a Soul 379

About the Author 384

Dallas P. Elkheart

Dallas P Elkheart

Overture

Congratulations on your decision to purchase this book.

"Bronze Bloodline of the Phoenix," is the story of Raven Reese, an unknown, unwanted and unwelcomed little girl, born with unique abilities. Raven faces many fears; however, the hardest obstacles will be herself and her decisions. Her intuition and gifts will make for some bad choices and give way to some even worse responses to certain situations. She will find herself in positions that force her to make choices; as her time is about to run out.

The hope is to help others learn how to define self-worth over self-value, to impart insight on handling specific lifetime problems and to hopefully tame predetermined judgments so quickly passed upon others, before knowing their real story.

Lessons that can be ascertained from reading this book were gained from personal experience, education, visions, and everyday gut intuition. I have seen many things from within the arena of life, as a prior teacher, business owner, parent, and now author. I hope you never have to experience similar situations and can instead learn from my hardships. Understand that one can handle situations without leaving horrible scars upon another's soul that may never heal.

Bronze Bloodline of the Phoenix

While this book may appear as fiction, the desire is to tell the story of Raven Reese to the world. It is based on real events and facts. Names and locations were changed to protect the privacy of the innocent and those that were not so innocent.

Keep in mind, as the reader of this story; there will be cliffhangers around corners that will bring packed suspense, excitement, surprise, and anticipation to the reader. It is worth mentioning that this book should enlighten the reader on the possible outcomes of temptation versus resistance, good versus evil, impulse versus rationale, contentment versus restlessness, but more than anything else, Raven Reese's unwavering tenacity to survive and soar in this world against all the odds.

Please try to remember, every action will be a cause for an opposite and sometimes not so positive reaction from someone else. Just make sure that your response to a situation does not cause someone else a lifetime of harm.

So, now that I have warned you, snuggle up, strap in, find a quiet place to read this book and be prepared for the ride of your life… and let's get this party started!!!

Dallas P Elkheart

"In a world where only strong wings can fly, a young girl born and given up to the serpents will learn that no one will groom her wings, (only cut them). She learns to fly from the bottom of the ocean as the underdog, seeking a place on the top of the mountain as a survivor. It turns out her bloodline will be the only key".

PART I: Four Branches But, Only One Leaf

Dallas P Elkheart

Episode I: A Boundary with no Barriers

On a scorching hot day in 1960, a bell rang out in the distance, with a loud and distinct call for supper in Cavalo, Mississippi. Bertrum Masson, an elderly sharecropper, stopped to catch his breath from the days' work, after toiling in his sorghum field. With the sun brightly beaming down on his back, he quickly pulls out a worn and tattered handkerchief from the right back pocket of his overalls. Bertrum wiped the sweat from his forehead and neck as he looked up at the sun.

Realizing it was the dinner bell calling the day to an end, he began to make his way from the fields. Walking toward the house, he dropped his head and stopped. He began to have deep thoughts about his wife Darla Masson, who died from pneumonia two years back. The bell tolled again, recapturing Bertrum's attention, and he continued to head slowly towards his house.

Bertrum and Darla had made this little *sharecropping shack* home for their not so small family. Two rooms of the house belonged to the children, one for the girls and one for the boys. The family seemed to enjoy sitting in Bertrum's and Darla's room (when she was still alive) by the potbelly stove and listening to the radio. In the summertime, the family loved having their evening meals on the front porch even after the death of Darla.

Bronze Bloodline of the Phoenix

He approached the front porch where his youngest daughter, Christine, was standing. She stood by the dinner bell, eager to greet her tired father as he approached the front steps of the sharecropping house he'd lived in for many years with his family.

As Bertrum got to the porch, Christine told her father, she had a surprise for him. He gave her a small smile but, said nothing else, and he made his way up the steps. Christine had prepared one of her father's favorite meals of hot buttery southern biscuits and old-fashioned sorghum syrup along with slab bacon. This type of meal was usually eaten by down-home folks in the south.

Bertrum was now the sole parent of 12 children, whereby he struggled to keep discord *out* and discipline *in* the home. To Bertrum's credit, the children would later grow up to become, mechanics, blacksmiths, singers, actors, and wives. Christine Masson was the baby of the family. She was a dazzling 13-year-old girl that stood about 5'5. She had a slender build, with an olive skin tone, big light brown eyes, and dark auburn hair. She wore it in a ponytail that hung down the middle of her back.

Bertrum was worried about this year's crop, being a sharecropper meant sharing the profits. Bertrum Masson knew he would have very little to share, but just like other impoverished families, he did not have much choice.

After dinner, Bertrum headed out to the old shed for his Blacksmith work. It housed his burro and sorghum molasses.

He needed to get horseshoes made that the neighbor ordered for the following day.

He thought that the sale of them might provide just enough money to buy the girls a little bit of dress fabric before school started back up.

~ ~ ~

All of the children, but especially Christine, enjoyed music and dancing. She spent her evenings listening to the small radio in a room she shared with six of her older sisters. Her older brothers were singers and had formed a band of their own, even though only the town locals knew about them. Christine was there biggest fan. Family outings and listening to different groups, led Christine's oldest sister, Bonnie, to meet a young man named Kevin Steel. Bonnie had decided to marry Kevin 10 months earlier.

Golden voiced Kevin, at age 24, stood six foot and four inches, and he was quite handsome with an athletic build, deep green eyes that seemed to resonate with his golden bronze skin tone, and dark brown hair.

He was the lead guitarist and vocalist of the group named The Master Stallions; they performed regularly at small bar's, especially a local one called, Club Aurora. He had become quite used to the active nightlife.

He often took gigs to make ends meet. Kevin's group performances at Club Aurora, attracted quite an audience, primarily females. Most could not help but gravitate towards Kevin; after all, he did consider himself to be a bit of a lady's man, plus a man of the world. This, of course, does nothing more than to lead him to believe that there are no boundaries.

Evidently, Kevin did not spend all of his free time at the club, and Bonnie had learned she was now two months pregnant. Kevin wasn't as excited about the baby as Bonnie. Christine's family wasn't excited either because they knew Kevin was not an ideal catch for Bonnie. Most men would go out and catch fish or hunt and bring home venison for dinner, but oh no, not Kevin. He would catch other things and bring them home to Bonnie, such as sexually transmitted diseases. The entire community knew of Kevin's infidelities with other women and late-night hours at the clubs.

~ ~ ~

Episode II: Midnight Encounter

Kevin Steel had gorgeous eyes, a voice of gold, yet, the problem began when he started to have eyes leering at Bonnie's baby sister, Christine. Unfortunately, he used his golden voice to whisper sweet nothings into a vulnerable little 13-year-old girl's ear. Bonnie and Kevin had never moved out of the house where Bonnie and Christine lived with the rest of the family. Kevin was just one more mouth for Bertrum to feed, as Kevin only brought a part-time musician's salary to the table, creating more strain on an already strained budget. However, Bertrum had given Bonnie and Kevin one of the bedrooms when they married, giving them a little more privacy.

With Bonnie now expecting in less than seven months, Kevin was feeling the pressure, and it was apparent he was never going to accept the responsibility of fatherhood. Bertrum and the brothers made it clear they despised Kevin, and it didn't push him to do any better by Bonnie. Christine was excited to be an aunt for the very first time since Bonnie was the first to marry. Up until then, Christine's biggest thrill came from throwing rocks into the creek down by the old oak tree. She loved the sounds of the birds singing and the water flowing. She even liked going to the old shed to watch her father work.

Other times, Christine would go to the creek after school. She would throw rocks into the flowing waters making a wish that one day she could find a prince charming just like her big sister Bonnie did. Of course, Christine had no idea that sometimes one must kiss a whole lot of nasty and slimy frogs and still never find that one that turns out to be their prince charming.

One evening after school, Christine went down to the creek to sort out a mishap that occurred in the hallway at school that day. She often used the creek as a place to think about things. Christine liked a boy from school, but he didn't like her back. Instead, he showed an interest in one of her classmates, who had now become her rival. Upon coming in from group practice over at the club, Kevin saw Christine sitting by the creek. This was the chance of a lifetime, so he thought, to talk to the teen without everyone hanging around and listening to them. Kevin caught Christine off guard since he had never hung out down by the river before. He struck up a conversation with her, which was fine for her since she was still upset about her situation, and she needed a friend to do some mouth bashing with about her troubles.

She felt that her classmate had stolen her honey right out from under her nose. Kevin, being the snake that he was, would say whatever he thought any young girl wanted to hear if there was something in it for him. It became a regular thing that after school, Christine rushed home, did her chores, and headed to the creek. Surprisingly, her old faithful friend Kevin would always manage to slither in at the right time. One night, Christine couldn't sleep, so she snuck out of her room and headed to her favorite place by the water. She sat there sobbing because she had gotten into a fight at school that day but was afraid to tell her father. Bertrum would be furious, and she did not dare tell her big mouth sisters out of fear it would get back to Bertrum. Kevin had a gig that night and came home later than usual. Before heading inside for the night, he decided to sit on the back porch and have one quick drink of firewater moonshine, before going to bed. Kevin overheard a whimpering coming from down the hill and decided to follow the sound. There, by an oak tree, was Christine at the creek sobbing her eyes out. Kevin took a seat by her and tried his best to console her.

She told Kevin that, she'd disclosed to the boy at school she liked him, and she felt she was the best choice for him and not her rival. Kevin explained to Christine that any boy would be lucky to have such a pretty little girl that had a crush on him. For Christine, that was all she needed to hear. In her mind, Kevin must be her frog, and all she had to do was kiss him, and he would turn into her prince charming. Christine felt so happy to hear a compliment that she went to kiss him on the cheek, but Kevin made a calculated move, and their lips met. After that, the meetings became more frequent, one thing leading to another, Christine would sneak off to the old building down by the creek where she and Kevin her prince charming, would meet, once everyone in the house was asleep.

One might think that Kevin Steel would have used better judgment than to have eyes for two sisters. Yes, Kevin was handsome, but just not that smart. He made the choice that he could have some cake while eating some too; he just didn't care about the lives he was re-shaping. Not more than a month after the midnight meetings started, Christine learned she too was now pregnant; how would she tell her family? How could she tell her sister, Bonnie? Would Kevin realize he loved her and not her sister Bonnie and leave Bonnie and become hers? She had a thousand questions running through her young mind.

Her family soon found out about the pregnancy, and everyone blew a gasket, especially Bonnie. Bonnie was devastated about Christine's pregnancy but moreover disgusted with Kevin. How could he be such a swine and sleep with her baby sister? As soon as everyone in the house found out that Kevin had self-indulged with not one, but two sisters in one household, the gig was up for Kevin; he'd humiliated the entire family. But old Kevin's troubles had just started.

~ ~ ~

Bertrum and the boys had a meeting one evening when everyone was out and about, and of course, it was about Kevin. This man had become like cancer to their family. With cancer, you know you have it; however, sometimes finding a cure for it isn't easy. One night while everyone was asleep, the brothers and their father put together a plan to remove this cancerous branch from their family tree. Three of the brothers snuck into Kevin's room, and while

Bonnie slept, they nabbed Kevin from his bed, putting a gag in his mouth and a sack over his head.

They whisked Kevin away in the dead of night. The males wanted proper retribution, for what this snake had done to the cherished gems of their family. So, they dragged Kevin out of the backdoor down to the secret meeting spot that started all this mess in the first place, the old oak tree down by the creek. Bertrum hoisted a stout rope with a pre-made noose over the thickest tree branch; they were prepared to end it all that night. Kevin Steel had disgraced not one but, two of his daughters and not one but, two of their sisters. Bertrum and his sons were hell-bent on removing this cancer that infected their family once and for all. As Bertrum placed the noose around Kevin's neck, the brothers were more than happy to hold old Kevin steady. Kevin tried screaming for his worthless life. He eventually managed to wake up Christine, Bonnie, and the other children. Christine bolted out of bed, beating Bonnie and her sisters down the hill where all the commotion was. That night was the precursor to the end, Christine would make a decision to do the unthinkable.

Episode III: Knocking on Heaven's Door

Kevin's muffled screams echoed into the night. Christine ran out the backdoor with her sisters as if an army had been called in from heaven. Christine threw herself at her father's feet, begging him and her brothers to spare Kevin's life. She sold her soul to the devil that night by telling her father and brothers that: "If they allowed Kevin to live, she would give her unborn baby away."

Christine's acknowledgment to her family and the entire world would prove to be a sealed fate for her unborn child. Her sacrifice for her lover was all too well received by her family, yet, the decision to allow Kevin to live would ironically be beneficial to the unborn child and rewrite this entire story. Some might say the birth of a new baby is a new journey for both parents and child. It is a time with thoughts of joy and happiness. In this case, it will be anything but that.

Bertrum made the decision to remove Christine from the site of public eyes. He found a place four hours and sixteen minutes away. He located a home for unwed mothers called Saint Broadrick's Home in Barrenfort, Arkansas. It was known to many as the *Broadrick House*. The home for unwed mothers was supervised by Nuns. This place was created for restructuring the lives of prostitutes and unmarried pregnant women, designed as a type of reformatory school in a home-like setting. This environment would become the new home for Christine and her unborn baby.

The plan was for Christine to give birth, give away the baby, return home, and go back to normal living as if nothing had happened. This way, the family's reputation would be saved.

Christine made the trip with only her father. The journey that was meant to take four-plus hours ended up feeling like a three-day trip for Christine. All Christine wanted was to be back at home with the love of her life. Once she arrived at her new temporary residence, the Broadrick House, Bertrum, and Christine got out of the car. He quietly got Christine's suitcase out of the trunk of his car and dropped her off and left quickly. She was left behind with strangers, a young and confused 14-year old girl standing on the sidewalk with one suitcase in her hand. The Broadrick House had a contract for the birth of all babies coming into the world with a hospital by the name of, *Peace Onyx River Hospital.* This would be the only place where Christine's new baby would be welcomed into the world.

While all of this was occurring, the paperwork for the adoption process had already begun for the relinquishment of her unborn child. Christine was sure Kevin would be hers alone now, and she just knew Kevin would be forever indebted to her for having his life spared. Therefore, he would be providing her with his full attention and undying and faithful love. After all, she had given up the baby for him. Kevin did not seem to mind that Christine was stuck in a home for unwed mothers since he also had a new baby about to be born to his wife, Bonnie.

Bronze Bloodline of the Phoenix

Christine sat day in and day out awaiting her delivery date, she anticipated her chance to be free of this burden, and get back to her stolen lover, Kevin. The day arrived for the baby to be born. They took her over to the hospital and prepped her for the birth, taking her in a wheelchair straight over to the birthing room. Christine gave birth to an eight-pound and six-ounce baby girl. The baby looked like both parents and was described by the hospital as a beautiful baby girl, with an olive skin tone, a head full of dark hair and appeared to be very healthy.

At the hospital, the nurses prepared to do what is typically done for a mother and newborn, which is placing the baby in the mother's arms or on the mother's chest, but, when they attempted to do so, Christine would not have it. She refused to look at the baby or even acknowledge it and wanted no type of interaction with this child. To do so meant, she might have a change of heart. Perhaps she felt as if seeing this baby would be a reminder of a border that should have not been breached either way. She refused to interact with her baby. As she promised, she would now move on because, in her mind, she heard a quiet voice speak and say: "I simply don't want this baby."

She chose the name "Bella Leia Masson." Once the nurses realized Christine would not show any interest in her baby, they quickly moved the baby to the nursery, never to be seen again.

Three days later, Christine was taken back to the Broadrick House, and the Nuns called Mr. Bertrum to come and pick her up. As Christine waited by the sidewalk with her one small suitcase, she stood there and found a rock on the ground, she bent down and picked it up and began to write her and Kevin's name in the dirt in big, bold letters.

She quietly sobbed as she wrote: *"KEVIN LOVES CHRISTINE."* Once Bertrum had arrived, Christine quickly took her foot and used it to erase her and Kevin's name. Bertrum picked her up on the same sidewalk where he'd dropped her off. The entire trip back home was a solemn one, overshadowed by the sound of dead silence.

Bertrum had more than enough time to cool off over the situation throughout the time Christine had been gone, but he just did not know what to say to Christine. She'd broken his trust. Christine also did not know what to say to her father. On the ride back home, Christine could not help but think about her regrets and all the what if's. What if…...

Bronze Bloodline of the Phoenix

PART II: Shhh, No One Will Know

Episode IV: Baby Talk

As Christine took the long ride back to her small world and home in Barrenfort, Arkansas, things moved in a whole different direction for baby Bella Leia Masson. The hospital prepared baby Bella for her new home with all the proper paperwork. Bella was being wrapped like a package and shipped over four hundred miles away. She was moved to an orphanage by the name of, *Enfant Laissé*, which meant in French, "a child left behind." Bella spent the next two years of her life in that orphanage.

Baby Bella was not your typical child. This baby was born with a little something extra, even though she would not learn of the many additional gifts she had until later. These things would help to groom Bella's miniature wings and make for one tough cookie, as they would all come together down the road to form an impeccable storm.

In the meantime, a couple in their mid-forties that lived three hundred plus miles away were battling their own storm. Horatio and Eliza Reese had the need to have a family of their own. However, Eliza had found that she would be unable to bear children and was well past her childbearing years. Horatio found himself to be both wealthy and tall. He had spent many years in the military as a drill sergeant. He was eventually honorably discharged and as a veteran enjoyed the benefits he'd earned.

Horatio began a new career at a prominent company specializing in medical supplies that paid very well. While earning such a grand income, he decided to buy a large ranch for his wife, Eliza.

They found a perfect 120-acre piece of land that had an orchard and plenty of farming land to earn a good living. They found an ideal spot to build a house just for Eliza. Horatio created a house that had all the bells and whistles that he thought homes should have. Most homes nearby were sharecropper homes and did not have indoor necessities or luxury amenities back then. Horatio wanted to make sure Eliza had only the best of everything. Everyone knew Horatio in that region, but they nicknamed him Big Fella; instead, they should have called him Big Money.

Eliza, a tall, full-figured and voluptuous military lady in her own right was a previous Women Airforce Service Pilots (aka) "WASP." Horatio did not mind that they would not have children, but Eliza did. She always dreamed of being a mother since she was denied the experience of being raised by a mom of her very own.

You see, Eliza's mother, Cassie, died giving birth to her. Chapman, who was Eliza's father, was left with raising his four children, Kay (the oldest), Wilson- a boy (next to the oldest) and Ilene (the middle child). Eliza was the baby of her family. Eliza's sisters had always had a beef with her because, they believed that if

Cassie had never had a fourth child, which was Eliza, Cassie would have lived.

Eliza had spoken with Horatio on many occasions about adopting a baby, but Horatio would only blow her off and quickly get on another subject. One day Eliza had enough of Horatio's avoidance of the conversation and put her foot down, demanding to extend the family. This behavior was very unusual from Eliza, considering she was somewhat the quiet child of her family and never really asked for much or made demands for anything. She had a need, and it wasn't being fulfilled. Reluctantly, Horatio said yes, and they began the process of adoption, which is tedious at best.

After months of paperwork, background checks, interviews with co-workers, neighbors, bosses and churches, the State where they lived, gave the clearance to place a baby in the home of the Reese's. Immediately following the phone call that the state had a child to be placed, the Reese's jumped into their new crème colored Chevy Impala four-door sedan and drove to Martin Bay, Mississippi to pick up the latest addition to their family. When they arrived at the orphanage after looking around a bit, they spotted a rambunctious little girl about five years old. She seemed to be a bundle of joyful energy, and they decided to adopt her.

One day Eliza was washing dishes and Horatio was sitting at the kitchen table reading the daily newspaper when the pocket-sized girl walked into the kitchen and stated: "I want some chew tobacco and I want some now."

Everyone was frozen with shock and bewilderment, due to the satanic voice that projected out of the mouth of such a seemingly sweet and energetic little girl. They immediately knew something wasn't right, and the fact that a 5-year-old would even have this type of demand was shocking.

Horatio blurted out to his little girl, "You ain't getting no tobacco," and he thought it would nip it in the bud. Eliza stood as still as water with eyes so large it seemed as if she saw a ghost, but it was merely the disbelief of hearing such a thing coming from a five-year-old child.

Well, the young girl was not going to take no for an answer. She came back with a thunderous voice so loud that the heavens may have shaken after hearing it. She stated in no uncertain terms, "You better get me some chew tobacco now, or I'm gonna kill you." It was at that moment that Horatio and Eliza both thought, "Boy, did we make a big mistake getting this little girl." Horatio said angrily and firmly, "Hell NO" and grabbed the little girl by the arm and looked directly at Eliza and said, "Call the state, right now."

As night fell, they knew the child had to stay one more night with them, and that was one of the longest nights ever. They slept with one eye opened in fear of what the child might do as retaliation for them not supplying her with chewing tobacco.

The following day, the state showed up to remove the child from their home.

Horatio and Eliza explained to them what occurred and that they could not have that type of behavior in their home. The placement of the little girl was terminated. Eliza went a few days and realized she still had an empty spot at her table, in her home and most important in her heart. In the following weeks, the decision was made that she wanted another child, but Horatio was reluctant to do so.

After all, a few weeks ago, a five-year-old child had threatened their lives over chewing tobacco. Eliza would not hear of such foolishness; every child cannot be like that one she thought to herself. "I want a child, Horatio," Eliza demanded. Turning to her, Horatio responded angrily, "No, and that's that."

She stood up at the kitchen table and said very vocally, "If you don't allow me to have a child, we will be getting divorced and quickly." Horatio sat stunned. He'd never heard Eliza raise her voice at him nor threaten him with divorce. He finally agreed to try adoption one more time for Eliza. The following day, Eliza contacted the state to schedule an appointment to find another child. They set a date for two weeks later. Horatio and Eliza took the trip all over again to the state office at Martin Bay. On this long ride, Eliza and Horatio had secret thoughts of the last experience and disappointment with the previous placement. Eliza expressed out loud: "Lordy, I sho hope this goes better and hope this one ain't an axe murderer like the last one."

Once they arrived, they parked their car and slowly walked toward the office door with trepidation. Upon entering the office, they were greeted by the social worker and then led to a large room with thirty beds lined up on a series of two walls. It reminded Eliza of a hospital. They saw newborns in their cribs and toddlers playing with others or nurses.

Eliza looked around, and the social worker asked them, "Do you see a child you might be interested in"? Horatio glanced around the room, as he was hoping to make a better choice this time. Eliza looked for a connection to another soul, and then she noticed, a tiny two-year-old toddler. The girl was not with other children but in a corner on the floor, and she was playing all alone with her toys.

The child was wearing a pair of small tattered black high-top shoes, with 3 buckles and straps. The child caught Eliza's eyes, and she knew, right then and right there. Her soul soared as she watched the baby girl. She pointed with her hand, her mouth opened and as loud as a sonic boom, she yelled out: "That's the one, That's the one I want."

That little girl ended up being "Bella Leia Masson," the same baby girl that was born to Christine Masson two years back, that no one wanted. Once all the documents for the adoption were complete, the Reese's would be allowed to leave.

They would take two-year-old, Bella Leia Masson with them. Horatio and Eliza named their new daughter Raven Gabriella Reese. The name would be a fresh start for a new life for little Raven. One of the biggest things that no one knew was, it would also open a door that no one would be able to shut, not even Raven herself would be able to control the uncontrollable.

Bronze Bloodline of the Phoenix

Episode V: Tainted Goods

Horatio looked over at Eliza, as they left the orphanage and noticed her face looked at peace, and she looked as if she was glowing, something Horatio hadn't seen since they first got married. Bella Leia Masson who would be only known from this point on as Raven Gabriella Reese took her rightful spot in the back seat of the family car. She was intrigued by the radio station Horatio played.

Raven heard a song called, "You ain't nothing but a Hound Dog." Well, when Raven heard this song, she sprung up from the seat and began to dance on the back seat. Horatio looked up at his rear-view mirror to check on baby Raven and behold, tiny Raven was in her own world, standing up on the seat facing the back window and dancing up a storm. He threw his head back while letting out a boastful laugh while looking over at Eliza and then he said, "That baby gonna be a dancer one day, that baby loves herself some music." Horatio and Eliza laughed so hard tears ran down Eliza's face.

Unexpectedly and rather quickly, things changed. Horatio heard a high-pitched sound, in the far distance, and so did petite-sized Raven. Raven stopped dancing, her eyes got big, and suddenly she yelled out, "COP, Daddy, COP." Well, this took Eliza and Horatio by total surprise, and as they looked up, a set of blue flashing lights with the siren blaring rushed past them. It was a police car headed to some other occurrence.

Horatio stated to Eliza, "That baby, must be from a BIG city to know about COP's, cause, she didn't say police, she said, "COP, Daddy, COP." Horatio continued the drive home while wondering to himself, "Where did this quiet and intelligent child get her street smarts from? Did she just call me daddy for the first time? Does she really see me as her daddy already?" After all, she was only two years old and had been in the orphanage for the entire two years, so she must have been around someone who had a run-in with the Cop's or saw something that happened in her short two years. At any rate, Horatio stated out loud with a smirk on his mug, "WOW, I'm sho glad it wasn't me those cops were after.

Eliza felt they needed to make one final pit stop before getting home. She could not get the picture out of her mind of those raggedy looking shoes that little Raven wore home. She asked Horatio to stop at the store before heading home.

They stopped at Eliza's favorite shop called Redman's where Eliza often shopped. They all went into the store together for the very first time as a completed family to purchase Raven's first pair of new shoes. As the sales lady went to try a pair of shoes on Raven's toddler-sized foot, everyone noticed something…

No one, in the area of the store, could believe what they were seeing. For the first time, Baby Raven Gabriella Reese would share one of her many secrets with the world.

Even though she was too small and innocent as a two-year-old to understand adults, she realized one thing, and that was, not every adult is kind to you. Sometimes big people can be unkind and untrustworthy, especially if they are mad at you, then they hurt you.

Eliza and the salespeople that were in the store that day, all began to shed tears as they asked themselves and each other the daring questions of, how could they? Why would they? Who would do such a horrific and despicable thing to a baby? Horatio's eyes, welled up with tears even though he was a hard-core, prior military man; therefore, he allowed no tears to roll down his face as he tried to maintain his manly persona. Yet, deep inside, his heart broke into pieces as he saw the harm that others had inflicted upon his new daughter. Baby Raven had held many pains quietly inside her tiny heart. The horrendous things that others had done to her at the orphanage before she met the Reese's were now, being felt by others.

Baby Raven's battle scars were not only encased inside her soul, but she carried them heavily on her chubby, yet, tiny legs, which seemed hidden by the oversize garments she was wearing. Someone, perhaps a caretaker, a guardian or someone who simply did not find small Raven to be worth much, had burned her with numerous cigarettes and cigars. There were more than 20 burns seared into baby Ravens legs. Apparently, someone used the burns as a form of punishment. Of course, she did not understand what all the fuss was about.

Why were all the big people crying over her and looking at her legs? She understood one thing though, she could comprehend for the first time in her little life, someone seemed to care for her.

Pondering the mean and horrible things baby Raven must have experienced, and observing her tattered and ripped clothing, the Reese's knew in their hearts that she would never have to do without again, she will be loved until they could love no more. The expression on the face of the salespeople in the store and the dismayed look in their eyes, told a different story, a story of righteous indignation and redemption.

As they fought back the tears, the thoughts of the horror this tiny two-year-old girl went through, they said, "this will be one of the luckiest and loved little girls in this whole world, thank God, the Reese's found her in time."

Everyone had the same idea and began to scamper through the store to find items for baby Raven. Eliza headed to the dress aisle to gather as many beautiful dresses as she could, dresses that would be befitting of a princess, and let's not forget the lacy little girls' underpants that were frequently worn by any ritzy female toddler in those days.

One sales attendant headed over to the shoes and socks aisle seeking stunning, yet colorful baby shoes and filigree socks to match for Raven.

Another salesclerk stood at the counter happily ringing each item up. Horatio posted himself at the checkout counter, thinking, "wow, this could take a while."

Eliza could only think about the outfits that baby Raven would get to wear to the fantastic social events that they would be attending. Then as quickly as everyone started their shop-fest, Eliza stood back, and as still as the night, she began to contemplate and mumble to herself. She looked at all the clothing and shoes on the checkout counter, then she glanced over at baby Raven and abruptly said, "Wait, no young lady of mine would be fit to meet the world without every girl's essential item, hairbows."

Without another word said, the salespeople and Eliza took off stampeding through the store like a heard of female elephants that would do anything to protect their young. They began to gather little girl hats with matching children's hand purses with lots of lace and pearls. In the south, ruffles and pearls adorned most of a female's dresses, purses and hats and the puffier, the better, that is, if you are really a "Southern Belle girl."

Eliza wanted her precious baby girl to meet the world, and she had to be dressed to impress. This intended quick stop ended up becoming an all-afternoon ordeal. Anxiously, Horatio stood at the register to pay for the items, and then it registered in his brain that his wallet was about to be a lot thinner. However, he thought peacefully to himself, "I don't mind.

The baby is getting what she needs, and Eliza is smiling," so it's all good. After the shopping spree had ended, Horatio and the family headed to the car and made their way home.

As the car pulled up into the driveway, the sun was setting over the horizon just below the fruit tree orchards in the yard. The air was heavy with the aroma of fruits such as apples, pears, peaches, plums, and figs. The pleasant bouquet of scents greeted them as they parked the car and began to get out.

Horatio and Eliza, exhausted from all the activities of the day, stumbled out of the car with packages in hand. Horatio opened the back door, but Raven didn't' move. She sat there in the backseat, as if in a hypnotic trance. But wait, what had she seen that had her under such a spell.?

Episode VI: Tattletale Delight

Raven sat there in a trance with her little mouth wide open, and her eyes did not seem to be fixated on any one thing. Her mind was engulfed, and eyes were engorged with all the beautiful things that were present in her new environment. Raven could not understand what all these things were. It was not like the place she had come from. Where she came from, nothing was yours, and now she had her new little world, all to herself because there were no other children around.

She sat in awe, looking at the big soft yellow-colored house that was trimmed in white with tons of windows. All she could think to herself was, "Do I get to visit here?" Then, there was the yard, which was extremely grand, well grand is putting it mildly; it was bigger than the toddler could wrap her small mind around. In this yard, she could see two oversized shaggy rug looking things, and, they made deafening noises when they opened their mouths. Now they were jumping all over her new mom and dad. Her eyes glanced over the yard, and she noticed all the trees and flowers, but wait, there was something else sitting between two of the trees that really caught Raven's eyes. A giant green swing set with white seats with a shiny sliding board. On the side of the swing set was a very petite sized, bright red three-wheeled tricycle and a little red "Flyer" wagon.

Horatio finally got Raven's attention, taking her tiny hand and leading her out of the car. Raven stood there, stunned.

Eliza approached Raven, kneeled by her side, and whispered softly in her small ears, "This is all for you and tomorrow you can come outside and play with all of this, all day long". Horatio and Eliza took Raven into the house to prepare supper, but first Eliza took Raven to see her new room.

As Raven walked with Eliza through the house, she could not help but notice the elegant hardwood floors, that had a sheen so bright one could see their own reflection in it as if they were at an ice-skating rink. To get to Raven's bedroom, one would need to go down to the end of the hallway past the bathroom. Raven had everything a tiny girl needed, right at her fingertips.

As Eliza gave Raven a bath and got her ready to go off to bed after supper, Raven became extremely quiet and stared blankly at the open bathroom door that led into the hallway. Eliza chalked it up as her child had such a long day and so many different experiences within that day, that she was merely tired and needed a good night's sleep. What was wrong with Raven? Why was she staring endlessly into the hallway? Eliza tried to gather Raven's attention, yet, Raven appeared to be frightened and distracted. Eliza turned around to see if Raven was looking at Horatio, but when she turned, no one was there.

What was she looking at, and what had she seen? Eliza squeaked a little yellow rubber duck that Raven had in the bathtub with her, which finally got Raven's attention. She dried her off and got her off to bed.

The following day, Raven awoke in time for breakfast. Eliza was a woman good at all things, and cooking was one of her outstanding traits.

Eliza walked Raven down the hall, past the living room, and before they made it to the kitchen table, Raven noticed that there was something that she had not seen last night. A piano was there that Horatio had bought for her before they brought her home from the adoption agency.

To Eliza's astonishment, Raven walked over to the piano, and sat down, placed her small fingers on the piano keys and began to play one of Mozart's piano pieces. Eliza seemed flabbergasted at the way the child played the piano with so much skill and emotion. Horatio, who was outside working in the garden, heard it. He stopped what he was doing and came running inside and asked, "who's playing that piano"? Eliza looked at him with amazement and a somewhat smirked smile, stuck her chest out proudly and said, that's my baby playing.

They looked at each other, trying to sort out how Raven knew how to play the piano. In the 1960s, orphanages spent their time running the establishment for homeless children, so, they knew Raven had not had any formal music lessons.

Right at that moment, Eliza made up her mind that she would put Raven into private music lessons to enhance her skills as a pianist. Eliza immediately set up music lessons in town for Saturday mornings.

Saturday music lesson time was unique for the two of them, since, this was their mother and daughter time together. After music lessons, Eliza always treated Raven to a special meal. Raven's favorites were burgers, fries, shakes and sometimes shrimp. Eliza made sure she could have all she wanted.

Saturday evenings were always reserved for visiting Eliza's sister Ilene. Eliza and young Raven would be dropped off by Horatio. Eliza and her sister would sit on the couch and chat while Raven spent time playing with her two cousins until Horatio would return. Horatio considered himself somewhat of a card shark and would play into the wee hours of the morning at the homes of some of his gambling buddies.

Horatio developed a pattern that everyone in the house learned to recognize. Everyone knew when Horatio returned whether he had lost or won his card games. If he lost, he would be in a horrible mood and start-up disagreements over seemingly nothing with Eliza, arguing all the way back home.

However, if Horatio won, he would be in a mellow mood and somewhat pleasant. When he won, he would give Raven anywhere from five to ten dollars to do with as she pleased the next morning.

When he wanted to stay gone for a couple of days over a weekend, he would come home on Friday after work, pick a fight with Eliza, grab his money, iron it on the ironing board, sort it based on denominations and then place it in a paper bag. Raven remembered seeing the steam coming from the iron and the unique smell that emanated as the hot metal pressed against the paper bills.

As time went on, Raven finally got a chance to meet more of her extended family. Horatio had two brothers and two sisters that lived relatively close to him, and one day, they dropped by to meet little Raven. Their names were Bill, Larry, Onie, and Olivia. Since Horatio came from a large family, these five siblings spent a lot of free time together, especially on Sunday afternoons, right after church. Raven's uncle Larry was her favorite uncle, as he had never been married, he lived across the street, and he had no children. He was like a second father to Raven. Raven would go outside early on a Saturday, dig worms and grubs with her uncle Larry or Horatio and when she thought she had plenty, off she would go trekking barefooted, to one of their ponds.

One Saturday morning, Olivia, better known to everyone as "Livi," stopped by the house to see her niece. The day passed by with Horatio, Eliza, and Olivia sitting in the oversized yard under one of many of the shade trees, while eating melon and telling jokes. Once the sun went down that Saturday afternoon, Eliza called Raven to get ready for her customary Saturday night bubble bath. She had to wash off the grit and grime from the mud pies, rolling around in the dirt, riding her tricycle and fishing.

This particular night, Raven's aunt Livi decided that she would prepare the bathwater and gather Raven's bedtime clothing while Eliza made a supper of fried southern catfish, homemade hush puppies, coleslaw and for dessert homemade fried peach pies.

Horatio was still working the farmland, and you could hear his tractor roaring far away as he plowed and prepared the fields for planting time. Eliza was a religious lady holding profoundly to her spiritual roots, and it so happened that Horatio's sister Livi was a minister in her church and felt even stronger about religion. Livi would get up every morning before the sun could rise, prepare herself breakfast, and began reading her Bible until the late hours of the night. Livi had never been married, but she had one child who was in his late fifties by now, but he lived far away. This helped to explain why Livi could not wait to help raise baby Raven and voice her opinions for the rearing of Raven. After everyone had supper that Saturday night, Horatio had come in from the fields, finished his supper and decided to relax and watch T.V. in the bedroom, while Eliza and Olivia gave tiny Raven her weekend bubble bath. They thought it would be a fantastic way to spend time with Raven and each other. Olivia sat on the right side of the tub and Eliza sat on the left side as they scrubbed all the dirt off of the two- year old, then out of nowhere the somewhat quite elderly Olivia opened her mouth and out flew the words, "Have you told her yet"?

This caught Raven's attention since the two-year-old was quite bright. Eliza's mouth dropped, and eyes bulged as she looked down upon the toddler, then her eyes grew wider with surprise as she looked over at Olivia and said innocently and tenderly, "told her what?" Everything went dead silent, and Raven's little head raised up and stated, "Mommy, told me what? What you suppose to tell me, mommy?"

This left Eliza in the position that if she would have had a rock to crawl up under and if she could be sure no one would find her, she would have found that rock to crawl up under. Eliza replied snobbishly, with her head held high and squinted eyes, she rolled her eyes to the side as she looked at Olivia and then she said in an almost whispering voice to Olivia, 'BIG Mouth.' Raven would not let it go. She continued to ask Eliza, "Mommy, tell me what'? Eliza decided that she would go ahead and tell her, even though she and Horatio had discussed telling the toddler a little later in life when they felt she would be able to understand. Eliza then looked at Raven and stated, "Sweetheart, we are not your birth parents."

Dallas P Elkheart

PART III: The Gift Bearing A Curse

Episode VII: Family Secrets

Eliza had tears in her eyes and, hurt in her heart as she listened to Raven. Eliza had hoped she would have more time before telling her little girl about her adoption. Raven took her aunt and mommy by total surprise. The toddler continued to play with her toys in the tub as Eliza held back tears. Olivia looked as if she had spilled the family's last container of milk on a new mink rug; Raven spoke as if she had lived her own life before by reincarnation, she said, "You're my mommy and, it don't matter what they say. "I know you are my mommy now." and continued playing in the tub.

Eliza could no longer contain her sobbing. Tears flowed as if water was trickling delicately down a stream. She took the sleeve that she had rolled up previously to bathe little Raven and used it to gently wipe her weeping eyes. Afterward, Aunt Olivia and Eliza tucked the toddler into her bed, and as the light went out and right before Eliza closed Raven's door, she looked back and said in a gentle, hushed voice, "That's mama's baby."

Around two o'clock in the morning, when everyone was sound asleep, something awoke Raven. She jumped out of bed, flung the door open, and bolted like a bear-footed baby lamb. Still disoriented, she ran down the hallway toward Eliza and Horatio's room, like a bat straight out of hell was chasing her. Cries came screeching through the halls as she yelled, "Mommy, Mommy, Mommy."

Eliza and Horatio sprang upright in their bed, and Eliza said in a panicky voice to Horatio," That's our baby, dear lord, that's our baby."

Both parents met Raven at the opening of their bedroom door. Raven jumped into Horatio's arms and was crying and mumbling so hard that, Horatio and Eliza could not understand her words.

They had no idea what had happened. Was there someone in Raven's room? Did she have a bad dream? Had she heard something? Unsure of what had happened, Horatio passed Raven over to Eliza and said, "I am going to see what's wrong with her," and he left and headed down the hall to Raven's bedroom. He turned on the light, he looked under the bed, he checked Raven's closet, he even checked an opening in her closet that led to an attic door.

After giving the room an all-clear, Horatio had Eliza take Raven back to her room, and they placed little Raven back into her bed. Eliza said, "There, there, baby. It was only a dream and we ain't gonna let nobody hurt my baby. Close your eyes, and I'm going to stay here until you fall asleep." Raven did not want to go back to sleep, and she fought it with everything in her little body, but the terrifying experience was too much for the toddler, and she drifted off to sleep. As Horatio and Eliza exited the room, Eliza looked at Horatio and said, "What in the world could cause that baby to be that scared?" Horatio stated to Eliza, "Ah, she probably had a dream about something that happened to her at the place she was at before we got her, and they both exited the room, but Eliza was not convinced. Had Raven had a bad dream? Was it more than a dream, was it a nightmare?

The following morning Eliza was still trying to organize in her mind what had happened that night. Olivia was still asleep and had slept through the whole situation. Olivia woke up, and Eliza was making breakfast and getting the family's clothing, ready for church services that morning. This would be Raven's first visit to become a part of the community, and it was going to be a special event for the entire family.

Olivia came into the kitchen and sat down for coffee. Horatio finished his cup of java and told everyone he was headed to the fields for a spell before church.

Eliza waited for Horatio to leave out of the kitchen door which led to the carport and from there to his tractor. As she heard the tractor pulling off, she looked back at Olivia and said, "Did you hear Raven last night"? Olivia stated, "Hear Raven? What do you mean? Naw, I ain't heard nothing, why?" Eliza told Olivia about the occurrence that happened that night with Raven. She asked Olivia if she had any idea about what would make a child act like that.

Olivia, older than Horatio or Eliza, believed in old school ways and she was one of the oldest in Horatio's family. She grew up with many sayings and many superstitions that came from many generations before her. The first thing she said was, "well, she might of have had a bad dream." Then she says, "Many things could have happened." She told Eliza, "That child could have some memory from what them folks did to her in that home, too." Eliza was still unconvinced Raven had a situation with either of these things the previous night. She said, "Well, all I know is this, that baby acted and looked like she saw a spook, but I didn't see nothing."

Olivia said, "You know, you might have something else, on ya hands too," and Eliza asked Olivia, "What might that be, you think?". Olivia said, "one out of every one thousand children born is born with a veil over their face." This was an old saying back during their lifetimes which had been passed down from generation to generation, meaning that some children are born with special powers, the gift of second sight so to speak of. Olivia was starting to believe Raven had more to her than meets the eye.

Aunt Olivia then said that people say that children, born with a third eye or second sight in this modern age, are known as "clairvoyant."

A Clairvoyant is someone born with mystical abilities; the ability to see or feel things either before or during an event. This is done by tapping into the sixth sense, one that most people are not aware of. Eliza stood silent after hearing what Olivia had to say about Raven's experience.

    She told Olivia of the first night she had brought Raven home and how Raven was acting while having a bath. How Raven had an uncanny look in her little eyes as she gazed into the hallway. She also mentioned to Olivia she thought Horatio was standing there, and that was why Raven was so struck by the open door that you see the hallway from, but that when she turned around, she saw nothing and just dismissed it as Raven was tired from the long day and needed some sleep. Eliza could not help but think to herself, what had really happened the previous night and was there something special about her child.

Episode VIII: The Chapel's Revenge

Eliza was not totally convinced Raven did not see anything. However, there was nothing to make her think otherwise, so Eliza proceeded to dress Raven for her first grand appearance and introduction to her new church community. This was a special event for everyone, but more so for Eliza. This was something she had always dreamed about, having a daughter to dress like a little princess, and knowing she would never be alone again. You see, Horatio and Eliza shared another family secret that Eliza never wanted anyone to know about, not even Olivia. Horatio was a big-time ladies' man, and if he saw a pretty face, he wanted it at all cost. He was having numerous affairs while married to Eliza, and he had managed to father an outside child with another woman. The child's name was Margaret, better known as Margie.

Of course, Margaret had been born to a mother that lived almost one hundred and fifty miles away, and Horatio had managed to form a bond with Margaret during her childhood. Margaret was nearly twenty-five years the senior to little Raven, and she never understood why Horatio would go out and get another kid. Understandably, there was a lot of animosity and tension from her towards Raven. She felt that she was more than enough; hell, she had no intentions of sharing her father with some kid, that wasn't even his bloodline nor hers.

Church services would soon be starting in less than an hour, and Eliza had to get Raven dressed quickly. Eliza, Olivia, and Horatio took little Raven to the car to head off to the church before services could start. At the church, all deacons and ushers were expected to be present before church services began, and if they were not all in place, services would be delayed until they arrived. As they pulled up in the parking lot of the church, it was a grand sight to see. Horatio stepping out of the car, dressed in his Sunday go to meeting best attire. Eliza was an usher in the church, so she was wearing her all-white dress, lacy white pillbox hat, white gloves, black stilettos and of course, she revealed her dark coffee-colored stockings, that embraced every curve of her long but well-built legs. Let's not leave out the fact, that Eliza would not be fancied entirely up for her prestigious church position without her signature deep ruby red lipstick.

Ushers were used in certain church denominations to assist in seating members and guests, sending out and taking in the church donations and providing some form of order and comfort, if required. Ushers took their orders directly from the pastor, and it was considered an honorary position to have within a church. As Eliza stepped out of the car, everyone noticed that something had changed, and Eliza was glowing. She grinned as if she was the cat, that had swallowed the only canary in the yard. What was different? Well, this Sunday she was looking as grand as ever, except today, she reached back into the car, and to everyone's surprise, she pulled out a package.

This package was wearing a lacy all-white dress with matching socks, an adorable little bonnet and she carried on her tiny arm a petite purse to match. The new addition or package, to the Reese family, had arrived and all of Eliza's love for her new little girl showed, especially in the way they were identically dressed in all white. Eliza stuck her chest out with pride, placed a stunning smile on her painted red lips, and without waiting for Horatio or Olivia, she strutted straight to the front door to greet the pastor.

At first, baby Raven was in total disbelief as she could see all the vivid blues, yellows, reds, oranges, and pinks that the women were wearing. She was simply captivated and mesmerized at the sight of all the colors, that seemed like a rainbow. Then she glanced over, and she became overly excited about all the other children that were there. She hoped that she would be able to play with them.

As the services began, Eliza as an usher was required to sit on the first seat at the front of the church, as all ushers were, and this meant that Raven must sit with her. The thing that little Raven did not understand was, when the pastor is preaching his Sunday morning services, that meant that all children must be quiet, sit still, and behave themselves. That was expected of all young children at church functions, and Raven would be no exception to the rule.

In Raven's eyes, there were children that she could play with, so while the pastor was preaching, Raven thought this would be a great time to get up and go visit some of the people her mother had introduced her to. Well, Eliza had other ideas about how this day would go, so the battle began. Raven jumped up from the front seat of the church bench and headed down the aisle to make new friends, and Eliza saw Raven from the corner of her eye and tried to reach for her before she shot off down the aisle running. Raven reached the back of the church and decided how much fun that was, so she made a b-line back down the aisle to the front of the church. She stopped right in front of the pastor as he was delivering his sermon.

Eliza gritted her teeth, and from the corner of her mouth the words, "Get over here" came out, but softly as not to disturb the services. Baby Raven thought to herself, "That was the funniest thing in the world, I never heard mommy talk like that before. She is so funny", as she giggled girlishly to herself. Well, Eliza wasn't laughing, and she did not find the humor in her daughter's behavior, after all, she and Horatio were prior military people, so self-control and discipline were mandatory in their household.

As Raven made the decision to make a run for it again, Eliza had had enough, but before Eliza could grab Raven and pull her out of the aisle, Raven had shot passed her again making a mad dash for the backdoor. Raven stopped as she reached the backdoor of the church and said, "Mommy, you can't catch me." This took

Eliza to a whole new level of motherhood. Everyone was watching, and Horatio was furious, but Olivia couldn't help but giggle a wee bit with the other church members to include the pastor. Eliza had a plan, and she planned to grab her child the first chance she could.

Raven took one more run for the road, so back down the aisle towards the pastor, she went, running as hard as she could to jet by Eliza. Eliza let her get past her with no problem, but as Raven high tailed it passed her again, Eliza suddenly slid to the end of the church bench on the inside of the aisle, and just as Raven headed back down the aisle, Eliza grabbed the end of Raven's lacey dress tail. Little Raven stopped dead in her tracks. Eliza grabbed small Raven up off the floor, stood up, raised up her index finger, and excused herself, straight to the back of the church with an arm full of one rambunctious daughter. This was a common occurrence back then in the church.

Today young Raven would receive her first lesson in meeting and greeting the public, with a class called behavior 101. Eliza took Raven and sat on the backbench, while Raven learned that that cute little lacy underwear could come down across your bottom half if required. The pastor proceeded with the services, and Eliza proceeded with serving Raven a good dose of, "Not today young lady, and not on my watch." After all, she was an usher, and one of her jobs was to maintain peace within the church, and today Raven would get two pieces of her mother, a piece of Eliza's mind and a piece of her right hand, right where the sun don't shine.

Episode IX: That Lady in Red

Little Raven Reese was growing like a weed and seemed to thrive in her new surroundings. Horatio and Eliza grew closer with the toddler until there was no mistaking it; they had accomplished their mission becoming a family. Raven took her piano lessons every Saturday morning like clockwork and Eliza made sure that she never missed a lesson.

By the time Raven had turned three-years-old, something had changed. Raven, would go up the hallway each night and Eliza would tuck her into bed, kiss her on her small forehead and tell her "Baby, Time for sleep, but first let's say our prayers." Eliza had such a deep-rooted sense of spirituality, and she instilled the same values into little Raven. Eliza had big dreams for Raven, and she felt that after a child grows up, no matter how far away they stray, if their home rearing were good enough, then a child would always wander back to their original roots.

Eliza had noticed that Raven was becoming ill quite frequently, so she took her in for a pediatric visit to the community family doctor. During the doctor's visit, Eliza was told that little Raven had to have her tonsils removed due to infection. Eliza set up the appointment to have the procedure done. The next three days, the nurses gave ice-cream to little Raven regularly. However, something happened to Raven during the procedure that produced a change that no one could see.

During Raven's stay, she shared a semi-private room in the children's ward. Raven's roommate would lay and talk with Raven all night long sometimes, which Raven loved. It was like having a little sister of her very own. On the night before they released Raven from the hospital, her roommate sat up in the middle of her bed, looked over at Raven and stated, "You got purple around you, so your name will be Violet. That's it; I'm gonna call you Violet". Raven had no idea what this roommate meant, but the roommate had no idea what changes would take place in little Raven's world after her statement. Not only was Raven growing on the outside, but something deeper inside of her was developing.

The next day, they gave Eliza the all-clear and told her that she could take Raven home, and so she did. That night Eliza took Raven to her room to tuck her into bed as usual. Eliza had placed a television in Raven's bedroom because she had noticed the child seemed somewhat skittish when she was in her room, and she thought that having the T.V. in there would help her sleep better. That night after Eliza left Raven's room, Raven fell asleep and around two o'clock in the morning, Raven woke again. She opened her little eyes and peeped from under the covers to see if it was her mommy that had come back, but there was no one there.

She closed her eyes again and hearing the sound again but somewhat louder than before; Raven pulled her covers high over her head. Now she was getting scared. The noise happened again, but this time, it sounded as if it was coming from the closet.

Raven could hear the movement inside the closet at this point and knew this was not her mommy.

Out of nowhere, Raven heard her closet door slowly open. She could hear the creaking sound coming from the door as it swung open gradually. She became frozen with fear and was too afraid to look to see what was coming from her closet, so she thought if she could close her eyes ever so tightly, and stayed well hidden under the covers, whatever it was, would not see her and go away. Well, that was wishful thinking on her behalf, because after the door had fully opened, things got quiet. Raven thought whatever it was, had to be gone by now, yet, she laid still.

As luck would have it, suddenly; she felt a cold hand grab her little foot and before she knew it, a second hand grabbed her other foot from the end of the bed and snatched her right out of her bed, pulling her to the floor.

Raven landed on the floor in shock, and as she looked up, she saw it; a lady standing over her in a red dress. The dress appeared to be flowing and see-through, but when she looked at the space where the face should have been, there was no face. She glanced down at the hands that grabbed her in the middle of the night. There were no hands. The only thing that appeared to be somewhat visible was a red dress. Raven let out a blood-curdling scream. She jumped up from the floor, and in the dead of night, the only thing you could hear was her bolting down the hall as her little bare feet hit the hardwood floor at the speed of light. She ran towards Eliza and Horatio's bedroom with tears streaming down her cheeks.

Horatio was a sound sleeper, but not Eliza. Eliza sprang up in the middle of her bed, flung her covers back over her feet and with her right foot, she kicked Horatio right out of his deep sleep and said, "Man get-up. Something's wrong with Raven." Before Horatio could get his eyes fully open to comprehend Raven's blood-curdling screams and cries, Eliza shot out of bed and ran as fast as she could to meet the toddler at the end of the hallway. Raven saw her mother and took a jump right into her arms, screaming, "That lady in my room mommy, that lady in my room. Make her go away, mommy. Make her go away".

Eliza embraced her daughter as tightly as she could and told her, "It's all right baby, mamma got you." Eliza could feel little Raven's heart racing at one-hundred miles an hour, as she held her close to her while caressing her small head against her shoulders.

Horatio, on the other hand, was furious that someone might be in his little girls' room and he jumped from the bed, grabbing his military styled assault rifle that he had brought back home after his time served in the military. He headed down the hallway and told Eliza to take Raven to the kitchen and stay there.

As he headed to Raven's room, he was sure that if someone had broken into his home, they would never make it out. As he entered the room, he did a basic military-style sweep of the room, clearing each area of Raven's bedroom, but at the end of the sweep, he found nothing.

Finding nothing in her room, Horatio checked the windows, and he even walked outdoors to check things there but found absolutely nothing there that was unusual. As Horatio walked back inside, Eliza was sitting at the table talking to Raven about what she saw.

Raven was adamant that she saw a lady in a red dress that pulled her from her bed and that the lady had no face or hands. Eliza did not know what to make of Raven's experience and could not help but think about what her sister-in-law, Olivia had told her, about children that are sometimes born with a special gift. Yet, Eliza was not sure exactly what had occurred. Was it just a bad dream or what? She also thought about the fact that Raven had just had surgery on her tonsils and perhaps it was and after effect that Raven was having from the anesthesia.

Horatio sat down at the table, pulled up his chair, and asked Eliza, "What the hell just happened here?" He told her, "I checked everywhere, and there was no one or anything unusual, so what is Raven saying that happened?" Eliza explained to Horatio word for word what Raven had told her. Horatio looked up at Eliza and then over at Raven and with a sneer upon his face, he said, "Hm, sounds to me like somebody seeing the boogeyman, huh."

Well, Eliza was not having that behavior or talk from Horatio, and it sent her into a fit of rage. She stood up, picked Raven up, and looked over at Horatio. She told him, "You sho got a lot of nerve telling that baby that. You ain't got no right to scare my baby like that." And then she took Raven over to the kitchen counter, set her upon it and said, "Let mama get her baby some cake. "That will make you feel better, huh?"

Horatio looked surprised as if to say, 'what did I do wrong?' He stood up and went into the bedroom and got back into the bed, telling Eliza, "Y'all turn off the lights when ya'll finish up in there." Eliza paid Horatio no mind, and she sat up with her little girl for the remainder of the night until Raven had fallen back to sleep.

What Horatio and Eliza did not understand was, their toddler was developing something more significant than fear itself. Raven was growing as a toddler, but her gift that aunt Olivia had mentioned earlier, was also developing. A gift that did not come in a package with a pretty bow. It would not be visible to the naked eye. Would this unique ability prove to be a gift later on down the road? Right now, it was a possible precursor to many things that a toddler would never understand. Would this gift leave everyone asking the question, "Are her abilities really a gift, or a curse"?

Episode X: Rollicking Raven, Hush

In the meantime, the toddler was learning about love, family, and how to finally be a child and experience all the things that an average child should experience at her age. Eliza saw that there was something special about her little girl and that the child could catch on to things fast, so Eliza and Horatio made the decision to let Raven start school at an extremely early age.

Most toddlers start pre-school at the age of around five or six years old, but Eliza would not wait that long to enroll Raven. She felt as if a child that could learn musical notes as early on as Raven did could certainly learn alphabets and numbers just as fast. In those days every culture had their own school system since integration had not yet occurred in the south, so Eliza had no problems enrolling Raven into her new school.

Raven would ride the bus every day to her new school, after all, Horatio and Eliza both drove the school bus every morning and then after dropping off all of the children to their prospective school systems, they would drive back home, change clothes and go to their daily jobs where they worked a full eight hour shift. After work was over, they would go back, pick up the buses and gather all the little children and drop them safely back at their homes. This was a daily routine for both Horatio and Eliza.

Dallas P Elkheart

As the toddler grew and the seasons rolled around, it was time for Horatio to spend his countless hours working his farmland. The one-hundred and twenty acres that he had purchased just for Eliza was a great source of additional income for the family. Horatio took great pride in growing his acres of watermelons, cantaloupes, potatoes, soybeans, and cotton. In the south, these crops grew readily, but they were usually not produced by or allowed to be provided by people of a particular heritage.

One day Horatio had hired a large group of sharecroppers to pick the cotton from his fields to prepare the bails for sale in the nearest town. The trick was, that the more cotton one picked in their bag, the more money they made for that trip, and the more trips one could make to the pay station in eight hours, the more money one would make for the full day. You were paid by the weight of your sack, which by the way was called a "Croker-sack," and it was made from a type of burlap for heavy-duty tasks and hauling of goods. Eliza was the perfect business partner as she carried such a soft-spoken personality that Horatio felt, who better than his wife to sit under the shade tree and give the workers water to drink and take the bags of cotton and weigh them in for payment.

It was on a Saturday morning, and young Raven had taken such a liking to two of the elders in the neighborhood. These two elders came from two different backgrounds, cultures and totally different belief systems, yet, Raven never saw the difference in either one of the men.

Bronze Bloodline of the Phoenix

They appeared to care significantly for little Raven as she felt the same about them. One of the gentlemen had tremendously wavy hair, and Raven seemed intrigued with his mane of waves with lockets of curls at the ends.

This gentleman was called by his nickname Kelly, and Raven adored Mr. Kelly. He would come over to help Eliza with the payments, water, food, and other things for the sharecroppers. Well, this day, Raven took it upon herself to go above and beyond the call of duty because in her little mind she had to look like Mr. Kelly and to do this, it would require something extra.

Raven had a head full of long hair already, however, Eliza always kept Ravens hair in neat little ponytails as most little girls wore in the 1960s, but that simply would not do for Raven.

Mr. Kelly never wore ponytails, and the toddler had to make some changes. When Mr. Kelly showed up that morning, Raven disappeared. Eliza searched for Raven to no avail, and after calling Raven repeatedly, the group working for Horatio and Eliza grew wearily concerned for the toddler and her whereabouts, even Mr. Kelly searched the farm over and over while calling out her name in vain.

Suddenly, out of nowhere, Raven darted out of the house, and everyone stood in utter surprise as baby Raven ran down to the field and jumped into Mr. Kelly's arms and yelled out loud, "Look, mommy, I look like Mr. Kelly now. See, I look like Mr. Kelly, mama." Everyone broke out into a laugh as they looked at Ravens hair and Eliza's face. You could have run Eliza over with a tractor and not had the same look of bewilderment that she had on her face that day. What Raven did was speechless to all. Back in that timeframe, households killed their own fresh meat, and if they slaughtered pork, fat from the pig that was leftover was melted down and a product called "Lard" would be created. Lard was used in cooking bread and for frying food items, and it was generally kept in a lard barrel for use. Raven had found a lard barrel down by the bottom cabinets in Eliza's kitchen and climbed to the sink, wet her long hair down and grabbed a handful of the lard and rubbed her entire head with it. This created wavy and curly hair for Raven. Therefore, she now looked like Mr. Kelly, and her mission was accomplished.

Eliza grabbed Raven up laughing all the way back to the house with Raven in tow, saying, "Oh my GOD, how I'm gonna get all the grease out your head." Of course, Mr. Kelly was quite impressed, that is, once he could finally stop laughing at Raven. Eliza took the time to wash Raven's hair and tried her best to remove all the greasy pork lard out of Raven's hair. In the meantime, the workers were hard at work, and Mr. Kelly took over the pay station while Eliza got Raven dressed and back on duty for play.

Bronze Bloodline of the Phoenix

Once things were back to work mode for everyone, Raven wasn't finished with her job, and could not help but be puzzled by all the Croker Sacks everyone had. The toddler was not finished for the day, by any means and she watched everyone pull the fluffy, white soft material off the plants and then shove it into a sack, but for Raven, the best part was that they took it to Eliza, and they all seemed to smile when they were walking away. Aha yes, Raven had a brilliant idea, why not grab a sack and go and see what everyone was making such a ruckus about, and that is just what the toddler did.

Without anyone noticing her mischievous behavior, she ran out the door and headed to the shed where the Croker-Sacks were kept; then she grabbed the smallest bag that her little body could carry.

Off she went, to the fields where the sharecroppers performed their task. Eliza was still searching for little Raven; however, Raven had a better idea about becoming a big girl, and once she reached the area that everyone was working in, she stood side by side with the workers and began to try to pick cotton with everyone else.

The workers seemed smitten with the child as she jumped right in as if she was one of them. They looked at their little work buddy with great admiration, well that is until Horatio spotted the small vermin and just about had a stroke as he bellowed out across the field with a deep yet angry voice," Eliza, get that girl out them fields, Right Now, I mean Right Now."

Eliza stood up, spotted Raven and off she flew running as hard as she could, almost as if the child's life was in danger. She made it to Raven and snatched her up into her arms, saying, "Child, your daddy about to have a fit. Come out these fields, right now." Little Raven was shocked and hurt, as she had just made some new friends, but for whatever reason, she was left to wonder, what had she done wrong.

She only wanted to be with everybody else. But why, why didn't Horatio want little Raven to be in the fields and why couldn't she learn how to do what the sharecroppers were doing? What Raven didn't know, and Eliza did know was, Horatio had a tough life, his mother was a sharecropper. She had raised all thirteen of her children as a single mother since his father and mother had divorced in his younger years, which left Horatio's mother to fend for herself and the young ones.

The way Horatio's saw it, no child of his would ever be subjected to the disheartening and demeaning work of a commoner. Therefore, he would have no child of his doing anything other than school, music, education, and a good career, end of the story. Of course, Eliza never saw things that way. She felt that hard work was good for the soul and a decent way to make a living and become a useful member of society. Then, again, Eliza never really agreed with a lot of Horatio's opinions based on the way he was raised and the way he viewed the world. Raven spent the rest of the afternoon in tears as her little heart could not follow the reasoning behind her father's decision.

In the following days, Raven finally got a chance to meet some of her new neighbors that she had never met. However, all the children in her neighborhood were years older than little Raven, and they were all either in high school, middle school, or elementary school. There was a family that lived right across the street from her, and they had four girls and four boys, all far too old to play with Raven, but that never stopped her from regularly visiting with their family. There was one other family that lived a little way up the hill from her, and when she finally got a chance to meet them, she realized that they had one girl and two older boys as well. Even though the older boys were not of playing age, the girl seemed to be quite playful and started to give Raven a lot of attention. Raven enjoyed playing with the younger girl even though the girl was seven years older than Raven.

The girl's name was Lettie, and she was in middle school. Lettie was not much for school and appeared to look more like a little boy, not a girl, but that never stopped Raven from playing with the young girl whenever she would come around. She always brought Raven snacks and toys and enjoyed combing Raven's long, thick, brownish-black hair. She would put bows on Raven's hair and paint her nails to make her feel special when she came to visit the toddler. Eliza never thought that any of the children around Raven was a threat to her because everyone knew all the children in that neighborhood and the parents. It was what Eliza didn't know, that would prove to pose the greatest threat to her family and more so, little Raven.

Lettie lived with her elderly grandmother, grandfather, and two brothers. The mother of the children had sent them to live with their grandparents for various reasons, and one of them would prove to be the most harmful to little Raven. Lettie would regularly come down to Raven's house when Eliza was home and take Raven outdoors to play and make mud pies.

One day, Lettie stopped by and asked Eliza, if Raven could come to her house for a bit and share some cookies that her grandmother had made, just for the toddler. Eliza being a trusting soul, happily agreed and Lettie told Raven to grab her toys, "And let's go eat some cookies."

Off they went down the road and up the hill to Lettie's grandmother's house. Once they reached the house, Lettie took Raven and asked the grandmother if she could take Raven to her room to play for a bit, and the grandmother agreed. The house that they lived in was ancient and drafty, so old that you could see through the cracks of the house into another room.

Attached to this house was an old storage room that the family used to store grain, flour, and other canned goods. From Lettie's room, one could see into the bedroom through a small crack in the corner of the wall, right where the large bags of flour were held.

That afternoon, Lettie told Raven that she was bored with playing in her room and asked her to come and go with her to the storage room where they could play a new game. Raven was only three years old and very impressionable, so she went willingly. Lettie took Raven's hand and led her out the door and around to the storage room. This storage room only had one way in, and one way out, no electricity existed in that part of the building. The only lighting was the bits coming from the outdoors, and in through the cracks of the door or between walls, so the rooms were quite drab, and Lettie closed the door behind her.

Lettie had taken a hand full of toys for the toddler to play with, so Raven sat down on the bags of flour and began to play quietly with her toys. Lettie made the decision that she no longer wanted to play with the toys and told Raven, I know, let's play mommy and baby, and you gonna be the baby.

Lettie picked Raven up and sat her up on her lap and told Raven, "Now lay down because the baby was wet, and I have to change your diaper." She took little Raven and laid her back across her lap, and before she even knew what was happening, the older girl started to pretend that she was changing the toddler's diaper leaving Raven to think it was a game. This started to feel uncomfortable, and it began to frighten Raven, especially as she tried to raise up, and she tried to push Lettie's hands away from her body, but the older girl was far stronger than the toddler, and she tried unsuccessfully, as the older girl held her tightly in place. Raven began to cry, and Lettie took both her legs, wrapping them around the toddler's legs and placed one hand over the child's mouth.

It all happened so quickly that she could not move or scream, so instead, she laid still and began to sob quietly, while Lettie did the unthinkable and unspeakable act of sexually abusing the toddler.

Lettie must have kept the toddler in the storage building for quite some time because once she had finished, it was getting late, and the sun was close to going down. She knew she had to get Raven back home before Eliza grew suspicious, so she quickly set the toddler up on the flour sack, pulled her bottoms back up and her little dress down.

She bent down on one knee, looked the toddler in her eyes, grabbed her with both hands and shook her while saying, "If you tell, if you tell anyone, your mama will take you back to the orphanage, and they will take all your toys away." She told Raven that it was ok and that she was only checking her to see if she needed a diaper change, and then she said in a snarling type voice, "Now wipe your face, and this is only our little secret." The toddler nodded her head but somehow, she was still gripping the little doll that she had brought with her as if she had a death grip on the baby doll. Lettie grabbed the child's hand and said, now let's go, I must get you home." And she walked the toddler back to her house.

Eliza was cooking dinner and had seen them coming across the fields from Lettie's house from the kitchen window. When they walked into the house, Eliza never looked around, but she asked, "Did you girls have fun?" Lettie was quick to say, "Yes, we had so much fun, can I take Raven to the house to play again soon? She likes our house, don't you, Raven". Raven looked at the girl, and before Eliza could look back to ask Raven if she wanted to go back over to Lettie's, Lettie looked down at Raven with squinted eyes and said under her breath, "Remember what I told you." Raven was terrified and said, "Yes, mama, I will go with Lettie." By this time Eliza had looked back to see Raven's response to the question, everything appeared ok. She did not understand just how terrified Raven was of Lettie. What the toddler did not know was, Lettie would become Raven's biggest nightmare and make the child the victim of sexual abuse over the next couple of years.

For the next three years, Lettie would come down two to three days a week to get Raven and take her back to her dungeon of a storage shed, where she became more and more dominant over Raven.

At this point, the grandmother had also become just as perverted, and Raven could see her watching many times at the things her granddaughter would do to her in the storage shed. She could not understand why no one would stop Lettie. Raven knew no one would help her and because she feared Lettie, Raven knew that she could never tell anyone about what was happening to her. Besides, who would believe her? She was only a young baby in most eyes. She often thought of telling someone, anyone, but she remembered how no one believed her about the lady in red from her closet, so she made the decision to remain silent and hold it locked within herself, hoping one day someone would stop Lettie.

By now, Raven would no longer cry, only grip her baby doll for comfort as these acts grew crueler and crueler each time. Young Raven had become a prisoner in her new world and learned to lock feelings and hurt inside herself. This would be the beginning of her learning to depend on only herself for help.

As Lettie got older, she dropped out of school, and her grandmother moved her away because she had now become pregnant by her own stepfather.

The fact that the girl up the hill dropped from school was the saving factor for Raven and the only way little Raven would be saved from further sexual abuse by the hands of her tyrant. Young Raven was now left with a deep painful, shameful and dark dirty secret and she would remain afraid to ever speak of it to anyone.

Bronze Bloodline of the Phoenix

This would become one of many private hells that young Raven would have to master if she was going to ever be able to grow and thrive beyond this point.

Eliza had pulled Raven from her school a couple of years early. Raven started school at the age of two, and she would have finished high school by the age of fourteen. At this age, she would not be able to get a job or register for college. Eliza finally put Raven back in school at the age of five. Eliza never knew that Lettie, the young girl she trusted with her precious cargo, was capable of such an unspeakable act and would harm her only little girl scarring her for life.

Now, young Raven was close to six years old and outwardly appeared to be a happy child. Schools in the south of Mississippi were just beginning to become integrated, and that meant Raven was now in school with other little children closer to her age and from different nationalities.

Raven was starting to notice things that made her feel like she was different than others as well. She could see that children from her own nationality did not want much to do with her. The girls seemed to show almost a dislike towards Raven, and the boys seemed to want to be around her and paid far more attention to her than the girls.

Raven did not seem to mind, as she remembered what girls were capable of and what the last girl that she trusted did to her, so she was not eager to have girls as friends anyway. Raven was growing slowly into a beautiful yet lonely little girl. Eliza was both a seamstress and a beautician. Therefore, she always made sure Raven was dressed in the best-tailored clothing and kept her long ponytails welled groomed, even though Eliza would wear handed down clothing herself. By this age, many mental, physical and emotional changes had begun to take shape in Raven's little life, internally and externally, far more than anyone could imagine. Tiny Raven was now like a dormant volcano. You see it's smoke, you feel the ground move, but when will it blow?

Bronze Bloodline of the Phoenix

PART IV: Changing of the Guards

Dallas P Elkheart

Episode XI: Revelation & Prophecies

Raven, a now lively and somewhat thriving six-year-old, was finding school quite exciting. Even though she had lived through some horrible experiences in her little life, she was finding coping mechanisms to help her learn to exist.

She was also finding other interests in things such as books and photos, especially photos. One day, Eliza was outside working in her garden where she loved to grow tomatoes, peas, okra, corn, and mustard greens. She took such pride in gardening when she was not working at her factory job in a small town about thirty-five minutes from their home. In the meantime, Raven was watching television in her parents' room and playing with her toys quietly on the floor. Raven noticed a book with many photos in it, pulled the book towards her, and began to glance through the pictures. She had always enjoyed seeing pictures of things new to her and many times; she would spend endless hours flipping through her mother's old catalogs as she would mark items with a pen or pencil and flip the pages down on things, she one day wanted to have.

As Raven flipped through the photos, one caught her eye, and as she pulled the plastic cover back to take the picture out, she noticed there was a little girl on the photo standing in front of a house she had never seen before. Raven turned the image over to see what was written on the back of it. She could see there was writing, but it looked as if someone did not want what was there to be seen. She could see where they had taken a pencil or pen and scratched through the writing on the back of the photo. Raven held the picture up high in the sunlight that beamed so gloriously through her mother's picture window in the bedroom.

She realized that she could not see what was under the scribble marks, and then she had an idea and tried something.

She was a bright young girl and would often think of things that perhaps other young children her age would not. She came up with an idea, and once an idea hit Raven, there was no removing it until she was satisfied. Raven found a sheet of paper, she crawled on her mothers' bed, laid the picture down on paper, and placed them both on top of the book. Turning the backside of the picture down onto the paper, she used two fists, then pressed as hard as she could in a side to side motion. Before long, she noticed that an impression was being made upon the paper. Once she was finished, she stopped and lifted the photo. That is when she saw a name had re-imprinted itself on the paper in Raven's hand. She could barely make it out, but there was a name on the paper and not only a first name but also the last name.

But what name did she see? Whose name was it? Who was the little girl in the photo? Where was this taken? Why was someone trying so hard to keep anyone from seeing the name? Was this a family member and what if any, connection was there to her?

All these questions went racing through Raven's little mind, yet, she believed that no one would answer any of these questions for her. If they could, who would she ask? And should she ask her mommy, her daddy or her aunt, Olivia? These were things that would perplex Raven the most. The name or letters she found on the back of the photo was Ell_ M_ ss_on, not a legible full name, but a name that would preoccupy little Raven's mind, for many years to come.

When Eliza came in from working in her garden, Raven showed her the picture and then she asked, "Mommy who is this"? Eliza looked as if she had seen a spook and took a giant gulp and sunk her shoulders inward, then softly said, "that was a picture of you, and they gave that to me when I got you."

What Eliza did not know was that this answer would open nothing but a floodgate of questions. Raven would seek the answers, but she would not be asking them from Eliza. Raven was a very resilient child and was not a child to take an explanation for what it was, as Eliza would soon learn. Raven was born with many gifts, but one of her best assets was the one thing that would one day keep her alive, and that was her tenacity.

Eliza walked away to put her garden vegetables up as she spoke under her breath, "My baby." As the evening moved into nighttime and Eliza ran Ravens bath water to prepare her for bed; Raven started to ask her mother questions about God. Eliza being the patient mother that she was, understood why her child had many questions, just as most young children do. Eliza went into her bedroom and told Raven, "I have something for you." Eliza pulled out a small bible and gave it to her daughter, saying, "This may help you answer some of your questions, and I pray I can help explain the rest."

As Raven headed off to bed and Eliza kneeled with Raven for her prayers, there was a sense of closeness in the air. Eliza felt her little girl was headed in the right direction and that pleased Eliza very much. They kneeled together and recited the prayer, "Now I lay me down to sleep, I pray the Lord my soul to keep, If I should die before I wake, I pray the Lord, my soul, to take, AMEN."

Eliza stood up, tucked Raven into bed and as she walked out of the room, she stopped at the door before closing it, turned around and smiled while moving her lips without the words being spoken aloud and said, "Thank you, Jesus, for my child."

As Raven had grown, so had a special gift that was unbeknown to anyone and that night it stepped forward and made itself known. As young Raven slept, she began to see a place in the countryside, that she was very familiar with since her godparents lived in that area, and in this dream, she saw buildings being torn down with city buildings being built in the places that she was familiar with.

The problem with her visions was, those types of buildings had not been designed yet, nor created in the area of the world that she lived in, so how could she see buildings that had not been designed being built in a small town that had never been developed?

Was Raven's aunt Olivia's old wives' tale becoming a reality? Was Raven born with a gift, or did she have a child's REM sleep dream? As Raven grew, she had many vivid and recurring dreams about places, people, and things that would leave her wondering and sometimes frightened.

By the time Raven had turned eight years old, she had developed other talents, talents that ordinary people do not have. Therefore, they cannot see it or hear it. One day after school, she took her standard route home on the school bus. She lived a reasonable distance from her school; it was a redundant routine. Raven would get home at about 3:30 every day, and many would consider her a latch-key baby because she arrived home much earlier than her parents.

This day started as any typical day, but it would certainly not end that way. It was in the fall, and the weather had turned quite cold by now. Raven came home from school one afternoon, and she had several assigned chores to do. After finishing her evening chores, Raven would do her homework first, and then she would gather her favorite friends, her puppies. They would gather in Eliza's bedroom and watch cartoons until her parents came home from work. She had two beagle pups that came from Horatio's bloodhounds that he kept for hunting. Raven and Eliza had created names for Raven's puppies. She had two twin boy pups, but they looked nothing alike, so they named them, Did-he-bite-you and Will-he-bite-you.

These two pups were her best friends. Every day that young Raven arrived home, the pups would lie at the end of the road leading to Raven's house, awaiting that big yellow school bus that would drop their little friend off. The pups would greet Raven with the same affections those other old, shaggy, rug looking things greeted her parents with when she first arrived at her new home, except these pups were all hers.

Raven and the pups walked up the long driveway to the house; she found the key that would be left just so she would not have to climb through a window, and she opened the door and was escorted into the house by her two pups. After finishing up her chores and homework that day, Raven went into Horatio and Eliza's bedroom to sit on the floor with her pups and watch cartoons. There was still almost forty-five minutes left before her parents would get in from work.

Raven would always close off the hallway door leading from her parent's room up to the hallway. She always had an uneasy feeling about her bedroom and the hallway. She was sitting by a small heater in her parents' room, and while sitting on the floor, playing with some old toys, she noticed her pups started to act strangely.

They would play around and then stop, their ears would go in an upright position as if they heard someone, but Raven continued playing with her toys. Out of the blue, Raven stopped, the pups stopped, and she heard a sound, but she could not determine just where the sound was coming from.

She knew she was home alone, out in the country with very few houses around them, so where was this sound coming from. After a couple of minutes, Raven and the pups went back to their routine, but within five minutes, the noise started again, except it was louder. Young Raven heard the loud noise again; she changed positions and ended up on all fours, just like her pups. Her eyes got as wide as a half a dollar, and she got really scared. The puppies, on the other hand, whined and began to pace the floor. Raven was trembling in fear and shaking so badly; she could no longer hold her toys. She thought that it sounded like a noise coming from the north end of the house, her room.

As she slid nervously over to the door, she placed her small head against the door with the right ear facing the door and what she heard was ghastly. She could hear something that sounded like it was sliding its feet down the hallway in a slow dragging motion. The crazy part about it was, by now the pups had become so unsettled that they were now scrambling and scratching at the kitchen door while whining to get out, not to mention looking back as if something was coming for them and they didn't want to be there when it arrived.

Raven pulled her head back from the door as tears began to well up in her eyes, but she covered her mouth so as not to let out a scream that would alert the intruder of her presence. It did not matter because while hearing the mysterious thing dragging its feet down the hall; she began to hear a whisper. The whisper was coming from the hallway, and it knew her by name, the wispy but masculine voice said in a slow, yet drawn out way, G-a-b-b-y.

Wait, that was her middle name given to her by the Reese's.' However, it knew her nickname; it was calling her, and the voice and name became louder as it approached the door. Raven was holding her breath with large tears falling, she was so frightened she wet her pants, and she desperately tried to scoot back on all fours. Finally, the unknown creature stopped at the door, and suddenly, she heard it as it appeared to slam on the door with a fierce fist, with such a force that she fell trying to get up and get out of there. The pups were in her way as she made her move towards the kitchen door. There were a series of locks on their kitchen door to ensure the family's safety, but these items also made it more challenging to get out of the way of whatever wanted Raven.

She fought to get to her knees and pull all three of the locks and chains from the door; the pups bolted in front of her tripping

Raven which made her tumble out of the house onto the front doorsteps. She quickly closed the door and could move no further. Raven sat on the steps of the carport frozen, too afraid to move. She was crying so hard that by the time Eliza's car had pulled into the driveway; she was crying only a dry cry; no more tears could come down her cheeks. The pain and fear of her experience were so real it continued to create a dry crying effect.

Eliza jumped out of the car immediately as she knew something was not right. She knew Raven should be inside since Eliza told her to stay inside with the doors locked every day after school until she or Horatio got home. Raven screamed to the top of her little lungs, "Mommy, mommy, don't let them take me," as she fell into Eliza's arms with her small head resting on the lower half of her mother's tummy. Raven acted as if she had just seen her savior for the first time saving her from the bad man. The child was left shaken, and Eliza was extremely disturbed by what had happened. Raven moved on and tried to put the incident behind her. However, Raven refused to sleep in her bed out of fear that the very thing that tormented her in the afternoon was still lurking around in her room. It was almost another two years before Raven would try to sleep in her room again alone. This thing harboring in her room, would gain strength and become bolder, for it was not finished with Raven, and there was nothing it would not do to stop her from ever getting away from its clutches.

Episode XII: That Old Devil

As Raven grew a bit older, she also noticed that the apparitions that she had been seeing, began to develop to be a bit stranger and become more detailed. Let's not forget that the thing lurking in her room began to grow more powerful and to manifest itself more frequently. Eliza and Raven would go to church on Sunday's, no matter what. Many times, they would have a Choir Day, and that meant they would travel to different churches around the city and Raven played the piano for their church choir. Oh, but Horatio was not a church kind of guy, so he would choose to stay home and work in his fields, work on his old tractor, or even relish the quiet time at home alone. One day after church, Eliza and Raven came home and as usual, they undressed and prepared to relax, that meant that Eliza would finish up cooking her Sunday dinner that she would leave simmering while they went to church.

That afternoon, after Eliza finished preparing supper for the family, the family thought it was a great evening to lie on the bed and enjoy watching Sunday television programs. Even Horatio would lay down with them, and Raven would crawl between her parents and get comfortable watching westerns or Star Trek. She was a western-style girl mostly and spent a lot of her time playing cowboys and Indians in her yard with a cowgirl suit, that Eliza had purchased for her.

Dallas P Elkheart

Horatio and Eliza had drifted off to sleep, being tired from the day's events while Raven was submerged in television. Raven noticed that she thought she saw movement in the hallway, so she scooted herself to the end of the bed to see what was there, but she saw nothing.

As she began to scoot herself back to the head of the bed between Eliza and Horatio, something caught her eyes. She noticed something small and red coming down the hallway. It appeared to be a little person about three feet tall, but the difference was, it did not have the face of a child. Instead of the face of a child, it had a face so grotesque, causing her to jump straight up in the bed. The figure ambled down the hall to the foot of the bed. Raven's eyes filled with tears as she looked towards her parents to see if they saw the same thing she was seeing. As the creature reached the foot of the bed, Raven drew both feet to her chest and wrapped her arms tightly around her knees as if to keep the beast from pulling her by the feet right to the bottom of the bed to him.

She tried to scream, to awaken her sleeping parents, but nothing would come from her mouth. She was frozen as if paralyzed, leaving her so terrified that she began again to wet her pants. Eliza and Horatio still sound asleep, as the creature started to reach towards the middle of the bed for Raven, but because of the creature's small stature, he could not grab her feet as they were still snuggled tightly to her chest. By now, Raven had scooted so far to the head of the bed, that the headboard had now become her backrest.

Raven tried one more time to scream, but nothing would come out. She felt helpless, terrified, and totally shaken by the event. After the creature could no longer accomplish his mission, he dropped his hands by his side, smirked at Raven with one eyebrow raised and turned to go back down the hallway where he came from, disappearing into her room. Eliza and Horatio opened their eyes and sat up as Raven whimpered and cowered at the head of the bed, but soon her voice had returned, and she let out a shrill scream. It was a long, scream of sheer terror. Horatio grabbed Raven, he shook her and called her name repeatedly to bring her back to herself.

Raven was screaming so loudly that she did not realize Horatio and Eliza were now awake. They tried their best to comfort the youngster. Raven kept saying, "It's me. They are after me; they want me. I don't want to go with them. No, No, No. Make them go away."

It was apparent something bone-chilling had just occurred in the Reese household, but Eliza and Horatio could see absolutely nothing that would have caused their child to be in this much distress. Raven continued to have these types of experiences, and her dreams at night became utterly terrifying. She was being tortured in her own home and her world. She had no one she could share her experiences with, not even friends, since the children she was growing up around, still wanted nothing to do with Raven, they felt as if she was a "Miss. Goody Two-Shoes" and they felt as if she was not part of their community. Raven was alone and lonely, and by now, she felt even more abandoned than ever before.

Raven turned thirteen years old, and she had met a young man by the name of Carlos. She met him through a neighbor that had married Carlos's older sister. Raven was smitten with Carlos. He was the first guy that showed her love.

She was at the age when she started to notice boys and boys noticed her. Raven was growing into a beautiful pre-teenager. Her eyes seemed to always catch every ray of the sun, and her personality was giggly, yet serious at the same time. She took great pride in her looks as Eliza would not allow Raven to go out in public any other way. Eliza always taught Raven to comb her hair and keep it neat, dress well, smell good and act like a young lady, sit like one and speak like you have some education and home training. Raven heard this daily.

Eliza was a down-to-earth woman, but a wise one as well and knew unless she taught her young daughter how to be, how to act and how to speak, it would make for a hard life, and she never wanted Raven to experience the life she had lived.

Horatio, however, saw it differently. He spent endless days showing Raven, how to repair things, build things, and do basic things. Horatio would say, "Learn to do things for yourself, and you will never have to rely on a man for anything."

He always said, "Otherwise, a man will always have the upper hand on you, and no man wants or needs, a needy person." Horatio had now become also quite critical of Raven, and if he showed her something once, he never wanted to have to show her twice. Therefore, if she did not catch it the first time, he would start to become angry with her and say, "You just dumb as a doorknob, you can't do nothing right."

Raven would feel awful as she loved Horatio and wanted nothing more than to prove to him; she was worth something and not just a pretty face. The thirteen-year-old endured more and more insults from Horatio, which Eliza was not aware of. Raven could not comprehend why her father who once adored her, was now being so mean to her and saying hurtful things, but life went on, and soon Raven began to believe many of the things that Horatio would say even when he would tell her, "You're worthless."

Some nights Horatio would sneak outside in the dark of night and go to Raven's bedroom window. He knew how frightened she was of her room, and he would not stand for a wimpy daughter. He would take his nails and scratch on her window screen and make ghostly sounds, then sneak back in and wait for her to show up screaming her fool head off as he would laugh and say, "See, when you bad, the boogie-man come for you."

This would make Eliza so upset that she would not speak to Horatio for days. She would try to explain to Raven that she was a blessing to them and tell her, they loved her.

Somewhere along the way, Raven's mind could no longer see the good, only the bad, and she fell into a depression. Eliza even tried to take Raven to a psychiatrist for some help, because there were a few times when Raven tried to end her life. She believed she was being tortured, and there was simply no other way out. Raven felt everything was closing in on her, from her father's insults and physical abuse, the hauntings in her room and the lack of friends, she saw no other way out besides to take her own life.

She would spend her afternoons after school at band practice or choir practice before racing home to talk for hours on the phone with Carlos. Carlos and Raven were now an item; he was now her boyfriend. Eliza would allow Carlos to come by on Sunday evenings after church and chat with Raven for about one hour in the front yard, only with adult supervision.

Carlos was smitten with Raven, and he gave her a dainty promise ring, with two hearts interlocked in silver. Raven felt like the most special girl in the world. Horatio was not so thrilled, because he thought his daughter was not ready for a boyfriend even though he liked Carlos. Eliza took it all with a grain of salt because she knew she had trained her young daughter well, and by now Raven had decided that when she grew up, she wanted to become a nurse.

Eliza was pleased as she had always referred to Raven as "Florence Nightingale," since Raven made it her mission to take care of people when they were sick or in need.

Raven now had in-depth dreams each night. Her dreams were repetitive; they always centered on her arriving at her church. She would see herself walking into the church and seeing a coffin at the end of the aisle. She would stroll down the aisle and see someone inside the coffin, and as she got closer, she would notice that it was herself, lying cold and still, then she would abruptly wake up, and the next night she would dream it all over again. This continued for over eight months.

One day, Raven was on the phone with Carlos after school, and he asked her a question that would alter her choices for years to come. Carlos was so in love with Raven, he had thoughts most teenage boys get, and he posed Raven with a question. He made a statement to Raven and said, "Raven, if you love me, then we should have sex."

This took Raven into a world that she hadn't yet thought of. She was still intrigued by her toys, school, music lessons, and the band. This was more than Raven was ready to deal with. Not knowing how to respond, she said to Carlos, "Well, if you loved me, why would you ask me that?" Carlos was almost two years older than Raven, and he was used to being around faster girls, so to him, Raven was a bit of a nerd.

After the phone conversation, Raven became distant from Carlos, and eventually, she would dodge his phone calls, because she did not want to think about sex at this point in her life. Raven then fell further and further into a depressed stage because she loved Carlos, but after the molestation event that happened to her with the girl across the street when she was little, she had never thought of venturing down the road of sex. Raven, wondered weeks later if she had made the right decision and if she would have said yes, would she and Carlos still be together? Carlos stopped speaking to her altogether, causing Raven to lose someone she felt so deeply about.

Raven's dreams became even scarier, because by now she was dreaming the same vision, but with a twist. She now saw herself, leaving the church in her family car, and she was sitting on the passenger's side.

The passenger side window would be partially opened, and she could now see a woman's hand, reaching into the window. The hand would grab her by the throat, and then she would wake up. She would gasp for air as if she was having her life strangled right out of her.

By now, each night would present three to four different dreams. Sometimes she could see her own funeral and then walk outside from the church and get into the car and see the woman's hand appear, sometimes she would see new buildings being built in an area where there was only farmland, and then a new dream started to appear. She began to see Eliza's body in a bronze colored coffin, lying beside the carport and she was wearing a bronze-colored dress, a hairstyle that Raven did not recognize, a set of beads around her neck.

Many unpleasant dreams disturbed the teenager, but she tried very hard to go on with her life as if nothing was happening. By now, she had made two new friends at her school, and both girls would become part of her life for the long-term. Raven had no clue that her life would take a turn for the worst. These two young girlfriends she had finally made would play a significant role in her life, in more ways than one.

Raven was also about to make one more friend, a young man that would become her private nightmare, and all but bear the mark of Satan. He would play such a role in Raven's life, that her life would never, ever be the same again. He would also bring a whole new meaning to the words "predator" as he would prove to tear the Reese family unit apart and take great pleasure in doing so.

Dallas P Elkheart

Episode XIII: Pre-Cognitive Nightmare

Raven visited two cousins over the summer before her fourteenth birthday. One of her cousin's best friend walked in. This young man's name was Toby Johnston, and he was tall, and not so handsome according to Raven, who'd barely noticed his skinny facial features that looked strange to her. Toby asked Raven's male cousin, "Wow, who is that"? Her cousin introduced them, and as far as Raven was concerned, that was the end of that because her female cousin had a crush on him.

She saw the world differently than most teens and never felt that a decision as to someone's worth or character should be based on the way they look. She also thought, the money they had or the things they possessed, should never be a determination of character either, and that everyone deserves a chance, but in this case, she should have thought a little longer and looked a wee bit harder at this young man. Toby was persistent in his pursuit of Raven, and eventually, she thought maybe she'd been wrong to judge his looks superficially.

As time passed, Toby being the sweet talker that he was, asked Raven, if he could come and see her. Toby was sixteen years old, and Eliza and Horatio had not approved him to visit Raven. Toby had convinced Raven to ask her parents on his behalf. Eliza wanted to know more about this young man, but Horatio had already heard about him through his gambling buddies in town, and the verdict was not good.

Eliza and Horatio wanted nothing more than to make Raven happy, and she seemed to be stuck on stupid with this young man. Nothing Horatio tried to tell her; would she hear, and she pled with Eliza about her love for this boy and for permission for him to be able to come to visit on Sundays after church.

Raven soon turned fourteen years old, the same age her biological mother was when she gave birth to her. Raven was hell-bent on doing things differently. Horatio had always taught Raven to be self-sufficient, and she wanted to make him proud, but that did not stop her from wanting to see Toby.

Eliza and Horatio sat one afternoon on the porch after work and discussed whether they should allow this young man to visit their Raven. Eventually, but not without reservations, did the parents grant permission for Toby to come to visit Raven after church only. It would be with strict guidelines. The rules Horatio wanted to put into place were straightforward; they would only allow Toby to come by on Sunday afternoons if Raven went to church that day. He could only come between the hours of two o'clock and four o'clock in the afternoon. They could only talk on the phone in the afternoons after school once Raven had completed her chores and her homework, and time would be limited to one hour.

While Raven did not like all the restrictions, she knew the only way to see Toby was to comply with her parents' wishes.

Raven and Horatio were still butting heads because of Raven growing into a teenager, and Horatio had already had a severe dislike for Toby. He felt that this boy should have approached him as most young men would have done, as an honorable man, and asked him for his permission to see his daughter. Eliza, like Horatio, did not care so much for Toby, but she was still willing to tolerate him because of Raven finally having someone in her life that appeared to make her smile. Raven suffered still from depression. Her and Horatio would periodically have substantial disagreements, and no matter how old Raven was becoming, Horatio's anger for others was being projected over to Raven. Eliza seemed to be caught between the two.

Horatio's unkind words towards Raven became increasingly hostile. Raven began to like herself less and less. What Horatio did not realize was, the more he criticized Raven, the more it made her turn to Toby. Toby knew Raven was now suffering from self-esteem issues which allowed him to cast his spell on her, more effectively.

Here was a young and naïve girl who craved her father's love and acceptance, but Toby was the only man she seemed to be able to please. Eliza would sit on the bed with Raven and talk to her about how much they wanted her. Eliza would let Raven know, that before she adopted her, she was so alone herself, but since she now had Raven, she was no longer lonely. She also would tell Raven how pretty and smart she was and that she could be anything she wanted to become. Eliza always instilled in her daughter, that she only wanted what was best for her, but Raven seemed to throw all of that out of the window, because the one person she wanted to hear this from, would never say it. She needed to hear it from Horatio. Raven spent the next four months drawing closer and closer to Toby. One day Toby asked Raven to go to a fourth of July concert with him, and he asked Eliza for their permission to take her daughter to this concert.

Well, Eliza said in no uncertain terms, "I have to speak to Horatio about this, I don't know." One week later, Eliza met with Toby and Raven. She sat them both down and said, "Horatio and I discussed the concert, and if you take our daughter to the concert, it must be in the daytime, and she must be home by six- o'clock, but she better come back the way you took her."

As Raven prepared herself for her very first outing, Toby was also preparing but in a different way than Raven was. He was preparing to make his first advance towards Raven; he knew now that Raven was desperate for her father's love; she would be putty in his hands.

The day finally came for the concert, and just as Toby promised, he came by in his baby blue LTD sedan; all decked out to pick up Raven. As Toby approached the door, to ask for Raven, Horatio stepped to the door instead, and said, "Toby, I am telling you now, you better bring my child back the way she left, or there will be hell to pay, and the price will be paid to me."

Toby's eyes got wide, and he looked like a startled deer caught in headlights. As Toby took a deep gulp, he said, "Yes, yes sir, I intend to bring her back the way she left, sir." Horatio finally stepped out of the way and called for Raven. As she walked out of Eliza's room, Horatio and Toby's mouth dropped. After all, Eliza would never allow her daughter to go in public dressed less than a beautiful young lady, so Eliza designed an outfit just for Raven. Eliza had painstakingly; hand made it for Raven's event.

She enjoyed customizing clothing to fit her daughter's shapely body. Eliza stood back and smiled as she said to Horatio and Toby, "Ain't my baby pretty." Raven became shy and speechless as she smiled and dropped her head and asked Toby, "You ready to go." The two of them left the house, walking hand in hand out the door to the car. Toby being the rat that he was, knew just what Horatio and Eliza expected to see him do. He opened the door for Raven, tucked her neatly into the car and off they went to the concert, or so Raven thought.

As they drove out of the country into the town Raven asked Toby, "So where is the concert at?" and he replied, "We'll get there, but first I must make a couple of stops."

Toby pulled up to a liquor store and told Raven, "You sit tight, and I will be right back." Raven had never seen a liquor store, and she thought Toby ran in to grab sodas. The naïve teenager sat in the car nervously awaiting Toby's return. Shortly after Toby returned to the car and said, "I have a surprise for you before we head to the concert." He cranked the car and drove off, but Raven was so nervous that she never asked Toby, where they were headed.

Toby drove the car down an old dirt road away from town. It seemed far away from anyone or anything. Raven asked Toby, "Where are we going? You said we were going to a concert. There's no concert here." Toby replied, "We're still going, but we're going to stop here for a bit." He stopped the car, reached under his seat, and pulled out a bottle of champagne. Toby told Raven to relax, "I got this," and he began to open the bottle. He took the first sip and then passed the bottle to Raven, not realizing she had let nothing other than milk or soda pass her lips. As Raven just sat there, Toby replied: "Come on, loosen up, have a swig, you'll love it." Raven told him, "NO, I don't want any," but Toby insisted that if she took a drink, she could forget all about the ugly things Horatio would say to her.

Toby had the right combination to convince Raven to do what he wanted, and she took her first drink of the devil's potion. Raven did not know Toby was only pretending to drink, but Raven was the only one drinking the champagne.

As the alcohol quickly took hold of Raven, she became a giggly little girl, all the age of fourteen and Toby knew, he had her where he wanted her. Raven felt the alcohol take effect and could feel her head spinning, but by then Toby had laid Raven's seat back and positioned himself on top of her. As she tried to move him back by pushing him off, the champagne had her in a giggly state of mind. Therefore, her effort was in vain, and Toby knew it.

She heard Toby whisper in her ear, "You're my girl, and when you love each other, this should happen. It's nothing wrong with it. I love you, Raven, I love you." But Raven never knew just what he meant. Not realizing it, Raven had now put herself in the devil's hands, and she would soon live to regret her choice. Toby made sure Raven's alcoholic beverage had taken its toll on her, and before she knew it, he had just undone everything in the world Eliza and Horatio had tried to do which was to protect Raven from this ever happening to her.

Toby was not a gentle creature in everyday life, nor would he be gentle with Raven. In his eyes, Raven was not only his girl but his property, and like a dog, he would make sure his property was marked. After he had finished with Raven, he rolled over, and tears ran down her face. She realized she would bear his brand secretly and for the rest of her life. She hated Toby for not stopping, yet, somehow; she felt crazy love for him. She was so confused. Toby's reward was that he had conquered a young virgin untouched by any other man.

Raven now carried the shame of this situation that she put herself into, and now she would have to deal with her parents at home. Her parents would ask her how the concert was, and the only thing she would be able to remember was the painful experience she encountered.

Toby later took Raven home, never having been to the concert and once they arrived Eliza and Horatio greeted Raven at the door. Toby, on the other hand, did what he intended to do and never got out of the car. He rolled the window down as Raven tried to make it to the door without allowing her shame to be seen, and yelled out, "Goodnight everybody. Hey Raven, I'm calling you tomorrow." As Raven walked inside the house, the first person to ask her how the concert was, was Eliza.

Raven pretended everything was all right, and quickly made her way to the refrigerator, opened the door and buried her head deep inside as if she was seeking a snack. Raven felt as if the entire world could see her dishonor. She said to her mother, "Ah, it was pretty good, but I did not know any of the groups."

A week passed after the incident and Toby was calling Raven more than ever now. It was almost as if he was now possessed and had an addiction to Raven. She would get home from school, and the phone would ring, and it would be Toby.

Toby would call, sometimes calling over five to six times a day in a four-hour time frame. It had become too much for Eliza and Horatio. Eliza was so perturbed with Toby and his constant and persistent phone calls she would tell Raven, "Girl, if you farted, that boy would know what it smelled like, cause he all up in your behind."

Raven was still having crazy dreams of her death, the church and a woman's hand strangling her through a sidecar window and the visions were now getting so intense she would awake drenched in sweat each night. Four weeks had now passed since Toby tainted Raven with his body and she was no longer sleeping well. One afternoon, Raven was practicing her piano for a piano recital in a few weeks and out of nowhere, she felt unwell.

She started to notice her mouth would become watery, and within a few minutes, she would feel as if she wanted to throw up, she would leave her piano and make her way to the bathroom. Every day at 4:00 in the evenings, the same things would occur as if it were a broken record.

What Raven did not know was, Toby put his brand on her as his girl, and he had also placed his label inside her because she was pregnant. Pregnant at fourteen, just as her biological mother had been. Was this fate? Was this a curse to reoccur over and over to each generation to come? Was history about to repeat itself?

Bronze Bloodline of the Phoenix

Would all of Raven's life be replayed like a scratched record, that remains in one spot and never moves forward? Is it possible that Horatio would blow a fuse and kill the young man that defiled his baby girl? Would Eliza become unhinged and lose her spiritual faith and her faith in her young daughter? Could Raven weather it out and give birth to the baby of a young man that came into her life for only one purpose? Should Toby, man up, and do the right thing by Raven and his unborn child and finally, did Toby love Raven as much as he proclaimed?

Dallas P Elkheart

Episode XIV: Somebody, Stop Him

Raven had a thousand questions running through her head, but, what Raven did not know was these questions would soon be answered. Many of the answers would not be the answer she was seeking. These things would create a recipe for one big pot of chaos. Oh yes, this meal would become anything but digestible and give a whole new meaning to the old saying, *Eating crow with no milk*. Eating crow with no milk simply means that one would somehow choke on their own unwise decisions. Once Raven's mother realized that Toby had done the unthinkable, she immediately called one of her sisters Ilene, to discuss what the family should do.

Raven quietly sobbed in her bed while she overheard her mother, speaking to her aunt on the phone. Raven was hurting because she felt guilty that she had let her parents down. She was more upset that she had broken GOD's will, and one of his ten commandments. Raven had decided that, since she had already allowed this to occur, she would just suck it up and make the best out of it. Raven always saw the world differently and trusted everyone she met. She believed if you loved someone and did your best to be the best, giving your heart, you could change the world.

As Raven reflected, a part of her knew that she was not like the woman who cared so very little for her and was so eager to give her unborn child away.

Raven had decided that no matter what, she would see the bright side of things and began to believe that for once in her life, she would have something that would love her and that she would love.

She refused to see things in a negative light, even though her future looked dark, she had decided that she would have her baby and finish school, become a nurse and a single mother. That was imprinted in Raven's head. Unfortunately, it was not so imprinted in everyone else's head.

One morning Raven overheard her mother speaking to someone on the phone, so Raven pulled up a chair and listened at the door. What she heard was heart-wrenching. She heard Eliza say, "My daughter is now pregnant with your son's child after I warned him not to bring her home with a baby, and what we want to know is what does he now intend to do about it? He is running up and down the streets declaring his love for my child, but where is he now?" Eliza meant business; you could hear the anger in her voice as she spoke. Apparently, the reply to her questions was met with high resistance and the mother of Toby, stated, "Ain't nothing he can do. "My son's going to college to be a doctor, and he ain't got no time for no babies." This outraged Eliza as she replied angrily and loudly, "You think my child has fewer dreams than yours? We set her to go to a university too and become a nurse, but no, your kid can't keep his pants zipped".

Then the magic words came flying out of Eliza's mouth, "My daughter deserves better than crumbs and we ain't having her tied down to your trifling son or your family. She will survive, and we will help her. Oh, and by the way, you tell your son, if he comes snooping around my house or daughter again, Horatio gonna shoot him, like the mangy dog that he is." Eliza slammed the phone down and sat in tears. Raven sat in tears on the other side of the door, neither one close enough to ease the others pain.

Eliza got up from her phone call and yelled for Horatio to come inside as he was working in the garden doing some chores for Eliza. Horatio walked inside, and Raven heard her parents pulling up chairs in their kitchen. Raven could not hear the discussion, but she knew it was about Toby and the fact that this was not what Raven's family wanted for her.

Two weeks passed by; the school was now out for the summer. Eliza and Horatio had contacted one of Horatio's friends from the town that was a registered nurse. Eliza came into Raven's room one day and told Raven, "We need to talk." Ever since Raven had found out she was expecting a baby, she had become seriously ill, she would stand up from a chair or get up from the bed in the morning, and she would collapse and pass out.

They had taken her to the physician, but the doctor had told Eliza and Horatio that the baby was taking all of Raven's blood supply and causing her blood pressure to drop dramatically each time she tried to stand up.

Eliza came into the room and sat on the edge of Raven's bed and said, "Your father and I have decided we want what is best for you. You are young, and you have your entire life ahead of you, and even though we know, you could have this baby and finish school and do great things. We have decided the best thing for everyone is to terminate this pregnancy". Raven sat straight up in bed and screamed, "NO, you can't do that." She pleaded with Eliza to let her prove she could have her baby and finish school and go to the university. Eliza responded to Raven by saying, "Raven, we have made up our minds, and this baby is making you very sick. Toby ain't handling a man's job, so your daddy and I have gotten in touch with a family friend, and he will be here in the morning to carry us to the location for the procedure."

Raven fell back in the bed and screamed with all of her might, "This is my baby, and I want my baby, you can't do this, you just can't." Ravens screams for mercy went unheard and fell on to deaf ears. Horatio and Eliza had made the final decision for Raven. They would consider nothing she had to say. As night fell, Raven could hear Eliza and Horatio making plans for the long trip the next day, leaving Raven to wonder where they were taking her and why was it such as secret. Raven could not sleep that night because all she could think was, "This is my baby, and no one has the right to be able to take it from me."

As morning dawned a new day, Raven dressed for the trip. She heard a car arrive at six o'clock before the sun had risen. Since they lived in the country, she knew it was the car that would take her away. She also knew that when she returned home again, she would no longer have her baby. As everyone prepared to leave for the trip, Raven and Eliza got into the back seat, and both Horatio and the male driver got in the front seat, and they pulled out of the driveway.

Raven expected to be at the location soon because she thought it would be in the town close to her. She was in for a shock as the drive would take four hours. They made the long drive with only the men in the front seat talking. Raven sat in the back seat with Eliza, staring out the side window, watching all the houses and things she passed as tears trailed their way down her young cheeks. She was feeling a pain in her heart that would live far longer than anyone could imagine. Her parents did not realize that their decision would scar her for life.

As Raven traveled, she realized the dreams she had been having all these months, had led to this moment. The images she saw in her dreams, now made sense. The church represented her religious upbringing. The coffin she would see herself in, described the death of her spirit as this event unfolds. The car, yes, the car she always saw in her dreams, that was parked in the church parking lot, by the front door while sitting at an angle, was the car that would take her away to this event. Eliza seated in the driver's seat of the car would be her mother taking part in this, but the hand she always saw reaching through the window of the car and grabbing her around her throat in a chokehold was a woman's hand, and now it made sense, her mother would play a role in the extermination of her unborn baby. To Raven, it meant taking another's life. How did Raven pre-see these things? How did she know in advance about the death of her baby and her own soul?

Was Raven born with a gift, or was this gift part of a curse? She tried desperately to figure this all out as they took the long drive to her appointment. Once the car arrived everyone got out except the driver, and they all walked into this clinic that seemed to have only strangers from all walks of life, but very few that appeared to be Raven's age. Soon after the arrival to the clinic they called Raven's name, Horatio never moved out of his seat, but Eliza took Raven and walked her to the door. They would not allow Eliza to come beyond the door for sanitary reasons and a woman took Raven's hand and told Eliza, "We gonna take good care of her," as she escorted Raven to her fate.

The nurse led Raven to the operation room and had her change clothes to a gown. They assisted Raven on the procedure table, and tears ran steadily down her face. She was frightened, ashamed, upset, and shaking.

The doctor seemed so uncaring as he told Raven," This gonna be over before ya know it. Just relax." It was like he was giving Raven a shot and that was it. Relax, but who could relax? What was about to occur was fifteen different flavors of wrong. Who could relax knowing they were about to kill her unborn baby? Relax Raven thought, what a joke. As the doctor began the procedure, Raven felt a painful tugging at her tummy, more pain than one could imagine and it seemed to go on for an hour, but within thirty minutes, it was all over.

Later they took Raven back to the lobby with her parents and told them," It's a done deal." Take her home, and she will be weak for a couple of weeks, but she will live." Raven was still teary-eyed as they left the clinic minus one person, her unborn baby. Her young heart sank, as she tried to wrap her head around what her parents had just done to her. As she got into the car to leave, the only statement Raven said, and she wanted to make it clear to all parties was this, "You killed a human being." "Y'all going to hell and you making me go with you. You killed my baby. I wanted my baby; I wanted my baby."

Horatio turned around in the car and said, "Hush Raven, you don't know what you talking about." Raven sank into her back seat in pain and cried herself to sleep as the long journey home began. Once they arrived back to her hometown, it was nighttime, and Eliza helped Raven to bed, but Horatio, feeling full of guilt, decided to go into town to play cards. Raven crawled into bed, and Eliza sat by her side most of the night.

About three o'clock in the morning, Horatio was still not back home, and Eliza had fallen to sleep sitting by her daughters' side. When she woke to check the time, she noticed Raven was sweating profusely and shaking uncontrollably as she mumbled in her sleep. Eliza jumped up to checked Raven's temperature. Raven was running a fever of 104 degrees by now. Raven mumbled that she wanted a pink coffin with native American attire for her services, but what in the world was this about? Eliza realized Raven had gotten some type of infection and she immediately ran to the phone to find Horatio. She called every number she had, but no one knew where he was. Then she called her sister who lived in town and told them, "Find Horatio, Raven is bad sick, and we need to get her to a hospital fast."

It took time, but they found Horatio at an unnamed woman's house, and he was playing, but it was not cards. They told him of his daughter's condition, and he rushed home as soon as he could. The car pulled into the driveway, and Horatio raced inside only to meet Eliza at the door carrying Raven in her arms. Horatio grabbed his daughter from Eliza's arms and laid her on the backseat of the car, and they raced to the closest hospital.

Raven survived that night, Eliza and Horatio were grateful to the doctors that saved their daughter. They all learned that night that the doctor that Horatio's friend picked to do the procedure was a quack doctor and had his license removed and Raven had contracted a blood infection that almost took her life.

Dallas P Elkheart

PART V: Fight or Flight

Episode XV: She's No Baby!!!

Many things changed for Raven, several months after the life-altering decision that Eliza and Horatio made for Raven, and after she was able to overcome a near-death experience. One thing that did not change was Toby Johnston. Toby wanted Raven more than ever now, and Horatio and Eliza wanted nothing to do with him or his family. They certainly wanted him to have nothing further to do with their daughter. A confused Raven wanted to see Toby still. She pled her case with Eliza, and Eliza spoke to Horatio about it, and somehow, they allowed her to go back to talking to Toby.

Toby had his prom, and he had asked Raven to go with him. She went with him even after everything that had happened. What Eliza and Horatio did not know was, Toby was now beating on Raven every chance he could. If he were mad at his family, his friends, from school or even about something Raven said, he would slap her and hard. Raven was still stuck on stupid over this boy and would not listen to a thing Horatio nor Eliza had to say about him.

Toby came to pick up Raven the night of the prom and without realizing it, she had her hands full again. Toby got as far as to town, and just as they were approaching his school to attend the prom, he pulled the car over onto the side of the road. He put the car in park and asked Raven if she knew that a certain boy liked her. Raven replied, "No, why?"

Toby reached over and slapped Raven with so much force, that her head hit the side window. For the first time, Raven stood up to Toby; she had now had enough of his abuse.

Tonight, was about to go really wrong, and the fact was, Raven had had enough of everyone's mistreatment of her. So, she jumped out of Toby's car and into the middle of the street. They were parked close to a library, and Raven went to make her way over to the library to call Eliza to come and pick her up, when Toby jumped in front of her and said, "You don't think you are just gonna walk away from me like that." Raven became infuriated at his snide remark and his possessiveness. She felt as if he had put her through enough. Raven pulled up her evening prom dress bearing her all-white high heel shoes and said, "Toby, I hate you," and she took her foot and kicked the window of Toby's car. He was furious, and he grabbed Raven.

As they began to struggle in the middle of the road while wearing a tuxedo and evening gown, a man driving a wrecking company automobile saw the disturbance. He was headed to pick up a stalled vehicle, and the man pulled his truck over. The driver got out of the car; he said: "Hey, you have no business hitting on this young woman, no real man does that." Toby's temper got the best of him, and he went to the car and pulled out a handgun.

Toby pointed the gun at Raven's head and said, "She's mine, and nobody tells me how to treat what's mine." Raven screamed, and the older man jumped in front of Raven and pushed her to the side and then behind him and said," Young man if you shoot her, you got to kill me to get her."

Under his breath, he said to Raven, "get in the car, get in the car, right now." Raven fearing for her life and the man's life, got in the tow truck. Toby did not know how to respond to it all.

Toby dropped the handgun to his side and jumped in his car and took off. The older gentlemen asked Raven, "Young lady, are you ok? Where do you live?" Raven told the man, "I'm' ok. Can you take me to my aunt's house, my mother will come to pick me up?" The older man did just that, and Eliza was called to go and pick up her frightened daughter. Raven never got to attend a prom, not even her own.

Toby refused to let Raven go. He was obsessed with Raven by now and snuck around to see her whenever he could. Raven and Horatio's relationship was even more estranged as Raven became Horatio's outlet for anger. No matter who he seemed to be mad with, Raven took the brunt of the blow, either by words, put-downs or worse. He became extremely violent to Raven and her mother. Horatio was verbally abusing those that should have been the closest to him.

If he came in from work and something had happened at his job, all it took was Raven to say the wrong word and Horatio would unleash his wrath on her, leaving Eliza to fend for Raven, creating an unsafe environment for herself.

This only pushed Raven closer to her controlling and obsessed boyfriend who seemed to enjoy seeing Horatio unleash his anger upon his own family. This made it so simple for him to step in as the good guy, and it made it seem as if he was the right guy to Raven. Raven began to sneak off to see him, even though Eliza felt as if it caught her in the middle of things.

Raven's school soon started back again, and Raven was now beginning the tenth grade. She had developed only two close friends throughout all her years in school, and she formed a tight bond with these two young ladies Megan Harrison and Jasmine Graham.

Both friends came from two different backgrounds, yet, they were the only ones Raven trusted. Much like Raven, Jasmine found much abuse from the kids at school and her family, and this bonded her and Raven close. Megan, on the other hand, did not live too far from Raven and they grew up together.

Everyone still rejected Raven at school and made fun of her because for some, her complexion was too light, and for others, it was too dark. Therefore, she found herself always alone, except for the two young ladies that seemed to accept her for who she was.

Bronze Bloodline of the Phoenix

Other children in school always made her feel less than human, and Raven suffered from self-esteem problems because of it.

Raven was picked on by the kids at her school for several reasons. Sometimes it was because of her lengthy hair, the way she looked, the way her mother fussed over her, the way she walked or about the way she spoke. No matter how hard Raven tried to fit in, she just did not seem to fit and could never please the girls at her school.

One could quickly tell Raven differed from other children in her school, and even she knew, she was. Raven always felt unwanted at parties and events and still was left out of most community events sponsored by other children or their parents.

Even against the odds, Raven Reese was turning to things that made her feel like she had value in the world, such as her piano, band and now she had entered beauty contests in her city. Meanwhile, things started to go from bad to worse between her and Horatio. One day Raven had come home from school early. With the upcoming holidays, the students were let out of school almost three hours before most local parents finished work. Raven came in from school around noon that day, and she remembered she had a band contest that upcoming weekend. She also wanted to try out for majorette at her high school even though no females of color would ever make the team, whether cheerleader, majorette or drum major, it was not allowed at her high school. Raven was still hell-bent on trying, anyway.

She came home and started to practice a tryout routine, where she would learn to twirl her baton, and as she stood in her mirror in her bedroom practicing twirling, she did not realize Horatio had arrived home.

Eliza was getting in herself, and as Eliza opened the door to come in, she yelled out, "I'm home, everybody." This distracted Raven as she tossed the baton up into the air in a twirling spin and to make it even worse, Horatio was coming down the hallway as the stick was about to land. Raven could not move fast enough to stop the twirling metal baton as it fell and as luck would have it, Horatio entered Raven's room just as it landed.

Oh boy, did it land, it landed right on Horatio's head, right across the top of his head and down into the bridge of his nose and this made him go berserk! He just knew Raven had to have done this on purpose and he flew into a stark raging fit.

Before anyone knew it, Horatio grabbed Raven by her throat and threw her across her bed and began to choke her, screaming, "You Bitch, You Bitch. You did that shit on purpose." Raven was now gasping for air as she tried to tell Horatio it was an accident.

Eliza heard the commotion and ran to Raven's room, and as she entered the door, she realized Horatio had choked her daughter so hard, she was losing consciousness. Eliza screamed, "Lord have mercy, let her go, Horatio, let her go, you killing my baby, let her go." But Horatio looked as if he had turned into a demon.

He had a glazed look in his eyes, with an almost wild look on his face.

Horatio could hear nothing that anyone was saying as he tightened his grip around Raven's neck. Eliza realized he had snapped and knew the only way to release his grip was for her to throw her body full force onto Horatio and remove his hands herself.

She came at Horatio with full force, as any mother would do. Eliza reached out, and with all her might, she fell into Horatio and tried to pull him off Raven, but Horatio was so angry with Raven he threw Eliza across the room, without releasing his grip on Raven's throat. Eliza landed in the corner of the room on the floor. Stumbling to her feet, she reached for her daughter as she realized Raven was unconscious.

Perhaps, Horatio released his death grip on Raven's throat because, he realized that his anger had created a situation where he lost control, and his overreaction may have injured or killed not one, but both women in his life. Eliza grabbed the teenager up and ran out the door to the car to save her child. Eliza took Raven's lifeless body and laid it across the backseat of the car, and to the emergency room, Eliza flew, driving well above the speed limit.

After administering emergency attention to Raven at the hospital, the doctors realized they would need to perform emergency surgery on Raven's throat to repair the damage caused by Horatio. Raven had survived yet another attack on her body, which put her into a total depression that would take her years to learn to deal with.

Once Raven healed from her surgery, she was more than ever determined to find happiness somewhere in her world, but unfortunately, Toby Johnston had stood idly by waiting for this moment.

Raven was now sneaking to see Toby every chance she could, even though he too was now verbally and physically just as abusive as her father was, so Raven had to pick between, bad and worse, not realizing Toby was probably the worst of the two. One day Raven began to receive odd phone calls, and these calls were coming from a young lady in the nearby town of Rochester, Mississippi. Each day after school, the young lady would call Raven and threaten to harm her or Raven's mother, because of Toby Johnston.

Toby Johnston could not see Raven as much as he wanted. Horatio and Eliza had put their foot down and tried to end the relationship, and it was with good reason. Toby was cheating on Raven, and he had gotten himself a girl on the side, because, he knew Raven's family would never allow him to have Raven outright. Toby seemed to take the girls threats against Raven seriously, so, he went to his older brother and inquired about a gun to protect Raven. Even though Toby knew who this young lady was. He also knew what the girl wanted and why she wanted to fight Raven. He pretended to be extremely concerned for Raven's safety. To Toby, Raven was ant bait compared to the girl he had become involved with.

He never bothered to tell Raven, that he even knew who the young lady was and what type of background the young lady had.

This young lady was Julia Jenkins, and she ran with a well-known gang in her hometown; her sister Lori Jenkins was her sidekick. Raven was now almost sixteen years old and weighed all of 110 pounds soaking wet. Raven always watched her weight. She had a part-time job at a local general store and was active in music and band which kept her weight under control. The young lady in question was very stocky built and weighed about two hundred and twenty pounds. The two young gang members physically outweighed Raven by two to one, which gave weight to Toby's worry about Raven's safety.

Horatio had heard about this young lady and her gang members. He did not realize his daughter would fall victim to manipulation based on hidden agendas. He was so strict on his daughter; he had hoped she would never involve herself with these types of people.

Toby and Raven met secretly one night and rode together into town to a local park where all the neighborhood kids hung out on the weekends. Before heading out for the evening and picking Raven up from work, Toby loaded his .38 snub-nosed gun. He placed it under his driver's seat, thinking that perhaps, just perhaps, there might be trouble.

Raven would not have to go looking for that trouble because that very night, that trouble would find Raven. As Toby and Raven pulled up to a stop sign; two large females approached the car. Ravens window was partially cracked, and both females made their way to the passenger side of the vehicle where Raven was sitting.

The older girl, Julia, had a nickname on the streets, and most gang members called her Baby-Cakes. As Baby-Cakes and her sister Lori made their way to Raven's window, the older girl grabbed the window and tried to pull it down and told Raven, "Get out of the car." This startled Raven, and it terrified her as she had never had to fight two people at one time.

Bronze Bloodline of the Phoenix

Toby told Raven not to get out of the car, but before Toby got out of the car himself, he laid the gun in between the seats on the console of the vehicle. Toby stepped out to address the two females, telling them to leave Raven out of this. Before he could finish speaking, the sister Lori grabbed Toby and took him to the ground. Baby-Cakes joined in and began to kick Toby repeatedly in the head, face, and torso. Raven was screaming as she did not know what to do, and she knew she would have no strength to take on these two females.

Raven could hear Toby screaming for his life. Not being very smart about it, Raven thought she had to help him because she just knew he would help her. That was the biggest mistake Raven would ever make. Why might one ask?

It was because, as she got out of the car, the fight had become so violent, numbers of people had stopped what they were doing, came out of the park building, out of the corner store and stopped along the walkway to watch. No one appeared to help Toby. Raven decided she had to break up the fight. But how? Raven looked around for a stick, an object, anything to use to stop the beating from occurring and then she saw it.

She saw the gun laying in between the seats, and she thought, the gun was heavy, she could use it to hit one girl and possibly distract them, but this would prove to be a horrible idea. What Raven did not know was that, before Toby had laid the gun between the seats, he had engaged the hammer of the firearm, and it was now locked and loaded. Raven did not know as much as she thought about weapons. Horatio had taught her how to use an A5 Browning Sweet Sixteen and a military assault rifle, both of which were used for hunting. She knew nothing about a .38 snub-nose revolver which was mostly used for personal protection and this one had a hair-trigger. Raven only knew she needed to help this young man before someone got killed.

One thing most people know, and that is, GOD looks after babies and fools, and Raven was no baby. She grabbed the gun and took the butt of the gun while trying to swing it at the bigger and older female, hoping that it might distract her so that Toby could crawl away to safety. Instead, the moment she swung the gun at the older girl, a shot rang out.

Everything went extremely quiet, "You shot my sister," Lori screamed. Raven went into shock. She looked around and saw a female laying on the ground. She didn't look for Toby to see if he was ok. She ran back to the car, laid the gun on the seat, and ran over to the female lying on the ground, who was Julia (aka) Babycakes. She got down on both knees and picked the older girls head up from the ground. Babycakes had on a white t-shirt, and every breath that she took caused blood to gush out in massive amounts.

As she held the girl's head in her arms, trying to stop the bleeding, she sobbed. Raven cried, "I am so sorry, I am so very sorry. I never wanted to hurt you. I did not mean to hurt anyone. I am so sorry. I was only trying to stop the fight, Oh GOD, what have I done?" By now, the police were arriving and so was an ambulance. They took Raven to the police station as if she was a villain.

The officers were kind, and they told Raven in the car that they did not believe she could harm anyone since her personality seemed so sweet and they could tell she did not mean to do it. Toby had successfully and single-handedly destroyed Raven's world and shattered Horatio and Eliza's dreams for their daughter. Not only did he get her pregnant, beat and abuse her relentlessly, but now, she might face a possible involuntary manslaughter charge, especially, if Babycakes died.

Raven who thought she was doing the right thing, but she was only digging herself in further and further with this boy Toby.

God must have had other plans for Raven because it looked as if he had sent one of his special angels so that they could watch over his young fool of a child. What Raven did not know was that the one bullet had actually hit Lori in the arm, passed through her arm and then struck Babycakes in the chest, only missing her heart by one inch. By the time Raven had gotten to the police station, Eliza and Horatio were there. The officer came in and sat down to ask Raven what had happened. He looked at Raven and said, "You must be a hell of a marksman because that one bullet hit both sisters in one shot." Raven broke down and kept saying, "I did not mean to do it; it was an accident. I only wanted to stop them from hurting Toby." That night they granted Raven permission to go home with her parents. Everyone was disappointed in Raven, but no one was more disappointed than Raven herself. She hated herself at this point for not listening to her parents about this boy.

Several days went by, Eliza received a phone call from the police station asking her if her daughter had been making calls to the hospital, but she replied, "No. She is on strict watch, and we do not allow her to use the phone." The reason the police wanted to know if Raven had made calls is, that Julia Baby-Cakes Jenkins was receiving hundreds of calls from people saying to her, it served her right, and they hoped she died. Apparently, Raven had not been Baby-Cake's only victim. Many others feared her intimidation, and she had already made a nasty name for herself in town. In the meantime, Horatio had had enough of Toby. He and Eliza hired a private investigator to find out the goods on Toby and the two females before Raven's court date. By Raven's court date, the community had finally rallied around Raven and her family.

Her parents had received numerous letters from church members, teachers, and other people of political status, stating that Raven had never been in trouble and would have never tried to harm someone unless they threatened her or as a means of self-defense.

On the date of court and right before court began, Raven's lawyer, entered the courtroom to speak with Raven and her family one final time before the hearing.

He had breaking news. The attorney had received his special investigation report back from the private investigator.

They had put Toby and his family under surveillance, and what came back was horrendous to all. Toby Johnston had set Raven up, that's right. He had set her up for the kill (no pun intended). The private investigator followed Toby for over three months and found that he had been secretly seeing Julia 'Baby-Cakes" Jenkins when he could not see Raven. Toby had told Julia that she was, in fact, his lady and that, Raven was an unwanted and unwelcome female that would not leave him alone.

This caused Julia "Baby-Cakes" to see Raven as her rival, and she was determined to remove any competition. The problem was that Raven knew none of this.

It was also found that Toby had requested his older brother to get the gun so he could keep it in his car, knowing that Raven would eventually be exposed to this weapon and possibly forced to defend herself.

Right before the hearing was about to take place, the two sisters' attorney approached Raven's attorney and asked Horatio, if he considered giving their family five thousand dollars, they would forget any of this ever happened.

The fact was, all they wanted was a small payoff because to go into the courtroom, it would bring much out into the open, and they needed to keep things quiet.

Horatio agreed, and they put Raven on probation for one year. She needed to finish school, stay out of trouble, and stop seeing Toby. This was the deal the courts made for her probation, and by now, Raven hated Toby with everything in her. She finally could see what everyone else saw, that he was a creep that destroyed her life, and she wanted nothing more to do with him. Oh, for the record, the sisters did live, but this incident did not slow them down. They continued to terrorize the community. Raven went home with Eliza that day, and she was more than ever determined to become a respectable young woman.

Episode XVI: Loud and Clear

Raven Reese was growing up, but through it all, she was still lonely. She so desperately needed her father's love, acceptance, and approval. Eliza always supported her daughter, gave her continuous compliments about her intelligence, looks, and personality, although it never seemed to be enough for Raven. Somehow, it was as if she needed to hear those three little words from Horatio, and everything could become whole again, but those three little words would never come soon enough. The three words that could have saved Raven from herself were: *I love you*. While not hard words to say, Horatio was never the type of man that could or would use them.

Horatio believed money, power, and name were all anyone needed to know they were loved, but not Raven. These things to Raven were only facades, and she knew none of these things would ever mean anything to anyone without true love from the heart. Raven learned to move on and could not wait to get out from under Horatio's dictatorship style rules. Raven had become quite close to a cousin of hers. This cousin lived in the next town. One day Raven was changing clothes to go to a family reunion while her cousin was there and when she came back to the room, her cousin commented to her.

He said, "Wow Raven, you really should think about becoming a model because you got the curves, the walk, and the look and I would think about it if I were you."

Raven smiled and shrugged her shoulders and said, "I am not model material." But her cousin insisted she was. She kept that in mind, but never took it seriously, and they all headed off to the family gathering.

What Raven did not know was, her cousin had predicted a career path for Raven that would come true some months later.

As time passed, Raven finished high school, but not without drama following her. Three weeks before her graduation was scheduled to occur; an incident would befall her. It almost derailed her graduation day. This time it had nothing to do with Toby Johnston. Raven went to one of her evening classes, and she and a young man at school had eyes for each other. There seemed to be a chemistry between the two of them that was obvious to onlookers. As she headed to her evening class, the young man that had eyes for her, passed her in the hallway and they made eye contact. However, he had a girlfriend that saw the eye contact take place. The problem was that different races and cultures did not mix. In the dirty south, this would be a cause for a race riot, and everyone tried to avoid it. Raven had never seen things the same way as others.

Raven moved to her locker to retrieve her class book before the bell rang. As she turned around to head to class, the young lady who saw the eye contact stopped her. It happened to be the same one who proclaimed the young man as her own.

She accused Raven and said, "I hear you like, Devin." Raven responded in a very nonchalant way, "Who wants to know?" Then Raven replied, "I think you should ask him." That set things into motion, the young lady that claimed Devin, had three other girls with her, so this gave her the courage to test Raven, and she pushed Raven into the locker. The coat hook caught Raven in the back. The pain unleashed a fury in Raven that resembled Satan; Raven had been abused all her life, but today, the world would see a new Raven, and she would no longer stand idly by and accept abuse and certainly not from this young lady. Raven's temper took over, and she struck the young lady in the face with a fist. This was the beginning of a horrible discord.

One's race had always been a severe issue at the school where she attended. Even though the schools were now integrated through mandate; the unfortunate thing about it was each culture stuck together and did not mix. Now you had four people fighting in the hallway from two different cultures; the young girl's friends tried to help her.

Perhaps everyone heard the ruckus and came in to see what was happening. Either way, before Raven knew it, both races had clashed, right there in the middle of the hallway and a full course all-out race riot had begun. Raven was still in the middle of her entanglement with the three young ladies in the hall where all of this started. This was when she heard the intercom as the high school principal made an emergency call to all teachers. He said, "All high school teachers to the hallway. We have a riot on our hands".

They expelled twelve high school students, including Raven. It looked like Raven had struck out again in life. Eliza and Horatio were furious with her about the incident. Raven should never have struck the girl back. Eliza tried to instill in Raven that if someone strikes one on the left cheek, one should then turn and give them the right cheek because of her religious beliefs.

Raven had a different spin on the whole thing. She believed if someone strikes either cheek, let them have it full blast, on any cheek. Raven did not realize it, but all the abuse that she had lived through, had turned her into an anger machine and made her very short-tempered. She went from never defending herself, to feeling like she needed to protect herself from everyone.

Somehow the things that Raven had lived through were changing her perception on the way she should handle situations. She believed that if she had defended herself from other people she met in her life, things would have been different for her.

They suspended Raven for three days, and she could not return to the campus until graduation night, but on graduation night, she did just that; she returned and walked the walk with her senior class.

As Raven heard her name called to receive her diploma, she walked up to the stage, and as she was accepting her diploma and a customary handshake, she was relieved that it was finally all over.

She was sure that many thought she would never make it that far. Ah, but she did. She was relieved that her school years were done and her years as a victim would soon be over, or at least, so she thought. But this would be far from the truth, as life had a few surprises left for young Raven.

Dallas P Elkheart

Episode XVII: A Million Pieces

After completing high school, things got better for Raven, as she could now take on a full-time job, working in the nearby town. Horatio wanted Raven to go into the military as her grandfather, mother, and he had done. Horatio offered to build Raven a large home on their property and told her she could build any home she wanted, all she had to do was live in the house once it was built. Raven had other ideas and wanted to see what the world could be like without the restraints of Horatio and his mean temper along with his foul insults on her and her mother. She loved her parents very much. Raven, needed to find peace in her life and a part of her still wondered, who was she really? What she really needed was the freedom to discover who she was. What made her tick? Her most significant factor was to piece together her life as a human being despite everything that she had been through since she came into the world.

Raven thought she was cursed because no matter how hard she tried to do all the right things, somehow everything she touched crumbled in her hands. She was still suffering from depression, and it would sometimes overpower her as she would look in the mirror and become unhappy. The depression would come, and it was not based on her looks, but from not being able to control her life, find peace, and make things run smoothly. She just did not know how to achieve two things in her life, which were her peace of mind and spiritual fulfillment, and this made her very moody. She eventually moved into town.

There, she would have conveniences not offered in the country to include many things she had been missing in her childhood. She missed the chance while growing up to go to movies with friends. Horatio took Raven to two films that she remembered in her lifetime. She also missed out on meeting new people and social interaction.

Raven also wanted to be able to have a choice of where she would be employed since mostly only factory jobs existed in her neck of the woods. Horatio had tried to limit Raven's opportunities from running all over the place, so she could not go to many places in town. After all, she might catch wind of his sordid affairs that he was having with numerous women while still married to Eliza. A lot had now changed, as Raven was now all grown up and she was about to be roaming in his playground.

Opportunities began to open for Raven, and she was offered a modeling position with a local company called Honey, Honey, and Rhythm. She seemed to have found something she was good at, as her cousin had previously mentioned to her during her high school years. She traveled with a group and grew very close to the coordinator of the group. She felt she was now on the right track to life and happiness. While modeling, she got many chances to show her talent as a swimsuit and clothing model. Raven felt as if she came from the 1950s almost a Deja Vu type thing, so she did quite well in her new career, that is until she met a young man by the name of Noah Evans.

Noah Evans came from a reputable family, and the family embraced Raven, especially Noah's mother. His mother had lost a daughter, and she had the same name as Raven. Raven even looked a lot like Noah's mother, so she was a good fit into the existing family structure. Raven's parents had helped her to get a car that seemed to fit Raven's personality. Raven, needed speed, and she ended up with a sporty race car, that was as exotic as she was.

On the first day that Raven met Noah, he told her that he was going to marry her, but she laughed because she thought to herself, "Silly boy, I just met you."

Noah knew something Raven did not know and against everybody's opinion, and her better judgment, she did just what he wanted. Three months later Raven Reese became Mrs. Raven Evans. Things seemed to go well, and she adored her new family. Her and Horatio's relationship seemed to get somewhat better, and Raven loved having Eliza come over to spend time together, and this caused them to get even closer.

Raven was quite proud to be Noah's wife and part of his family, that is until the first fists flew, three months after they were married. Raven and Noah had a quaint apartment they now lived in, and she was taking a bath one afternoon when Noah went on a complete rampage over a friend of his that had made eyes at Raven the previous evening.

Raven denied seeing such activity in her presence and told Noah that he was really paranoid of his own friends. He should know her better than that. Raven stepped out of the tub to dry off, Noah flew down the hallway, and suddenly, Noah hit Raven in the face so hard that it knocked her backward and she landed in the tub flat on her back.

As Raven stood up and realized she was bleeding from both mouth and nose, Noah picked up his jacket and walked out of the door, leaving her to recover from the bruises and pain all alone. As time went on, the beatings became more and more intense. Raven, once again, found herself under the thumbprint of another abusive man. She was hardworking, and her in-laws had been kind enough to give her and Noah a building. She had come up with the idea of a business. Raven and Noah quickly took an empty building and turned it into a thriving business; a community center for young kids. She also took on three part-time jobs while she and Noah ran the business.

Raven, much like her father wanted to become successful and respected in her community, and she loved people and making them happy.

Their marriage continued, and she held down the business venture and her part-time jobs. The lack of taking care of herself as she took on numerous missions, created a cocktail of lousy health problems. One of which would show its ugly face and soon. That night, as she left her business to go to her night job, forty-five minutes away, she realized that she had not eaten in almost three days and felt a bit weak.

Raven had gone days without food and was living on coffee, soda, and tea, not because she was on a diet, but because she wasn't taking care of herself. Once she arrived at her job, she began her regular 10 pm to 7 am shift. She had landed a position in the ob-gyn department at the hospital and sometimes worked the nursery, it was right up Raven's alley.

She remembered what it was like to be an expectant mother and tried to show empathy for the mothers-to-be. Raven adored children and enjoyed the nights that she found herself on the shift in the nursery. Besides, she wanted to go to nursing school to become a registered nurse.

She had no idea tonight would change many things in her life and send her spiraling into a whole new direction. As she was taking a nebulizer machine in her hand to one of her assigned patients that night, she began to feel lightheaded. As she approached the patient's door, she passed one of the on-duty physicians and gave him one of her more infamous smiles and hellos. Just as she passed him, it happened. Raven began to shake uncontrollably dropping the machine she'd held so tightly onto the hospital floor before she fell to the ground, right behind it.

The on-call doctor immediately pivoted and bolted towards Raven. He yelled for help from the staff on duty.

Hospital staff carried Raven to a nearby nurses' station where the on-call doctor administered assistance. Raven woke shortly afterward with a look of bewilderment in her eyes, and she looked around as she asked, "What happened? Where am I?"

The doctor replied, "You are ok. You had a nervous breakdown in the hallway, just as you passed me, and I am glad someone was there for you". He went on to say, "You look like you're under a lot of stress, and this could be part of the problem. The doctor asked Raven if she was eating right, and Raven replied, "When I am hungry, but honestly, I am never hungry." He also told Raven that her body was malnourished. He said to Raven, "Young lady, I am sending you home for bed rest for four days, you can return to work after that."

Raven checked out from her job and headed home for the night, but she thought perhaps she should spend some time with a dear friend and relax over good conversation and cocktails, so she called her best friend, Megan Harrison. Raven and Megan had become inseparable and were close to each other's families since early childhood and were like two peas in a pod. The two of them agreed to meet at Raven's house in forty-five minutes, which was the time it took Raven to return to her home from work.

Megan was in Raven's driveway as Raven pulled up to park, which made Raven smile. With both of their busy schedules; they did not get to spend much time together, and this was a chance to catch up and get some laughs in. Raven shut off her car and jumped out as the two girls met in the yard greeting each other.

Raven opened the front door; they flipped on the light and sat down for a moment before deciding how they would spend the evening. Noah was supposed to be working at the family business, or so Raven thought.

The two girls sat down on the couch, and Megan made a statement to Raven that halted everything. Megan commented, "Wow, them some cute Nike shoes you got there." This remark stumped Raven because, for one, she still had on her hospital uniform with hospital-style white nursing shoes on and for two, she said to Megan, "Nikes? Girl I don't wear Nikes, I wear Adidas".

Megan reached down underneath the edge of the couch, where they were sitting and pulled out a pair of size six Nike sneakers. Raven snatched the shoes out of Megan's hands and said, "What the hell is this? I don't wear a size six. I wear a size eight, and I don't wear Nikes, I wear Adidas". Megan looked as if a brick had hit her and Raven became enraged as the two girls looked at each other, and Megan gave Raven the eye. The eye was a look that said, 'Let's go and see,' without one word being spoken between the two girls.

Raven jumped up and led the way as both girls crept up the hallway, searching each room, room by room until Raven reached her bedroom. Yes, the bedroom that Noah and Raven shared as husband and wife. What she would see, she was not ready for. As Raven reached her bedroom door, the door was slightly ajar, leaving just enough room to see inside the room without having to open the door and what Raven saw was appalling.

She saw Noah in their bed, but he was not alone. In fact, he had his first cousin in bed with him, and both parties appeared to be engaged into a full sexual bliss, not realizing Raven, and now Megan, was standing in the doorway.

Raven cleared her throat, to attract the attention of the forbidden love that was taking place in her bed. Noah quickly turned his head and, wow and behold; he saw not only Raven but Megan standing in the bedroom's door with a look that could have killed. Raven yelled, "How could you? After all, you have done to me, now this."

Megan tried to control Raven by grabbing her arm and saying, "Oh my god, girl, let's go." Raven would not hear of it.

There were things Raven needed to say, and she was going to be heard. No one, nor nothing would be able to stop her this time. Right before Raven could spout her anger, Noah jumped out of bed. Raven saw him lunging towards her to grab her before she walked away. The girls quickly turned and exited down the hallway, with Noah running behind Raven in nothing more than his glory, not even a pair of underwear, as he pled his case to Raven, "Raven, you don't understand. I can explain,".

This set Raven off, and she stopped just short of the fireplace, near where they had just found the pair of size six Nike sneakers.

Noah and Raven reached it simultaneously. He grabbed her arm, spinning her in an about-face position. Raven yelled, "You son of a bitch! Let my arm go." And Noah said, "But baby, I can explain." Without thinking, she reached to the mantelpiece, on the fireplace. On this mantelpiece sat a trophy that Noah had won for the man of the year award. In Raven's eyes, and at that moment he was anything but a man of the year, despite his typical charm and good looks.

She grabbed the trophy, and before she knew it, she smacked him hard while saying, "The only talking you can do, is to my attorney. Don't call him; he'll be calling you because I am so done".

Bronze Bloodline of the Phoenix

For the record, the blow Raven landed on Noah went right across his shoulder blade as she turned and walked away. The following day, Raven came back, packed all her things up to leave and did so. She called Eliza to tell her what happened and that she had just left Noah, but to her surprise, Eliza replied, "Yep, I totally understand because I just left Horatio, too." Instead of being shocked at the fact that her parents were now no longer together, both, Raven and Eliza laughed, and Raven stated, "Geeze, what took you so long?" Eliza replied, "I guess I was waiting for you," as she laughed. Eliza made the statement, "If I only knew then, what I know now, I would have left your father years ago." An issue that should have had both mother and daughter in total tears now became the one thing that they bonded over. Eliza moved out the next day to her own place, and Raven decided that this would be an excellent time to get into nursing school.

The mother and daughter that had lived through hell together had now become so bonded, that nothing but death would separate them at this point. Sometimes, fate can play a dirty trick.

After Raven separated from Noah and Eliza left from Horatio, a new life began for them both. Raven still had vivid and reoccurring dreams of her mother, in a bronze-colored coffin. The fact was that Raven had now progressed from dreams to night terrors.

But the real terror for Raven was just starting. Raven and Horatio had now become more at odds than ever before. Raven felt that her father had driven Eliza away from him after forty years of marriage. She wanted answers, and she would get to the bottom of it. In the meantime, Raven had moved away from the city where she and Noah had lived.

Their divorce not yet final, Raven had begun a new life in Rockford, Tennessee. Rockford was an excellent place to start fresh in Raven's opinion. It had numerous hospitals and medical training and a University that she felt would be advantageous to her career choice as a registered nurse.

Things were finally coming together for Raven, and her life was finally on the right track. However, one day, Raven called Eliza to chat with her. As she heard her mother's voice on the phone, it did not sound the same. Raven could barely hear her voice, and it sounded like Eliza was sleeping. Raven asked her mother, Mama, are you okay?

A weak and timid voice replied, "Yeah, baby, I'm okay, "but Raven knew her mother, and she knew her well enough to know, something was wrong. Without a goodbye, Raven, told Eliza, "Mama, I'm on my way home. I'll be there in less than an hour."

The one-hour trip Raven mentioned was generally around a one hour and forty-five minutes' drive time, but as soon as Raven got off the phone, she called Megan and explained, "Meg, something is wrong with mama, and I'm on my way home. "Meet me at her house."

Raven walked out of her job without as much as a goodbye to anyone, didn't stop at home to pack even, and jumped in her sports car and down the highway, she went. Raven needed the actual speed from her sports car now, because, to her, this was a life or death situation. Raven pushed the pedal down to the floor, hitting speeds of one hundred plus miles an hour. Thank goodness it was a straight highway with plenty of flatlands around. As Raven arrived at Eliza's house, she saw that Megan was already there in the driveway waiting for her.

Both girls jumped out of the car and headed to the front door to knock, but to no avail. No one answered, yet Eliza's car was in the driveway. Raven told Meg, "You go to the windows on the left side of the house, and I will go to them on this side of the house and see if we can find mama. Megan agreed, and as the girls went to turn around to see if they could find Eliza, the door creaked open.

They stopped, and what they saw was frightening. Eliza had always been a large and tall woman weighing around 320 pounds of curvy, solid but healthy, woman. The woman that answered the door was all of 90 pounds soaking wet, and so fragile that she could not hold herself up. Raven jerked the screen door open and grabbed Eliza, putting her in her arms to pick her up, and the girls made their way into the house.

Raven carried Eliza to her bedroom, Eliza was extremely weak, and Raven was extremely emotional. Raven could hardly believe her eyes. She told Megan, "Call 911 now," and then as she laid her mother in the bed, she realized her mother had soiled herself. Raven could not contain her tears, as she scrambled to gather soap and water, to wash her mothers' body and put her some clean clothes on as Eliza had done for Raven for so many years.

The ambulance arrived and took Eliza off to the emergency room as Raven followed in her car. What Raven was about to find out that day would change her heart and the way she would perceive people or trust them. They admitted Eliza to the hospital in the city where Noah still lived. Noah and Raven were still legally married but separated at this point. At the hospital, Raven sat in the waiting room along with Eliza's two sisters Kay and Ilene, Raven's aunts.

The doctors came out to speak to the family, and Raven noticed there was one doctor that spotted her out of the crowd. He walked over and asked Raven if he could talk with her briefly. He explained to Raven, "We have seven doctors working with your mother, and none of us can seem to find a thing wrong with her." He then told Raven the most shocking thing in the world to a teenager, which was, "I will say to you, the best thing to do is to take your mother to a two-headed doctor, and he might fix this thing."

Raven stood there dumbstruck because she had actually heard of such a thing, but never, ever used one or dealt with anyone who used one.

A two-headed doctor or root doctor is more commonly known in southern witchcraft, and they practice hoodoo based on a system of pure magical doings. Raven did not believe in such things, even though she had heard Horatio mention it many times during her childhood. The doctor told Raven someone that knew about this stuff was responsible, and it would take someone that knew about this stuff to fix it.

Raven stood as still as a zombie herself as she tried to wrap her head around this piece of information. She asked the doctor what they were about to do with her mother now. The doctor told her they were about to take her mother to surgery, and it would be a while before she could see her. Raven said to the doctors that she would run to the store up the street, grab gas and a change of clothes really quickly at her x-husband's house and head back. The doctor told her that was good since she could not see Eliza until she went into recovery.

She thought that she would first run to the store then head over quickly to Noah's. As she pulled into the gas station and got out of her car, she saw Noah. Noah had overheard Raven would be getting gas for her car, and he made the trip there. He yelled across the parking lot, "Hey Raven," and Raven responded, "What?"

He then yelled again across the parking lot, "You need not go back to the hospital because your mama is dead." Raven did a double take at Noah across the parking lot, and she said, "WHAT?" He repeated, "Don't go back to the hospital, your mama's dead."

Raven stopped breathing for a second, and then she let out a primal scream, no one that heard it could forget. With the force of an elephant, she screamed to the top of her lungs, "NO! Oh, dear God NO!" as she grabbed her car door and fell to the ground in sobbing tears. That was it. Her world was no more and life as she once knew it, could never be the same.

Eventually, Raven picked herself up off the ground with the assistance of store customers at the service station, and after paying for her gas, she crawled back into her drivers' seat. Raven dropped her head on the steering wheel and just screamed, "Lord, have mercy. Why, Jesus, why?"

You gave me my mother, so I would not have to be alone in the world, and now you take her from me? Why, God, why? My first one didn't want me, so I lost that one, and I finally get one that wanted me, and you take her from me? Why Jesus why?

It was as if she believed somehow, GOD was responsible and that he cared nothing for her, but she could not have been more wrong. She was young and hurt, and she would learn why all these things were happening only to her. What she did not know was that later he would have a plan, far more significant than she could ever imagine. She continued to scream and talk to GOD while laying her head across the steering wheel of the car. She could not stop crying, because now not only was her heartbroken but so was her spirit.

It took Raven some time to gather herself, and as she slowly drove to Noah's house, she saw numerous cars parked already in the driveway. Among those cars was Megan's. Yes, Megan. She had already heard the word, perhaps before Raven did and knew Raven needed her at that moment.

As Raven got out of the car, numerous well-wishers and concerned people met Raven in the yard with hugs and kisses, none of which Raven wanted. She went straight over to Megan, and as Megan tried to console Raven, not even that was enough.

Raven must have been so distraught that she forgot Eliza had just died and she asked Megan to walk with her to make a phone call. They entered the house and made their way to the telephone; Megan had no idea what Raven was doing. Raven decided that she would pick up the phone and dial a number, and as the phone rang, and no one answered, Megan, asked Raven, "Who are you calling?"

Raven told Megan, she needed to talk to her mother, and she was calling her to see what she should wear to the funeral services. Megan then realized Raven was not at herself. Once Raven got no answer on the phone, and as she was about to hang up the phone, Raven was shaken back to the reality that her mother had just died.

Eliza used to always tell Raven, "If you ever need me, just call my name and the only way, I don't come, is if there is no life left in my body." Raven then realized, her mother, her heart, her soul and her only real friend was gone. The only person who she felt ever really loved her through it all and that she loved with every part of her fiber was gone. Gone forever and nothing could undo that. Raven began to cry uncontrollably and inconsolably for the dream she had dreamed since she was a little girl, had just come to pass.

The day of the funeral was one of the saddest and most painful days for Raven Gabriella Reese. Raven sat in the front row of the church, looking upon her mother's body. She was totally numb to everything around her to include Horatio, who by the way, seemed to be just fine. During the services, Raven could not handle the pain and burst into tears as Horatio leaned over her shoulder and uttered one of the coldest things that she had ever heard from anyone, friend or foe. Horatio whispered into Raven's ear, "STOP acting a fool," and when she heard those words, her heart turned to ice.

As far as Raven was concerned that was it, the final straw because she felt that her father had dishonored her mother during their marriage. Even now, he would dare to dishonor Raven's pain at the services with such an insensitive remark.

Days passed, and rumors began to circulate about Eliza's death. Stories that Horatio may have played a role in Eliza's death were all over town.

Eliza had left a will specifying items that were to be left to Raven. Eliza's two greedy sisters tried to accuse Raven of killing her own mother, this way they could take everything from Raven. Eliza wanted to make sure that even though she had very little money because Horatio had taken it all, she tried to leave Raven something to remember her by. In this will, she left her car, some smaller items and a death benefit to Raven of three thousand dollars. Eliza's two greedy sisters, especially Ilene, were hell-bent that Raven was not their blood and deserved nothing from their sister.

Kay and Ilene had never really seen or treated Raven as a member of the family. They had continuously reminded Eliza and Raven that she was merely an adopted child and nothing more. They swarmed into Eliza's home like buzzards on fresh meat to take everything of value, from pots and pans to clothes and perfumes.

Eliza had a little pink nightgown and, an old driver's license that she kept in her bedroom drawer, and that was all that Raven ended up with, of her mother. They even took the car.

Yes, they took the vehicle Eliza had left for Raven. The two sisters also went to court to fight Raven for everything Eliza owned. They tried to make Raven testify in court that her mother was insane at the time of her death, but Raven was not about to dishonor her mother with that type of lie, and she would not hear of such a request from anyone.

Raven, felt as if her mother's memory was more important, and she was not about to lie about her mother's mental state. Besides, Raven wanted her mother, not her mother's things. Raven knew there was a difference between how she felt and how her aunts felt about possessions. As far as Raven was concerned, if her greedy aunts needed Eliza's items that badly, they could have them and good riddance. She would treasure those two items she'd received for the rest of her life.

Raven spoke to Megan about the rumors of Horatio having something to do with Eliza's death. Raven and Megan were thick as thieves, and together they were about to unmask one of the most baffling and unsolved mysteries, that the south had seen in a while. Raven got wind of an old root doctor that lived in a small town not that far from Horatio. She and Megan went to see this man and see just what they could find out. Raven never believed in hoodoo or voodoo, but things were different now. She needed to know the truth once and for all. Raven's mother used to tell her, Ilene and Kay, her two sisters that, "If anything should happen to me, look at Horatio.

He did it, and he fixes me food sometimes mostly stew, but I get sick when I eat it, and it always tastes funny." Raven could not get that out of her head, and she was determined to find out the truth. Horatio and Raven had not spoken since Eliza's death. Raven was still furious with Horatio and was not about to let him off the hook so quickly.

They drove around town one day until they found the home of the man that they were told about. Raven wanted to know if such a thing existed and could it be powerful enough to take her mother's life. As the two girls pulled up to the house, they got a very uneasy feeling.

The yard was not like a typical yard at an average home. This yard had things in it that spooked both girls. The girls got out and went to the door and as Raven rang the doorbell and elderly man opened the door. Raven and Megan explained why they were there and that they needed some information that he specialized in. To both girls surprise the elderly man knew Raven already by name. The girls were a bit taken back, as they wondered how this man knew Raven. Who was he? What was his connection to Eliza or

Horatio? They would soon learn that there was far more to the story than either girl knew.

The elderly man said to the girls that not only did he know Raven's parents, but that he was a relative of Horatio. Horatio had purchased the items required from him. He stood up from his chair and then left the room, but upon his return, he came back with some of the items. He unrolled the items from a dark paper type of material, laid all the things on a table and began to explain just what Horatio had purchased and, how Horatio had used it to hurt Eliza.

The bottom line was this, Horatio had an affair with Eliza's first cousin, and Eliza had found out about it. That was why she left Horatio saying, "if I knew then, what I know now, I would have left him a long time ago." This affair had gone on for years during his marriage to Eliza, and once she found out about it, he could not have her defiling his name in the public eye, so the most accessible route was to take Eliza out of the picture.

He was to use the pink powdered substance that the elderly man sold him, to mix into food and feed Eliza. This had left Raven feeling like she was between a rock and a hard place. Should she take this new information and go forth with it and destroy her father's name? Should she hold on to the information and remain quiet, but allow her mother's death to go unsolved? What should she do? Raven was confused by now. The actual death certificate showed no known cause of death and classified it as natural causes.

During this time, Raven had personally confronted Horatio about his involvement with her mother's death, but he outright denied it in front of Megan. Raven was only eighteen years old, and she was afraid that the authorities would not take the information seriously.

This was not a good day for Raven nor Megan. Megan tried hard to understand what she had just learned from the stranger.

Raven changed in a matter of seconds, after learning the heart-wrenching truth about how she really lost her mother, "With this knowledge that Raven just gained, she could no longer go back to the way she saw the world. To Raven, she now believed that life was short and too short for strife, discord, and unhappiness. After she just learned how quickly someone else could make the determination that another's life is not valuable, not worthy, and thus disposable, she was more determined than ever, to live her life to the fullest.

As Raven drove back home with Megan, they discussed the new information they had got. They tried to sort things out and make some sense out of it all. Megan had to drive because Raven was far too broken and disturbed, plus her eyes were so swollen from crying that she could not see how to drive.

Raven sat in the passenger seat for the ride back with tears in her eyes just like a rainy night, and in her heart, there was no room for moonlight, nor stars.

She made her decision that she would go back to Rockford, and she would rebuild her life and make Eliza proud of her. She also decided that from now on, she would feed Horatio with a long-handled spoon.

She felt he was much too dangerous to trust and even though the rest of the world saw Horatio for the person he portrayed in public, she, Megan and her deceased mother knew him for the cruel, heartless and cold man he was.

The following week, Raven packed her final goods and headed to Rockford to make sense of all the things that had happened to her in her short eighteen years of life.

She hoped that at some point, GOD would forgive her for things she had done previously in life and, that she could forget what happened to her when she was young. She hoped she could gain some form of peace in her young heart, yet her trust had been broken in man, and her heart had been finally shattered in a million pieces, none of which anyone could ever fix.

She now understood, that her mother, the only person who would ever groom her wings, was now gone, and she was now alone in a crazy world, in a world that would never do anything but clip her wings.

Raven always knew that love was important, along with life and family. Both of which she never knew until Eliza found her. Horatio in Raven's eyes saw only two things, which were money and power, and she felt as if this was what he was living for. Raven saw Eliza as a kind, loving and wonderful woman that she so wanted to grow up to be like. This was a woman that Raven believed GOD wanted her to be like, and she knew in her heart that she would spend the rest of her life trying to do so.

One thing Raven was adamant about, and that was, she wanted to find a mate in her life that loved her, not just someone she loved, not like Horatio. One that served GOD and not money or things. Raven was now on a mission to find happiness, a lifetime mate, and she wanted children, yes lots of children. She felt as if she had been cheated out of the chance to be a mother and a good one, just like Eliza. Now, more than anything, she wanted to build a life for herself. But where should she start?

Dallas P Elkheart

Episode XVIII: Sister Margaret

Raven returned to Rockford, Tennessee to pick up the pieces of her life. She had a sister living there. Her sister's name was Margaret, but everyone called her Margie, and she was Horatio's birth child, and, Raven was Horatio's adopted child. She had never spent much time with Margie. For one, she was more than twenty-five years older than Raven. Therefore, the gap was tremendous, and there was just not much that a young child would have in common with a much older sister. Especially when growing up in two different households and being raised by two women with opposite beliefs on child-rearing.

Besides, Eliza never allowed Horatio to take Raven too far from her since she knew Horatio had a thirst for other women. One time, Eliza did allow Raven to visit Margie at a younger age, but Raven was twelve years old at that time, and the meeting went terrible the first time.

Horatio was a veteran, and the veteran's medical facilities serviced many of his medical issues in Rockford where Margie lived. Once Eliza allowed Horatio to take Raven with him to see her and they met in the hospital's lobby. Raven was very excited to meet her half-sister as she grew up alone with no one to have those late-night chats with, and she missed that part of life.

Upon the meeting, Raven eagerly ran toward her older sister, before Horatio could even introduce them. Raven had never met a stranger in her life. She saw everyone as a friend, which will prove to be her worst characteristic down the road. As she ran towards Margie, the feeling seemed not to be mutual, and as Raven approached her, they exchanged no hugs.

This took Raven by surprise, and her feelings had become stepped on in her eyes, as she had always dreamed of having a sister and now that she realized she had one, that sister wanted nothing to do with her, and to her this was hurtful.

Raven smiled and said, "Hi, Margie" and instead of receiving a hi or hello back Margie stepped forward and said to Raven, "I am not used to anybody calling my Daddy, Daddy", but to Margie's surprise the quick-witted pre-teen came back with a jolt and said, "Well, you better get used to it, cause he's my daddy too". The two half-sisters got off to a rocky start, but Raven was now eighteen years old and never really felt as if she should have been kept apart from her sister, therefore she was eager to embrace her again. She hoped Margie was just as keen to embrace her.

Raven moved there only taking a few items of clothing, and she took the car that Eliza had bought for her when Raven was married to Noah Evans. As Raven arrived at Margie's, she seemed to be greeted differently this time, and Raven felt as if Margie was glad to see her again.

Margie had invited several of her friends over to meet Raven as they had never seen her, only heard the things Margie told them about the teenager. Margie would always make snide remarks about Raven to her friends in her presence. She would say things like, "Look at my baby sister, ain't she beautiful? Daddy spoils her rotten; it seems like to me". Or she would say, "My baby sister is beautiful. She looks just like me, huh?"

Either way, it would always leave Raven feeling less than, but then again, she was used to the remarks and ridicule. If she were not getting verbal abuse from Horatio, she surely would get it from the other kids when she was in school.

Raven had toughened up a bit, but she was still quite fragile and very naïve all while being still compassionate and desiring love and acceptance in the world in which she had no choice but to be in.

One morning Raven had talked to Margie about going to school, but Raven did not know her way around town, so Margie told her she had a male friend that she knew that could take her over to the University to register for school. Raven was thrilled, and for whatever reason, she felt as if she could trust her big sister and that she would never harm her. Horatio was dead set against Raven going to live with Margie. Even though this was his biological child, he found great distrust in her abilities to look after Raven and begged Raven not to go there to live with her.

Raven was stubborn, which was another one of Raven's characteristics that would prove almost fatal, and she went against Horatio's wishes once again.

Margie called her friend to set up the date and time to take Raven over to the Rockford University to register, and when the day arrived, Raven noticed Margie became somewhat irritated with her. Margie had asked Raven about a black dress that had come up missing, and she wanted to know if Raven took it. Raven had no idea what she was referring to, and so she replied, "No. What dress?" Margie said, "The dress was in my daughter's closet yesterday, and now it is gone. Raven was very hurt that Margie would ever think that she of all people would steal a dress. Horatio and Eliza had gone through meticulous measures to instill in Raven values of honoring your own words, taking nothing that did not belong to you unless you pay for it and to treat other people, as you would have them to treat you.

By the time Margie's friend had arrived, Raven had decided that perhaps after she registered for the University, that she should move out and get her own place. Raven went to get into the car with Margie's friend, Raven also took the few belongings she had and told Margie she would be back for her car later. As the car pulled off, Raven sat in the front seat with this total stranger, and she could not help but notice the old brown Cadillac that Margie's friend was driving. It had a very musty smell to it which caused Raven to roll her window down during the ride.

Everything was quiet as the stranger took Raven to the University to register. After Raven had completed the registration process, she felt good about her decision to go to college, and she believed her life was about to go in the right direction, eventually.

The stranger picked her back up, and Raven told him, "Could you please take me back to my sister's so I can get my car?" The stranger nodded his head in a yes motion, while never uttering a word. They headed out of the driveway, and Raven assumed that she would arrive back at her sisters in less than twenty minutes. On the drive back, Raven began to see things that she did not remember seeing on the journey there, and she politely asked the stranger, "Is this a new way back to my sister's house?", as nothing was looking familiar to her.

The stranger did not answer and continued his drive. Raven asked again, "Where are we going?" By now, they were in a strange neighborhood that looked nothing like her sister's neighborhood, but this time the stranger came from under the seat of his car with a gun in his hand and as he pulled up to a stop sign, all hell broke loose.

Raven now found herself at gunpoint, by a man she did not know and in a town that she did not know. The stranger told her, Look, kid; you look like a friendly kid, but I got my orders. Raven asked the stranger with tears in her eyes, rolling in a stream down her cheeks as she swallowed with a hard gulp, and breathed heavily", "Please Mr. if you just take me back, I won't say a word.

Let me get my clothes from the back of the car, and I won't tell anyone". The man told Raven, "Look, kid, if I don't do you, they gonna do me, I got my orders." Raven now realized she was in big trouble, more than ever and Horatio could not help her, nor did he know where she was. The driver told her that he was told not to bring her back, that she was to be found floating face down in the Mississippi River and to dispose of her clothes so there would be no trace.

Raven saw the writing on the wall, and it sounded like someone had taken a contract out on her life but, who? If not Margie, then who? As the car came up to the last three stop signs that Raven could see, she could see hundreds of trees. It looked as if a river and forest were somewhere close by. She realized they were about to leave where all people were as soon as the car passed the next three stop signs. In her eyes, there was no way out of the vehicle as it never really came to a full stop, so Raven looked over at the gunman, and she looked at the two stop signs and then again around the area to see what she could do.

Whatever she could do, she knew she had better do it and fast, because her time was about to run out, and so were her options. As the car went pass the next stop sign, but, before getting to the last one, she knew in her heart, it would be now or never, and in the twinkle of an eye, she made a decision that would eventually save her life. She knew Horatio could not save her now, because only the driver and her sister knew where she was and without assistance, she was now helpless.

Refusing to give up, or in, on her life, Raven made a snap decision, and as the car pulled up to the next stop sign, she turned her back to the car door on the passenger side, leaned on the door and pulled the handle. Raven allowed the weight of her body to fall from the moving vehicle as the door flew open with the car in motion. Without thinking twice about the possible outcome of being injured, she allowed her body to hit the hard pavement, she knew now was not the time to grow feathers, except if she intended to take flight, to save her own life.

So, she decided if she would ever have wings, right about now would be the place to fly. She rolled out of the car and to her feet. As she took flight as a 747 aircraft with full fuel on a nonstop mission. She began to run as she remembered something Horatio used to teach her.

He tried to teach Raven about how to handle specific situations. He taught her that, if she needed to run from the enemy, never, never run in a straight line, "They cannot shoot a zig-zag target, and even if they do, you stand a better chance of survival." Raven did just what Horatio taught her to do, and she moved at the speed of light up the street. Horatio also informed her to always run towards lots of buildings and lights, "There you will find people and perhaps help, "so again, she did just that.

While in motion, she saw a big street that looked like it had hundreds of cars passing on it and she realized it was a highway interstate, and there should be people there that could help her. In the same breath, the gunman was in hot pursuit of Raven as she could hear the squealing of the tires coming right in behind her. He was not about to allow his victim to getaway. He had someone he was going to have to answer to, but his mission was not as detrimental as Raven's was. As Raven made her way to the edge of the highway, she heard squealing tires as they headed at full speed behind her and just as she hit the main road; she saw a corner store, so she shot to the store and through the doors.

As she opened the doors and jetted threw them, she fell across the countertop as the two workers stood at a standstill. Somehow, one worker behind the register knew something was wrong, and she immediately asked Raven, "Do you need somewhere to hide? Is someone after you?" Raven was so out of breath that all she could do was a nod as she cried and the worker told the other cashier, "call 911".

She ran from behind the counter and grabbed Raven by the arm and led her to the back of the store. The only problem was, the back-exit door was blocked with goods and on the left was a tiny bathroom. The store clerk led Raven into the bathroom and said,

"Lock the door behind me. Don't come out until you hear the police and get up underneath the sink and stay quiet".

Raven did just that, and as she locked the door behind the clerk she crawled underneath the bathroom sink, and with her knees, in her chest and arms wrapped around her knees, she tried to sit as still as possible, but she was so terrified, she could hear her teeth clattering together.

Everything got quiet in the store, and she knew the gunman was there. He had found the store that Raven ran into. It petrified her that he might kill both workers if he wanted her bad enough, then what?

After what seemed as if it was an eternity, which was probably eight minutes, she heard a bang on the bathroom door. "Open, ma'am, open up the door, it's the police." Raven's heart dropped, but then she heard it again, and she realized the cavalry had arrived. Fright and sheer terror prevented her from standing up to open the door, so, she crawled on both hands and knees to the door and tried to get it open.

The door flew open, and there stood a black uniform holding a sniper rifle in his hands, the difference was, he was also wearing a badge. She tried to stand up, but her knees buckled, and she fell into the officer's arms. He grabbed Raven and told her, "Ma'am, it's ok. We got you. You're ok". They led Raven out of the bathroom to the counter to talk with the police. During this time, she learned they had just passed the gunman, and as they were responding to a shooter call there at the store, he jetted past them, the cashiers could not give them a description of the car the gunman was in, so they did not recognize him or the vehicle when they crossed each other's paths. They asked Raven, where she lived so they could call her family to come and get her, and she responded to the officer saying, "I only have a father, and he lives about three hours away from here."

The officer told Raven it was ok; he had an idea, so he put the young girl into his squad car and took her to a restaurant. This store was a combination of a grocery store and restaurant, and the owners were friends of his. He asked them to look after Raven until they could reach Horatio, but Raven was in shock and could not speak, so she sat in a chair at the store for the remaining part of the evening, never uttering a word to anyone.

She stayed with the store family for two days, as Horatio prepared for the long drive to go and get his baby girl. While the family that took Raven in, were extremely kind to her, Raven was mentally not capable of trusting anyone again. She had become needy, and apprehensive of people by now and was just far too fragile to accept the attention that the family gave her. Horatio was furious at Raven and Margie, as he had warned Raven to stay clear of Margie.

He believed she was jealous of Raven and could even cause her harm, but he never, ever thought Margie was capable of this. How Raven wished she had listened to Horatio, and she was angered at herself that she trusted people so much, yet, her heart was way too kind to see the other side of people, and with everything she had already been through, she still did not have the gift of discernment.

Horatio came to pick up Raven and take her home, and for once, they were happy to see each other. Raven was so lost; it seemed no matter how hard she tried to start over; it was as if an invisible force was bent on keeping her from reaching her goals. But now the question Raven had to ask herself was this, was it fate or, the lack of faith, that stopped her from obtaining happiness? She knew that she had some serious soul searching to do.

She went back home with Horatio. She was reluctant to live there again because of the hauntings that had taken place at her house in her bedroom back home. Against her better judgment, she went back to try one more time. One evening, Raven had cleaned the house, wash some clothes and fixed supper, since Horatio had gone into town to handle some business. She thought to herself that it would be nice to help her father put some organization to the house. Since Eliza had left him and then passed away, Horatio had done little with the house. He had believed that Eliza was haunting the house because he had told Raven that every night, he would hear something moving around in Eliza's bedroom.

Bronze Bloodline of the Phoenix

As Raven was cleaning the house; she took a break and went outside to gets some fresh air. She went under the shade trees that Horatio and Eliza enjoyed sitting under when she was a child.

Once she got outdoors and sat down on the old swing glider, she noticed no neighbors were home at any of the surrounding houses, and it appeared as if she was all alone on the hill where the house sat.

She laid back and closed her eyes, but, as she did, she began to hear whispers around her. Although she knew no one was around and they lived in the middle of nowhere, she could hear the whispering getting louder. She opened her eyes wide as saucer's, looked straight ahead and sat up startled and said out loud, "What the hell? "She was afraid to turn around because it sounded as if it was coming from behind the house. She mustered up the nerve to turn her head to see if she could gather which direction the voice was coming from, and that is when she heard it. It was loud and clear what the voice was whispering. It was whispering her name out loud. The voice wavered in the air, and as the breeze blew, it carried the name. The whisper was soft and flowing; one might envision it as a long and sheer yellow dress that is displayed on a lifeless silhouette, caught in a gentle breeze.

Raven, could hear the voice coming closer and closer to her and she looked around as if she was looking for somewhere to hide, but where could she hide? No neighbors were home, Horatio was not back yet, and Raven felt that to run inside the house would be to run towards whatever was calling out her name. Raven jumped up from the swing and ran down to the street by the mailbox and stood there, looking around to see if she could find anyone who could help her.

Just as she reached the mailbox, Horatio's truck rounded the corner. Raven knew she could not tell her father, so she pretended to be checking the mail. She now understood more than ever before, she could not stay with Horatio, too much had happened, and she was surer than ever, more would be on the agenda if she remained in that house one more minute.

Once her father pulled into the driveway, she told him that she was going to stay in town with some friends, but she would come up each day to help him with daily tasks and check on him.

Raven simply refused to stay with Horatio, so she moved back into the small town, which was about 45 minutes away from Horatio. Raven had a female cousin that she cared for deeply, Jene. Jene had been there through most of Raven's tough times, and Jene was Raven's cousin on Horatio's side of the family. Raven spent a lot of her free time with her and her family. She felt as if she could find her way on her own. After all, she was, on her own.

PART VI: Love You up, Love You Down

Dallas P Elkheart

Episode XIX: Look Ma, No Hands

Raven now knew she was on her own. She found an apartment and focused on her modeling career while working full-time at a local restaurant. She had landed this position on a fluke. One day she and Megan, her longtime friend, went out for dinner, and after placing their order, the waitress later brought the first part of the order to the table. The waitress served the drinks they had ordered, which were a Coke and a Pepsi. The waitress did not label the soft drinks before bringing them to the girl's table, and she had to determine which drink belonged to which girl.

What the girl did to determine which drink was who's, was inexcusable. She took each soda off of her tray and placed it underneath her nose, and the top of the glass touched the waitress's upper lip, then she took a great big sniff and said, "Ah yes, this is the Coke," and then she repeated the same action for the Pepsi and then she sat the drinks before each girl. It mortified Raven at the girl's methods of identification, and Raven quickly spoke up and stated, "I don't want the glass after you just stuck my soda up your nose." Megan followed up with a similar statement. The waitress then said to the girls, "Well, what's wrong with it?" Raven responded quickly and said, "Really? And you don't know?" Raven immediately asked for a manager so, the girl left to head back to the preparation area to get one, but not before mocking the girls in the back of the restaurant. She laughed loudly as she told her coworkers, "HA, HA, HA, and I asked them, what the hell is wrong with the drinks?" This infuriated Raven, and as the manager approached the table, he asked the girls what had happened.

Raven was a people person, and she loved good conversation, and even though she had not finished college yet, she carried an excellent sized vocabulary and was well-spoken for a young lady. She told the manager that was not how you deal with customers, and the manager replied, "Do you think you would have been able to handle it in a better way?: Raven smiled, sat back in her seat with tons of confidence, and stated, "Absolutely, The customer should be treated with the utmost respect. The manager looked at Raven and then said, "Do you think you could do a better job?" Raven looked at him and said," Of course, I know I could."

Without hesitation, he told Raven, "Then you're hired, and she is gone." Raven's personality had just landed her a position without even applying or interviewing by being herself in a public place. She was outgoing, outspoken, and her personality for the first time drew a positive response from someone and not a negative one. Raven was ecstatic over all of this and could not wait to start her new job and show the world the real Raven Reese.

Raven had been at her new job over a week when one day while working the day shift, one of the night shift employees showed up to work. He had changed from night shifts to daytime shifts and would now be a co-worker with Raven.

The manager gave Raven more responsibility, as he watched how well she handled herself and the customers. The customers had grown to love Raven and would ask specifically for Raven's tables.

Raven made a killing on tips because of her wittiness and smile. This same wittiness and a smile would also captivate the new co-worker. His name was Eric Anderfal. Eric was still in high school and was almost two years younger than Raven. However, they seemed to blend like they had known each other all their lives, and Raven became smitten with Eric.

He was a very handsome young man, with a haunting smile, a romantic voice and had an athletic build as he was in numerous activities at his high school. Girls seemed to gravitate towards Eric, but Eric seemed to gravitate towards Raven, and it was certainly no secret that Raven had become consumed with Eric's charm.

Raven and Eric soon became inseparable, and by the summertime, they got an apartment together as Eric was nearing his graduation and going to a university was on his agenda. Raven loved the idea. Eric had become Raven's best friend, and the love between them seemed to be so tight that not even Eric's friends nor family could separate them. Eric's family and friends had told him, that they thought Raven might be too advanced for him. They felt that he was too young for Raven because she had been married previously.

Eric did not hear a word of what they had to say. He had fallen in love with Raven, and he would allow no one to destroy that for them. He was very protective of Raven. She saw him as a kind and gentle soul, one of which she had never experienced, which drew her even closer to him. They both worked long hours and pooled their funds together for their new life. Eric's friends rarely saw him anymore, for he spent endless hours with Raven.

They both seemed to have a lot in common as Eric had a stepfather, that was cruel to him. It was because Eric was the only child in the family that was not of his own flesh and blood, and Raven could identify with him since she and Horatio faced many similar situations. Eric had several brothers and sisters, but he was the oldest and the only one born to his mother before she met her new husband. Eric and Raven had already begun a search for a university that they could attend, and Raven loved the idea of them both pursuing educations for themselves since they both wanted to become successful.

Both Raven and Eric were sharp dressers and enjoyed flaunting their styles together at parties. After applying to three different universities, they both received a letter from Staten Maze University. It was further down in the south than where they lived, which meant more than four hours away from their hometown, a perfect distance from their families.

Raven received a phone call from the university, and the band director had caught wind of Raven's application and took an interest in her. He wanted to offer Raven a full scholarship to Staten Maze.

He explained to her, that since she had been a musician from the age of two and a band member at her high school from the fifth grade through graduation, she would make an excellent candidate for a scholarship. The university would pay all the fees for food, room, and board. The only requirement they had was that Raven had to play in the jazz band during offseason, perform on the field during football season and do parades during the remaining season, and, she would need to maintain a C average or above to keep her scholarship.

Raven jumped at the chance to see her dreams of having an education come true. The first thing she asked the band director was, "If they could enroll her in nursing school?" She explained how she had no family, and she was a loner, but she told the band director about Eric. Raven had seen Eric as her family and Eric saw Raven in the same light. The band director quickly said yes, they would enroll her in the nursing school program and that numerous students attend their university as couples, and sometimes they would graduate from the university and get married. This was just what Raven wanted to hear as she and Eric had big plans for their future.

The two lovebirds headed off to college in the car Eric owned; Raven didn't have a car after a few mishaps that had occurred.

The school year began, and things were finally on the right track. Eric had earned a position on the university football team, and Raven had landed a spot on the dance and majorette squad at Staten Maze University. She was popular among many at the university, but unfortunately, she was still not popular among the females, not even her squad and team members. They often teased her because they said, she acted like she was from another culture and not theirs. The university also had her nationality incorrectly listed on all her records. It may have been a mistake, or perhaps it was on purpose to fulfill a quota.

Raven called Horatio to see how things were; the phone rang, and Horatio picked it up on the third ring. As she listened carefully, she could hear a baby crying in the background, but she ignored it and asked how he was doing. Instead of him asking her how she was, he immediately went into a rampage over why she was in college, and he told her, she knew she was not smart enough to go to college. This hurt Raven, she tried to ignore his unkind words and went on to tell him about the school band, her travels, and Eric, but she heard the noise in the background again, and she asked him, who was there. He said, "Oh a friend of mine," and Raven replied, "Does she have a baby?"

Horatio told her, "Yes, and, please mind your own business." His comment threw her back, and she then apologized for asking. He then told her, "if you're calling for money, I ain't got any to give you. This girl here needs milk for her baby." Raven was floored as she had only called him to ask how he was doing and had no intention of asking Horatio for anything. Raven was independent and never tried to ask people for help. In her eyes, if she did not have it and could not work for it, then she would do without. Raven had now taken a part-time job on campus with one of the doctors.

She blurted out without thinking, "You know what, I wanted to see how you were doing, but you're still that same, mean, cold-hearted man I knew." She went on to say, "You will never change, so, I'll tell you what: you'll never have to worry about me calling you again." Raven told her father, "I don't want your money, nor do I need your money. If I ain't got cash to buy things, I will do without it, but you'll never have to worry about me again. You will need me before I ever will need you, and that is a promise." She slammed the phone up and began to cry. She was hurt, and she realized at that moment, she was still alone, and apparently, she would always be by herself. Raven felt, as if the only person in her life, that seemed to love her was Eric. Raven could see how Eric showed her real love every day and every moment. Her heart always told her, that she would never forsake him for anything nor anyone, because he was everything to Raven. She believed if you had someone faithful, you should remain loyal to them.

Raven and Eric were always together whether walking to class, eating meals or, traveling because he was a football player and she was a majorette and dancer and, the band performed at the games.

Even at night, either Raven or Eric would continuously sneak over to each other's dorms and spend the night together. They never missed a night in all the years they were together. Remember, they refused to allow anyone to keep them apart. Unfortunately, that mentality would not last forever.

No one knew a lifetime of change was about to occur. It had been three years now, and Eric and Raven were going stronger than ever until the football team had a trip that the band would not be making. While Eric was away, there was a young man by the name of Jordan Jackson that also was a band member, and he had eyes for Raven.

While Eric was away on the trip that the football team took, Jordan Jackson, stopped by to see Raven. They called her down to the lobby of her dormitory. She greeted him and asked him, why was he over at her dorm, and she jokingly said, "Lost your way to your girlfriend, huh?"

They both laughed as Raven was on friendly terms with his current girlfriend and saw Jordan as no threat. That was her biggest mistake because Jordan saw this as an opportunity to complete his scheme. Raven was still somewhat naïve and never saw it coming. As Jordan joked around with Raven and pretended to talk about an upcoming show, the band would perform at, Raven took him seriously and continued the conversation. After about fifteen minutes, Jordan leaned in to tell Raven something in secret. When he leaned towards her ear; she leaned in too.

Out of the blue, he threw his arms around her, and with his mouth, he grabbed her neck and sucked as hard as he could. Raven punched Jordan in the shoulder as she fought to pull back and push him off her, but the damage had been done.

She pulled back and realized her neck was in pain; she cursed at Jordan and asked him if he had lost his mind? Jordan threw his head backward and laughed, but the trick would soon be on Raven and Jordan knew it. She did an about-face walk towards the stairways going back to her room but not before giving Jordan a piece of her mind. He only laughed louder as he exited her dorm. She got back to her room and prepared to go to practice with her dance squad.

She got ready but noticed she was in pain where Jordan had chomped down on her neck, so she went over to the mirror, and in horror, she saw it. Jordan had grabbed a hold on to the side of her neck so hard in a sucking motion that a hickey was forming.

Raven almost died, and panic washed over her because she saw the purple spot forming on her neck. Raven ran down the hall to her good friend Sandy, and she told her what had happened with Jordan as she wept through the story. Sandy cringed, "Eric will be pissed, really pissed, and he will never believe you." He probably did that on purpose because everyone knows Eric, and Jordon knows how he will react.

Raven had always been truthful and faithful to Eric, but what should she do now? She thought repeatedly, was Sandy right about this?

Should she tell him the truth, and would he believe her, or would he think she was like everyone else and a cheater? Sandy came back into her room after telling some other girls on the hall what Jordan did to Raven, and her answer dazed Raven. She said, "Ok girl, we don't think you need to tell him because he might think you did something and not believe you when you tell him what Jordan did." Sandy went on to say, "Just wear a turtleneck sweater at practice today, and by the time tomorrow comes that stupid thing will be gone, and Eric will be ok." So, she listened to Sandy's lousy idea.

There were a few things Raven never considered, and they were that Eric and Raven had been like glue for over three years, and numerous females had a crush on Eric. Raven also forgot about the fact that most of her squad disliked her and spoke ill will behind her back and did not feel as if she deserved Eric. This would be a mistake that pushes Raven to the brink of doing the unthinkable. While at practice that afternoon, the word came in that the boys from the football team were back on campus and Raven needed to tell Eric the truth because she loved him, and she never wanted to hide anything from him. Would it be a big mistake?

The truth only works well when you have two people who are mature enough and know each other well, but Eric was younger than Raven and had not developed the gift of discernment. He had not developed the skills on how to determine the truth from a lie; therefore, that afternoon would become painful for both lovebirds.

Someone had told Eric the news as he got off of the bus, that Raven had cheated on him, and Eric could not make his way to the band hall fast enough. As practice was taking place with the squadron, Eric flew through the practice room door and went straight to Raven, but before she could say a word, he drew back and slapped her so hard, you could hear it down the band hallway. He stated, "You cheated on me. You don't love me. You cheated," and he walked away.

Raven embarrassed and crying simply could not believe what had just happened. Someone she knew had just set her up, and it worked out just as they planned because Eric Anderfal, her heart, and soul, had just left the building and her life, forever.

Believing that she had betrayed him when he was not around, he had shown Raven that he could now date other girls and knew that would get her goose. Just letting her see him with someone else as he had already pictured her with someone else. He was hurt, and he wanted to hurt her, the same way he was hurting. It devastated Raven. She tried to tell him the truth, but he would not listen. One day Sandy came by Raven's room and told her, to get dressed, that she needed to show her something.

As the girls walked the campus, Sandy took Raven to a female dorm, and when they walked in, Raven almost collapsed as she saw Eric in the lobby with another girl. He saw Raven, but he pretended as if he didn't. He appeared to be taking pleasure in rubbing it in that he was no longer hers because, in Eric's mind, she had betrayed him in the worst way. Raven went back to her dorm and sunk into a deep, deep depression. She could no longer sleep, nor did she want to be in anyone's company. Raven no longer trusted anyone and certainly not Eric Anderfal.

Raven attempted to commit suicide that night, but it was unsuccessful, and as her days turned into night, she realized her relationship with Eric was over, just like that. All the things that they had gone through together were pointless because one person destroyed two lives and made Raven the laughingstock of the campus in her eyes. She was now all alone, and her grades began to suffer for it.

The summer came, and school was out. Raven went to Minnesota to get away from everything and everyone. She moved to Minnesota and quickly found a job working in a lab where she made new friends and tried dating some, but it was not to be. The school was close to starting up again, and she had to decide whether to go back and face her demons or quit and try to start over, but Raven was no quitter, and she went back to Staten Maze for the fall.

The first day back to Staten felt strange to Raven. As she stood in the mix of everything, still heartbroken but trying to get in the groove, she felt someone watching her and as her eyes glanced over the crowd that was when her eyes locked with the culprit.

The culprit was a tall, very well-built and muscular young man, with wavy black hair and a smile, oh yes, that smile. He had a smile that was as bright and genuine as any night star filling the night. Raven caught her breath for a minute, as the young man had taken her breath away and then she realized, the attraction was like a magnet between the two of them. But who was the guy? She had never seen him on campus, but oh, he had seen Raven numerous times on campus. This young man that caught her eyes was Wyatt

Bronze Bloodline of the Phoenix

Adams. Matter of fact, he was on the same football team as Eric was. The bad part was both guys knew each other.

    Raven had been so smitten with Eric that she never noticed other guys on the campus that were attracted to her, especially Wyatt, but things were now different. Eric had moved on. Raven was feeling like somewhat of a celebrity on campus because of all the newfound attention. The thanks had to go to the backstabber that set Raven up, set her up to lose Eric that is. Raven was now solo, but somehow it still felt strange. Raven was so used to being with Eric, and she felt crazy, and if felt like she was cheating on Eric. Maybe the closure that Raven sought between her and Eric would come, but it might not happen for years down the road.

Dallas P Elkheart

Episode XX: Right, Out of The Skillet

Wyatt Adams approached Raven, and soon, they were becoming close. Wyatt explained to Raven that he was in love with her, but there was a slight problem. The slight problem, putting it mildly, was more like a nine-month problem. In fact, several weeks before Wyatt drew Raven's attention, and they became an item, Wyatt had learned that a girl he had a short fling with was now carrying his child. Raven did not know how to take this as she wanted no man, with children attached, yet, the situation with Wyatt seemed different. Raven was falling for Wyatt, and this made it hard for her to see anything other than the present feelings. He was expecting a baby, but she knew he was in love with her, but again, in the same thought, Raven had always wanted to be a mother, and she even thought that perhaps this would be a chance to be a mom, in a funny kind of way, without having to worry about having children of her own.

Raven had learned through all of her years that she, much like Eliza, may never be able to bear children because of the abortion Horatio forced her to have. Doctors had told Raven that during exams and numerous exploratory surgeries, it looked as if someone had thrown a bomb inside her body. The doctor that performed the abortion had, in fact, completed an unauthorized medical procedure on Raven, leaving her tubes totally destroyed and unrepairable. Raven saw the chance to help Wyatt with his situation, and she told him that she would be by his side as long as he needed her.

Wyatt not only needed Raven but had become obsessed with her and possessive about her. Wyatt and Raven grew closer and closer as the months went forward until one night, Wyatt could no longer contain his feelings for Raven. As they laid side by side in his dorm room, Wyatt looked over at Raven and said, "I don't want you to ever leave me.

I am so in love with you, and I am afraid that if you found someone else, you would leave me." He went on to tell Raven that while she was with Eric, he used to be so jealous of seeing Eric with her. He waited for the chance that Eric would do something stupid like letting her go, and he saw Eric's slip up as his gain. Raven had never had a man tell her this, and to her, it seemed so sweet that he loved her so much. Well, if she would have looked closer, what she might have seen was not just a man that adored her, but one that would do whatever it took to keep her, even kill.

Wyatt awaited the answer from Raven, and as she looked into his eyes, she could see a man that she loved. Wyatt and Raven soon left Staten Maze University to marry. Raven was excited and felt she was making the right decision, or was she?

Once they both left the university, they moved to Davison, Mississippi, and there they began their life together. Without a college degree, both Wyatt and Raven took jobs to make ends meet.

They were in love and money was not their primary forethought at least not until Wyatt brought up the discussion about Raven having his child.

He would sometimes make bizarre remarks to Raven when she would be in the kitchen cooking. He would stand back looking at her and then walk over to her, grab her in his arms and say, "I need you to have my baby, and I will make sure you get pregnant."

Raven often thought, "What an odd statement to make." She would tell Wyatt how she wanted that too, but they may have to go about it differently. What Raven did not understand was that Wyatt felt, that if he could impregnate Raven, Raven would never think about Eric again. Wyatt often mentioned Eric and how he felt like Eric still wanted Raven and he would never give her back. Plus, he would say, he was going to do something Eric never could, and that was to give Raven a baby. Raven never really took Wyatt seriously and felt as if he had some type of childhood or manhood thing he needed to overcome.

Several weeks passed, Wyatt would not let it go and asked Raven to set an appointment with a fertility specialist for them both. The only option for them was to use in-vitro fertilization. It would cost them between $10,000 and $15,000. Since she and Wyatt wanted children badly, they took out a loan and Raven made the call for an appointment.

By now Wyatt had already become a father, and the new baby seemed to take everyone's attention including Raven's, but the baby's mother was insanely jealous of Raven and Wyatt's relationship. Yet, Raven had fallen in love with Wyatt's new baby. The day came when Wyatt and Raven saw the fertility specialist, and he told them that he could assure them they would become parents with the procedure. Even though Wyatt had a mediocre job as did Raven, they dug deep into debt to make both of their dreams come true.

Soon they began to follow the guidelines of the doctor, and the medical team was able to finally fertilize not one but three of Raven's eggs with Wyatt's sperm and create three new embryos. They received a call telling Raven they needed to come back to the hospital for the transplant. Raven and Wyatt were ecstatic as they were about to do the impossible.

When they arrived at the hospital, the staff prepped Raven to transfer her and her husband's new life into Raven with the clear understanding that all three embryos could take, and they could be expecting one to three new babies soon.

Wyatt pressured Raven and still was not satisfied with the fact that his sperm and her eggs had turned into three embryos now inside her body, as he still wanted to be sure they took, by still trying to impregnate her while awaiting the results. He told Raven, he wanted to be sure he had planted his seed, so she is with him for life. Raven felt Wyatt was overly obsessed with her becoming pregnant.

The day for a blood test to determine if she was now pregnant with Wyatt's child or children came. After giving blood, they left the hospital and headed home, and by the time they had arrived back at their home, the phone rang. It was the hospital calling to congratulate and tell Raven, that she was not only to be a mother, but she was also carrying triplets, and yes, all three babies had taken.

Episode XXI: Hell's Gate

Wyatt overheard Raven as she shouted out with jubilation because she had just learned over the phone, that she was about to become a mother. "I'm pregnant; I'm pregnant, we're gonna be parents." Wyatt ran up the stairs to see if he heard Raven correctly, he said, "What? You joking, right? You kidding me. Stop playing, girl you play too much". Raven, with tears in her eyes, said no, "I am not joking, kidding, or playing around. I am genuinely expecting a baby, but Wyatt there is a problem." Wyatt stopped dead still and said, "What's wrong?" Raven put on her sad face before bursting out in a laugh and saying, "The question is, where can we get three cribs? It's triplets". Wyatt fell across the bed in sheer joy as he grabbed Raven in his arms and said, "We are finally tied together forever." Raven hugged Wyatt back as she thought to herself, this time, things would be different, and no one would take away her child. At least, so she thought.

One day Wyatt came home from work, and he was frustrated with his job. He felt the job paid so little, but having three babies would cost so much, and his daughter had needs. The baby's birth mother had to take Wyatt to the court of child support, and Raven made sure that the child's mother received her money like clockwork.

During his frustrated rant, Raven was upstairs and came to the top of the stairs to quiet Wyatt down as he was loud and slamming things around. Raven was a secluded person when it came to her business and did not want the neighbors in the apartment next to them to hear the ruckus.

Wyatt became angry and felt Raven had no right to ask him to calm down in his own house, and he flew up the stairs. Without thinking, Wyatt pushed Raven. As he pushed her, she was standing close to the top of the staircase, and with the shove, she lost her footing.

Raven tried to maintain her balance and Wyatt saw that he had pushed her too hard, he also tried to break her fall, but it was not to be. Without a word, not even a scream, Raven fell backward, headfirst down two flights of stairs and landed on her side with her face upwards. Wyatt ran down the stairs as he screamed Raven's name, but it was too late. Raven was bleeding profusely as Wyatt grabbed her up and took her to the hospital.

The doctors saved Raven, but not her unborn triplets. Once again, Raven had a dream in the palm of her hands, but life snuffed it right out from under her. The doctor hospitalized Raven for three days, but during that time frame, Wyatt was nowhere to be found. Raven later learned that the night she lay in the hospital alone, Wyatt was at a nightclub.

Once Raven was well enough, they planned an evening out at a club. As they were preparing to go out that night, Wyatt told

Raven how beautiful she was and how he knew every man in town envied him and how he was glad Eric Anderfal had walked away so she could be all his. They left for the club, and upon arrival, Wyatt got out of the car with Raven and walked into the club. He was used to the way Raven would get stares from other men when they were out in public. Raven, on the other hand, never saw herself in this light. She spent years alone without receiving compliments from others, and when she did, she would only say thank you and shy away and drop her head. Wyatt made Raven feel special true enough, yet his compliments would sometimes make her feel creeped out as they sounded like someone obsessed with looks.

    Tonight, at the club, Raven and Wyatt had been there for almost two hours with no problems, that was until Raven had to use the restroom and told Wyatt she would be right back. As Raven made her way from the bathroom, she then noticed as she opened the women's door to leave, a man's arms stretching from one side of the entrance to another and a line of ladies that seemed to be waiting for a chance to go to the restroom.

    It was Wyatt, and the reason the bathroom had gotten so quiet was that Wyatt had made his way down the corridor hall to the ladies' restroom and blocked the door as each female left.

    That's right; he blocked the door so no one else would be able to enter it. Raven was furious and asked Wyatt, "Wyatt what the hell is wrong with you? Why would you do something like that?"

Wyatt's response was, there was a men's restroom a few feet away, and he was not allowing anyone to get in to harm Raven. Raven left without another word to Wyatt and requested to go home. All the way back all she could think of was, what a crazy thing Wyatt had just done, and who the hell does that?

From that day on, things got even stranger. Raven tried to rebuild a relationship with her father again after years, but Wyatt would make sure that never happened. When Horatio would call to speak to Raven, he would deny her access to the telephones and tell Horatio; she was not home. The fact was, Raven would be sitting right there next to the phone, but that abuse had got so bad, that she began to fear Wyatt and for her life. On numerous occasions, Wyatt would tell Raven that he would rather see her dead than to allow her to leave him for some blonde-haired, blue-eyed man.

One day, Raven and Wyatt were having a conversation and, came up with an idea to go into law enforcement together, and Wyatt and Raven had decided to both enter the police academy.

As each day passed and Wyatt thought more and more about it, he no longer wanted Raven to go into the academy as there would be too many males there for his liking. When the time came, Wyatt went into the academy but refused to allow Raven to register to do so.

Bronze Bloodline of the Phoenix

After nine weeks the training was over, and Raven found herself married to one of their town's newest officers, but she would soon be in for the doozy of all times for her life was about to go from bad to worse. Upon graduation day, Raven, Wyatt, his family, and some of his new fellow officers, walked through town right after leaving the ceremony. As they passed three young men in a store, one of the young men made a statement out loud as Raven passed by with Wyatt and his friends and family. The young man turned and said, "Wow, she is beautiful," but, the young man did not realize he had just said the wrong words to the wrong guy's lady. Wyatt sprang into action and immediately grabbed the young boy up by the throat and pinned him against the wall of the store. Wyatt replied, "Boy, you don't know me. I will kill you if you look at my wife again." Raven stood there, helpless. Raven felt sorry for the young boy, and she tried to draw Wyatt's attention by calling his name in a calm voice.

She said, "Wyatt, Wyatt, baby. It's ok. He's young and doesn't know any better. Let him go," and then she said solemnly, "Please."

Wyatt must have heard Raven's soft voice, or perhaps he felt as if he had gone too far, or just maybe he spared the young man's life, either way, Wyatt, released the death hold he had on the boy as the young boy's body slid to the ground. Raven was both embarrassed and upset that her husband could become this type of man.

Their marriage was now on the rocks because of Wyatt's wondering eyes, and Raven had begun to see things in her dreams, again. Nightmares that were warning her of things to come. She had one dream that disturbed her so severely, that she had prayed about it to find out what it was trying to tell her. Usually, she would have had Eliza to fall back on as her mother was her best friend in the world, yet with Eliza now gone, Raven leaned more each day on her faith.

Raven had a neighbor who lived across the street from her that she had drawn close to, kind of someone to talk to about their marital problems. While at work one day, her neighbor made an upsetting phone call to Raven. She began to ask Raven if she could take off work and come home. Raven did not understand why she needed to take off work, but her neighbor soon explained it to her. Wyatt had recently taken a night shift position, as an officer and Raven had locked in a job at a local bank as a new account's agent.

She told Raven that she wanted her to come home now, but not to go the front way, she wanted Raven to take the back-road home. Raven was confused and asked why, the neighbor responded, "You need to do it, and you need to do it now."

Raven hung up the phone and made an excuse to her manager as to why she needed to leave. The manager allowed Raven to go without hesitation, and she jumped into her small car and headed home quickly. Upon arriving, she did just what the neighbor said and took the back-way home, but she was not prepared for what she found.

As she pulled up to her house and walked to her door, Wyatt greeted her. He wanted to know why she was even home. Raven tried to go pass Wyatt and into her own front door, but he blocked her and said, "Go back to work," but Raven did not listen. She knew something was up and pushed passed Wyatt, and as she tried to step up into her door, a woman greeted her. Yes, Wyatt had done the unforgivable, he had an affair in Raven's home and bed.

The affair resulted in Raven and Wyatt's separation. She started to feel as if life had it in for her. Wyatt and Raven stayed separated around three months before Wyatt could no longer live without Raven and he wondered who was she now seeing? He eventually moved back home, and they tried once again to patch things up, but it would never last.

One night, not even one week after Raven and Wyatt tried to reconcile, he was back at it again. Raven and her co-worker headed out for a couple of hours, but Raven wanted to stop at the corner store to get a pack of cigarettes. Her co-worker had driven that evening, so they left Raven's car parked at home. As they reached the corner store, Raven told her co-worker, "Stop right here. This is good. I can get a soda and smokes at this store". Once the car stopped, they both noticed a police car in the parking lot, but that was not unusual.

Raven walked into the store, and as she headed to the counter, she gasped as she noticed the girl behind the counter. That girl was not alone.

There was also another reason she gasped, and that was because no one other than Wyatt himself was embraced with the cashier. Raven tried to remain calm, but she had taken all she could stand of Wyatt's infidelity; she walked up to the counter, and calmly asked for a pack of smokes.

Neither person behind the counter said a word and Raven tried not to look at Wyatt. Wyatt never moved a muscle as if he was a stuffed doll sitting on a shelf. The cashier handed Raven the pack of smokes; Raven paid the cashier and turned around and walked out the door.

The ordeal was over as far as she was concerned. She was done with the craziness of Wyatt's womanizing days. The trick was, Wyatt was not finished with Raven, not by a long shot and she would soon learn just how crazy Wyatt Adams could become.

~~~

Wyatt was used to everyone obeying his orders as an officer, and he would not have it any other way in his home. Days past by and Raven never mentioned what she saw, but it was apparent Wyatt was no dummy, and he knew she would plot to leave him.

Raven got off work the following evening, and she came home to fix supper for both of them. Wyatt also seemed to be in a good mood, and the couple sat at the dinner table, making jokes and laughing together, right before the mood shifted. Raven told Wyatt, "Wow! Not bad for plain hotdogs, huh?" Wyatt responded, "Yea, these sure are good. "Raven made a mistake and said to Wyatt, "Yep, you'd better eat yours fast, or I just might eat yours, too."

These were the wrong words and as soon as she had said them, Wyatt's face changed, and his eyes got wide, and he sat up in his chair and said, "If you touch my hotdog, I will kill you." Raven did not think twice about it and thought Wyatt was joking when he made the statement.

Raven loved to joke around and have fun, so assuming things were good between them, she reached over as if she was going to touch his plate. Just as she reached, Wyatt took his rigid fist and struck Raven in the face. Wyatt punched her so hard that it knocked her from the front room into their living area more than fifteen feet away.

Raven was wearing braces, and the outcome showed. With blood running down her entire face, she could not tell where the blood was coming from. Usually, when Wyatt would beat Raven, he would go and stand over her as he kicked her in her head, face and stomach, calling her worthless. The enemy always stands over its victim once its prey is down and Wyatt knew the game as he defiantly saw Raven as prey.

As Raven struggled to get away from Wyatt before he began his routine of stalking and beating his prey mercilessly, she made her way to the bedroom. Wyatt being an officer, kept a Colt 45 and a Remington 870 Shotgun in their bedroom along with his walkie talkie.

Raven got herself to the foot of the bed and managed to pull herself up on the bed. That is when she realized, she would no longer accept Wyatt beating her. Raven reached for the Remington 870 Shotgun, loaded it and sat on the end of the bed. She knew that he would follow her, and this time, she would have the control to stop him.

In the past, she had gone to his superiors and tried to get help, but the brotherhood of officers will always supersede common sense. Therefore, there was no help for her. She had gone to his parents and tried to talk to them about Wyatt's abuse, but they blew it off and told her, "You know he doesn't mean it." One day she even took it a step further and reached out to the association of Internal Affairs, but while she was on the phone speaking to them, Wyatt showed up and showed out. He beat Raven in the middle of town, in broad daylight while Internal Affairs was still on the telephone, listening to the beating. So, you see, Raven knew no one would help her. She refused to tell Horatio about Wyatt, as she remembered the grief all her ex's had brought him in the past, so she remained quiet and dealt with it herself.

Again, God had bigger plans for Raven. While Raven sat on the bed waiting for Wyatt's usual punishment, she thought back over everything that he had done to her. She remembered a time when she purchased a pair of $12.00 walking shorts after work at one of the department stores, and once she arrived home, Wyatt beat her then forced her to return them to the store.

Raven's mind flooded with things that she had lived through with Wyatt. She also remembered back on a time when Wyatt got angry with her because he was sure that a blonde-haired and blue-eyed man had made a pass at her. This, in Wyatt's eyes, called for a step further than a beating. For this incident, the punishment was to strip Raven down and take his handcuffs and chain her to the refrigerator. He left her there for three days with no bathroom, no food, and no water. He gave her nothing for sustenance in those three days. On another incident, he was angry because Raven was ten minutes late coming home from work, and he believed she must have been cheating with a blond-haired blue-eyed man. To Wyatt, this required an unusual punishment, and he waited until she came home and as she was walking into the door, he grabbed her and slapped her a few times, stripped her clothing from her and threw her outside of the home and locked the door, leaving Raven cold, hungry and naked for an entire night.

After these memories of horror flooded her mind as she waited for Wyatt to walk through the door, a miracle occurred, and for the first time in the three years that Wyatt and Raven had been married, he did not follow her. Eventually Raven fell asleep, and Wyatt went off to work his midnight shift as usual. This was the best thing for everyone because before the sun rose, Raven had awakened in a different frame of mind.

As she stood up and looked into the mirror, she said out loud in the mirror as if she was talking to herself; I can no longer do this and then she looked at her mouth and saw it was ripped to shreds and said, "No, I *WILL*, no longer do this.

A change was about to occur, and she would, for the first time, take steps to resolve her own problems. Raven knew Wyatt would get off and be coming home soon from work. She made a mad dash to the bathroom, washed her face, grabbed her toothbrush, she slid on her t-shirt, blue jeans, and tennis shoes, grabbed her purse and keys and walked out of the door for the last time, at least so she thought. She drove to a payphone and made one call before she hit the road. She called Horatio, and she told him, "Daddy, I need $10.00 and please do not ask me for what, I will explain later. Horatio made the four-hour drive to Raven just to bring her the $10.00.

Raven took the money and put $9.00 worth of gas in her small car and used the other $1.00 and purchased a pack of

Bronze Bloodline of the Phoenix

cigarettes. She jumped back into her car and drove off into the sunset without a second thought. Raven had made up her mind, that she could do bad all by herself and would no longer allow the abuse to continue.

Episode XXII: Under Your Nose

Raven had made up her mind that she was sick of being everyone's punching bag as she drove off into the sunset, she feared that leaving her town would mean losing her job at the bank. She decided to take a few days and get away and come up with a game plan, plus she knew as soon as Wyatt found her missing, he would come looking for her.

After the fourth day in Tennessee, Raven remembered she had an old college friend that had a sister who lived in the town in which she worked. She called her friend up and told her the situation with Wyatt. Raven's friend told her, to go over to her sister's apartment, and she and Raven could share the rent allowing her to stay there. Raven drove back into town and headed to her friend's sister's apartment, not realizing Wyatt had gone on a crazy stampede, and he had the entire police force at all four precincts' looking for her.

Raven arrived that night at her friend's sister's apartment. Apparently, her old college friend had already called the sister and explained everything to her about what Raven was going through.

Everyone got comfortable for the evening, and later someone suggested perhaps it would be a good idea for everyone to go out for drinks. They all told Raven they had a favorite hangout that they knew police officers never frequented. This made Raven feel a little more at ease, and everyone agreed to head out.

They decided to take Flynt Barnes car, which was a friend of the sister that Raven would be now living with as they knew Wyatt did not know him or his vehicle, and they all felt as if Raven would be safe. Once they all arrived at the club, Raven could not believe how much fun she was having. She felt free, freer than she had ever felt, and unencumbered by problems, exes, and drama. Around three o'clock in the morning, they all headed back to the apartment. Once they arrived there, Tamara headed over to the couch and fell asleep, and Flynt's friend headed home. Raven decided to lay on the floor for the night and watch T.V., and shortly after she began to watch a show, Flynt came over and laid on the floor beside her.

That night as Raven lay there and began to think about everything that ever happened to her, she became overwhelmed with emotions and tears began to run down the side of her face. Flynt noticed Raven sobbing, and he took his hand and gently wiped her tears away, placed his arms around her waist, and said gently to her, "You're ok now. It's over; close your eyes and rest your mind".

Flynt told her that he was going to stay the night and would not leave her side. This was the beginning of something bigger occurring as Raven could feel his spirit as he laid next to her, and to her, his caring actions felt genuine.

Perhaps, she needed another soul to feel all the pain that she was in and fill the empty void she now had in her heart. She knew she had to leave Wyatt for good. ~~~

Raven came in from work one afternoon, and the gang all decided to have dinner together at Ravens and Tamara's apartment. The guys were somewhat good cooks, so they offered to bring potluck, and the girls would do the rest. After dinner that evening, everyone hung out, listening to music and chatting and then…

Knock. Knock. Knock. Tamara went to answer the door, but before she did, she decided to look through the peephole. When she peeped out, she quickly jumped back and gasped.

She turned around, and her face had gone pale, she looked at everyone and moved her lips, but not making any sounds, she said, "It's him."

Everyone sat up quickly as Flynt asked the question, "Who's him?" Tamara said," Wyatt." Wyatt was knocking on the door so hard you could hear it across the complex. Bam. Bam. Bam. He hit on the door with a hard bang as he yelled out, "Raven, I know you're in there. I just want to talk to you. We have to talk about this".

Flynt's friend quickly said in a whisper of a voice, "No Raven, don't. It's a trick." Flynt agreed and told Raven, "Don't, please don't. Don't go out there". Tamara moved away from the door and went over to Raven, grabbed her and placed one hand on her shoulder and another on Raven's chest and said, "No Raven, don't trust him.

He's lying. Don't go out there". What everyone did not know was, Raven was still very much in love with Wyatt, and she had hoped and prayed that he would change. Raven stepped away from Tamara as Wyatt beat at the door incessantly calling Raven and pleading with her to talk to him.

Raven trusted that Wyatt wanted nothing more than to talk to her. She knew in her heart they would eventually have to speak. The problem was, everyone in the apartment knew that Wyatt was taking the breakup hard and they could hear the desperateness in his voice as he shouted out for Raven.

Raven stepped passed everyone as they pleaded with her not to open the door but just as they shouted out, "Raven no please don't," she took the chain off the door, and before she could open it, Wyatt pushed his way right through the door.

He quickly snatched Raven and pulled her outside the door, grabbing her as if she was a rag doll, and then he threw her across his shoulder. Raven screamed as she fought the massive yet, powerful officer, but it was futile. Wyatt, a bodybuilder, spent all his free time preparing his body for his position as an officer on the police force. Her small body frame was no match for him.

He carried Raven down three flights of stairs while she fought and cried, begging Wyatt and saying, "Please, Wyatt no, please, dear God no." By the time he had got Raven into his car, everyone in the complex had been alerted. Everyone watched helplessly, as he held Raven down in the car by both her wrists with one hand and steered with the other hand. Her screams could be heard echoing through the parking lot, as they sped out of sight.

Raven's roommate and friends called 911, other citizens in the same apartment complex were also making the same call. Wyatt arrived back at the home that he and Raven once shared, he pulled up and dragged Raven out of the car by her legs. Raven continued to try and fend off Wyatt, but he had a firm hold on her, and there was no getting away this time. He pulled Raven through their front door as neighbors looked on just as helplessly as the citizens in the complex where Raven was kidnapped from. Wyatt dragged her through the door, locked the door, and let all the blinds down. Raven was terrified as Wyatt came after her. Raven shot through the kitchen and into the doorway of the bedroom.

Wyatt flew towards Raven and took her down with a football drive, causing her to land off the edge of the foot of the bed. She saw nothing but rage in his eyes as he said to her, "Baby girl, you ain't never leaving me, and this, I know."

The more Raven tried to push Wyatt off her, the more he slapped and punched her.

He seemed to find pleasure in watching Raven trying to get out from under him as he laid across her body with his body pinning her down. Wyatt raised up and grabbed Raven's face and positioned her eye level with his and said, "Can't no other man get what's mine." He then stripped Raven of her clothing and raped her. Every time she would yell for help, Wyatt would punch her in her face and tell her, "You're my wife. I can do what I want,". Every time she screamed how much she hated him, it only made him smile, and each time she would try to get out from underneath him, he would slap her harder and say to her, "Naw, you ain't going nowhere, you're mine."

Raven was screaming for help, and it seemed for a while as she was in the entire world alone, but just as she was about to give up, she saw it. Raven began to see blue lights outside her window as Wyatt was raping her. She then heard the sirens, and they seemed to be louder than she was, and she could see the blue and white lights outside her bedroom window, as she screamed for help. Someone had heard and seen Wyatt kidnapping her, and numerous calls came in at the same time to 911, and the police had been dispatched. The problem now was, it was not just the police outside Wyatt's door, but it was his police chief and numerous colleagues with a megaphone. He raised up and zipped up his pants and pulled Raven off the bed and threw her a towel.

The chief of police used the bullhorn on the police car and told Wyatt to come out and to let Raven go, but Wyatt was not hearing it, not at all. Wyatt grabbed Raven by the arm and dragged her to the kitchen so he could peep out of the window and see who was out there.

The chief continued to order Wyatt not to do this and how he should remember his job and that he should not risk his career for this. Wyatt broke a glass on the floor and picked up a large chunk of it with his right hand as he pulled Raven over to him and shoved her against the wall by the front door.

He placed the broken glass against her throat. At the same time, he heard his supervisor's voice call him down again, telling him to let Raven go and save his career. Wyatt looked Raven dead in the eyes, as he placed his forehead to hers and in a deep and gut-wrenching voice he whispered to Raven, "I love you up, I love you down, and I'll love you six feet in the ground."

This made Raven realize that this man was about to kill her to keep her from ever leaving him. She began to plead for her life by telling him Wyatt, "Baby, please don't, please don't do this. We don't have to be like this". All Raven knew was, she needed to survive this night, and to do so, she would have to convince Wyatt they had a chance to be together.

Wyatt's chief made one last plea, for Wyatt to release Raven unharmed, and this time, Wyatt snapped back to himself. He slowly allowed the broken glass to fall by his side as tears ran down his face. His grip had softened, and he began to caress Raven's arm and say, "I can't lose you; I love you, Raven; you don't understand."

Wyatt released Raven. The blue brotherhood protected him once again, and no charges were filed.

PART VII: Now, Which Way Do I Go

Episode XXIII: Lord Hear My Cries

Just barely having survived Wyatt's horrendous attack on her life, Raven left the home that they once shared as a married couple, upset, in tears and shaken, but still alive. Apparently, during the attack, her roommate Tamara and both young men had driven over to where Wyatt held Raven as a hostage during the standoff with police. They had patiently waited in a distant and safe location as they held on to hear the outcome of the confrontation.

Raven left the scene and rode back to the apartment with her friends, yet somehow, things would never be the same for her now.

~~~

Months went by as Raven had now formed a relationship with Flynt Barnes and eventually, they moved in together in a one-bedroom apartment in the same complex. As time went on, that relationship began to bear the same resemblance to Raven's past relationships, as it soon turned violent and Raven was no longer happy with Flynt. He too, had become dominant, possessive, and extremely combative. Raven saw this relationship as toxic and had begun to think of things and her future in a different light.

One-night Raven had heard about a university football game that was occurring in the town she lived in. The game was against the old university that she and Wyatt once attended.

Raven and some of her old college friends all now lived in the same apartment complex and had started to spend a lot of downtimes together. They had all decided to go to the game to support the old *alma mater*, which meant one's old university, school, or college that one once attended.

Everyone had become excited about the big game night since it would be the biggest one of the year. As the night came for the game, everyone seemed to be having a blast, and one of Raven's friends noticed that none other than Wyatt himself was sitting not too far away from the group.

Raven and Wyatt had not seen each other in quite some time; even though they had not filed for a divorce yet, they were still somewhat in love with each other. Don't get it wrong, Raven and Wyatt were intelligent, good people, the problem was, they just were not good together.

Wyatt spotted Raven like a leopard spots its prey, as she made her way to the concession stand for refreshments and he quickly made a B-line towards her. They both struck up a conversation, and one could tell, even though Raven was aware of Wyatt's temper, she was still very much in love with him and had a hard time ignoring his charm. Once the conversation was over, Raven made her way back to her friends, and the night went on, drama free.

Even though one of Raven's friends, who was a young lady by the name of Lula, told Raven that, she knew Wyatt was still in love with her, but this could prove to be risky. Raven heard what Lula said but blew her off. Obviously, Lula sensed something that Raven of all people did not pick up on, which was a dangerous situation.

As the night ended, Raven and her girlfriends made one last stop before heading back to the apartments but, Raven was unaware that Wyatt, had followed the girls back that night.

Once the girls pulled into the parking lot, so did Wyatt. Raven and her friends got out of the car and headed up the stairs to their apartments. Just as they did, Wyatt called out Raven's name. Mind you, Raven still had a thing for Wyatt, and she had not learned that she, plus Wyatt spelled trouble.

Raven told the girls, "You guys go ahead," and that she was going to see what was up with Wyatt. The two of them stood by the car talking, Raven foolishly let her guards down, and without any warning, Wyatt once again grabbed Raven and began to confess his deep and passionate love for her. Raven did not want Wyatt to touch her, even though she did want to hear what he had to say, and as he grabbed her, she pulled her arm away. This set Wyatt off, and without thinking, he caught Raven with both hands and flung her across the hood of a vehicle.

Raven was fighting desperately to release Wyatt's grip while telling him to get off her, and it seemed to give Wyatt more strength, and out of nowhere, Wyatt took Raven's head and slammed it into the hood of the car, while he confessed his undying love for her.

The residents in the apartments had heard the commotion and several of them had already called the police for a domestic violence scene, that appeared to be taking place in the parking lot.

In the meantime, Raven struggled to raise her head as Wyatt pounded his fist brutally into her head. As Wyatt noticed blood streaming from Raven's left ear, he slowed down his beating just enough for Raven to free herself from his grip and bolt towards the apartments.

She ran as hard as she could while begging for help and she managed to make her way to Lula's door. As Raven banged on the door screaming for help, Lula heard it, quickly unlocked the door, jerked Raven through it and, shut and locked it behind them.

Lula asked Raven if she was ok and she began to check Raven for wounds. Before either girl could determine the extent of Raven's injury, there was a loud bang on Lula's door, and it was Wyatt. He had chased Raven, but she had not noticed, and now her assailant was on the doorstep. Lula heard Wyatt screaming out Raven's name as he pounded on Lula's door, and she told Raven, "Don't move and don't say anything."

Lula responded to Wyatt's banging by saying, "Wyatt, stop hitting my door, Raven don't want to see you." Wyatt returned to Lula that it didn't matter what Raven wanted, he was going to see her, one way or the other.

Lula knew that she and Raven were now in an awful situation, and Lula managed to get to her purse, and without warning, she pulled out a lady's small firearm. Lula pointed at the door as she told Wyatt, "Get away from my door, and I mean now."

Wyatt had always been stubborn and believed he had the control since he was a police officer, and he took his foot and proceeded to kick the door. Lula took one step back and said, "Wyatt, get away from my door. I got a gun, and I will use it if you don't leave, and leave now". Wyatt and Lula knew each other from the university, and whether it was the fact that neighbors had called the police or that Lula had warned him that she had a gun, Wyatt made the decision to leave. Raven knew that night, Wyatt would one day find her and kill her. She was now no longer, going to allow herself to put others in harm's way.

Episode XXIV: Dream in Color

Now that Raven had finally understood she would never be safe if, Wyatt had access to her, she had no choice but to go to GOD in prayer, about her troubles. She sat down one evening with one of her college friends, Lula and both girls discussed all that had happened in Wyatt and Raven's relationship and just how dangerous things had become for her. In the previous month with everything that Raven had dealt with in her life, she had seen a psychiatric doctor for him to help her deal with her misplaced life, especially since Eliza had died a few years back and Raven was all alone. What the doctor told Raven was, if she were to get away from everybody, she might realize she did not want anybody in her life for a bit.

Raven took the doctor's advice to heart and spoke with Lula about it, but Lula had a different take on it. Raven had told Lula that she believed she was too good to the men in her life. She went onto say that; she thought she gave way too much of herself to them and that they always took advantage of her because of it. Lula's take was different and, what she told Raven was this, "No, that is not it at all." Lula said, what needed to happen was that she should not stop all the things that she was doing for a guy but, change who she does it for and find someone that is worthy and appreciates all the things that are done for them. All of this now started to make sense to Raven.

After she spent a couple of weeks really thinking long and hard about everything that ever happened to her, thinking about the loss of Eliza, her strained relationship with Horatio, all the failed relationships and abuse in her life, Raven came up with a decision.

The decision was a drastic one and a major one. Raven wanted to see her old friend Megan from back home, and she needed to see her father, so Raven planned a trip. She set up a trip to drive almost four hours home to see both Megan and Horatio, but first, she wanted to spend some time with Megan. She called Megan and told her she was on her way home for the weekend, and Megan agreed to meet Raven. She took the drive along the lonely highway and had almost four full hours of thinking time, and by the time she had reached Megan, she knew in her heart what she had to do. The girls met each other at a small coffee shop in town, which was one of Raven's favorite hangouts. As the two sat, laughed and chatted, Raven blurted out abruptly, "Meg, I'm leaving."

This caught Megan totally off guard, and she stated, "Leaving, but you just got here." Raven replied to Megan, "No, silly, I mean, I am leaving the state." Megan sat dumbfounded as she was not sure that she heard her best friend right. Raven looked over at Megan and said, "Well, crazy girl, say something," as she smirked at Megan. Megan looked at Raven and said, "Don't you think you're just a little extreme with the Wyatt thing." Raven went on to tell Megan that "No, I am not leaving the state because of Wyatt; she was leaving the state because of herself."

Raven tried to explain to Megan that she needed to find herself and regain some control over her life. She felt as if she has never really had control over her own life and things had spiraled into a state of unease, unrest, and with far too much discord. Megan looked over at Raven and asked her, "So, where to?" Raven replied, "What?" Megan asked Raven, "Where will you go?" and without hesitation, Raven stated, "The military."

Megan sat straight up in her chair, turned her entire head towards Raven, and said with a bizarre and puzzled look on her face, "Do what?" Raven replied again, "The military." Megan sat still in pure shock, as she could not believe at the age, they now were that Raven would contemplate such a thing.

They were both now twenty-eight years old. Megan told Raven, "You can never keep up with all the teenagers in there. "You know most of the people that go into the services, are right out of high school, and we are anything but out of high school, and we are certainly no teenager." Somehow, this did not faze Raven, as she had always been a strong-willed, headstrong and tenacious female and once Raven sunk her claws into something, there would be no one who could release her grip on it.

Raven knew that she needed to tell Horatio of her decision and hoped that he would be proud of her for making this choice. Horatio had already been saying to Raven, that he believed that unless she left that town, he thought that, Wyatt would not rest until he killed her. Horatio had now thought Wyatt had mental issues and feared for Raven's safety. Even though Megan did not like the idea, she had no other choice but to support Raven's decision and hope for the best for her friend. Megan agreed to go with Raven to break the news to Horatio, but first Raven had a pit stop she wanted to make.

There was a lady in town who was an elder in the community, that was born with a special gift. She had the gift of precognition, which is someone who can foresee future events, and Raven was curious to see just what the elder had to say about her future. The girls took off and headed over to see the elderly lady to get a reading for Raven. As they pulled up to the house, Raven noticed some weird-looking objects on the lady's front porch and Megan made a statement to Raven and said, "Maybe we should just turn around and leave." The porch was adorned with small stuffed animal carcasses all over the front area and by the door. The girls made their way through the open door, and a charming elderly woman greeted them. The woman appeared to smile and smirk as if she was expecting them. The two girls walked up to her and introduced themselves.

The lady looked at Raven and said, "Yes, I have been waiting for you," which caught Raven and Megan off guard as they had only decided to come within the past two hours, so how could she know they would arrive? The lady asked Raven to take a seat at a table she had prepared for the reading. Raven reluctantly pulled up a chair as did Megan. The elderly lady took Raven's hand and began to run her fingers through the lines of Raven's palm.

She told Raven that her future was about to change and that there was a man that would bring positive changes in her life. She went on to say to Raven that she would meet this man and very soon. Raven, being curious, asked the lady, how would she know that the man that she would meet would be that man? The lady told her that, the man that she would meet would wear creases in everything he wore and that he would be tall, dark and incredibly handsome and, well-groomed.

This was funny to Raven, and she laughed because she had heard of this expression only on the television and movies and everyone meets a tall, dark, and handsome man in the films.

The elderly lady then stopped Raven's laugh dead in its tracks, because she told Raven, "You will know him because he will place a ring upon your finger that will be no less than two carats" and that, that man would become the father of her three children.

To Raven, this was the biggest crock of crap she had ever heard as she already knew she could not have children, so she knew this elderly lady was full of it. Afterwards, Megan could not help but be curious about Raven's reading, and the two girls talked and laughed about it all the way to Horatio's house.

As they both arrived at Horatio's home, he seemed to be pleased to see his daughter and greeted both girls with open arms.

The girls walked into the house with Horatio and sat down with a crazy look upon their faces. Horatio noticed the girls looking as if they were both up to something, and he asked, "What ya'll up to, ya'll grinning like a Cheshire cat." A Cheshire cat was one of the mythical creatures from Alice in Wonderland. Megan could not wait to see Horatio's reaction to Raven's decision and blurted out quickly, "Rave's got something to tell you, don't you Rave?" Raven had planned to tell Horatio, but she was trying to wait until a little later in the visit, but since Megan could not hold water, Raven decided, why not tell him now?

Raven looked at Horatio and said, "Daddy, I got something to tell you, I have decided to go into the military." Raven waited to see a pleased look upon her father's face, but he said, "What? Are you crazy? Nobody goes into the military during wartime".

You see, the United States had entered a war campaign called "Desert Storm." It started on August 2, 1990, and Raven had already decided at the end of June to go in on a delayed leave. It horrified Horatio that his daughter would choose to do such a thing at this particular time.

Horatio had served during World War II and knew she might be called to put her life on the line. He wanted her to get away from Wyatt, but sending her to war, was not quite what Horatio had in mind.

He became angry, and in a thundering voice, he told Raven, "Damn Raven, the older you get, the dumber you get." Nobody in their right mind would sign up for the military service in wartime.

This was not the reaction she hoped to get from her father and again, instead of telling her how proud he was of her, he threw insults her way. This time Raven did not argue with Horatio. Instead, she stood up, looked over at Megan, and said, "Let's go Meg."

Whether Horatio meant to insult Raven with his hurtful words or not, no one would ever know, but this statement cut Raven to the quick, like a knife. As Raven and Megan walked out the door, Raven was now more hell-bent than ever to go through with it, sign up, swear in, and, earn her place in the United States Air Force as a soldier, just as her mother Eliza, father Horatio and her grandfather Chapman did in the United States Army so long ago. There would be no one or nothing that could or would stand in Raven's way. Raven did not know that her entire life would lead her to the fate and event, that would change the game of life forever.

Dallas P Elkheart

Episode XXV: Blue Angel's Prayer

Without hesitation, Raven and Megan left Horatio's house and headed back to town because Raven had a few things she had to do. One of those things was to put some closure to her relationship with Flynt Barnes. To her, it just was not working out for them, and she needed to let him know that she had decided to join the military and would be leaving. The one thing that she would not do was, tell Wyatt about her leaving. She already knew that he would never stand idly by and allow her to go without a fight.

Raven wanted to drive back to her old stomping grounds to pay her former roommate and college friends a visit and meet with her recruiter, so off she went on the long journey. While driving back down the highway on the four-hour trip, her memory went through the reasons that had brought her to this life-altering decision. Raven, thought about a conversation that she and Wyatt had a while back when he told her that the reason he married her was, he had always wanted to be married to a Hawaiian girl, with beautiful skin and long hair and to him, Raven fit that description and made his dream a reality.

Raven remembered how that made her feel, which was used, and she finally realized love was not part of the marital equation, only her looks mattered to Wyatt, and he did not know the meaning of love.

This pained Raven as she loved Wyatt, but the mental, physical and verbal thing, had driven her love to the back burner, and she would rather be alone, then a doll on a shelf, for some man's eye candy.

As Raven went by to tell everyone of her decision. They were all thrilled for her, all except, Flynt that is.

Raven met with a recruiter and did all the things that were required to join the Armed Forces. She even had to get a waiver, since she was right at the cut-off point based on age. Raven had signed up to become a proud member of the United States Armed Forces, and she left on December 11, 1990. Now she was set. Raven had just taken a new step in the right direction, and she knew that with the strictness of the military and base security, she would never have to worry about Wyatt again.

~~~

The night before Raven was to leave, one rule of going into the military was, that the recruit needed to spend that last night in a hotel before becoming an active duty member. So, Raven did just that.

That night, while not being able to sleep, she fell to her knees in tears as she realized life had dealt her so many blows that she was beaten, bruised, and empty inside. Raven began to pray as she had never prayed before. She went to GOD, totally empty, with tears in her eyes like a fragile piece of crystal glass, that had all the water poured from it, yet, still remained damp with teardrops. She spoke to GOD and said, "Lord, I come before you empty, with nothing left to give you. I am beaten, worn out, and I am defeated. So, my lord, I come before you and ask if you could, one day send me someone that would love me half as much, as I could love them and, I will never forsake him. This I pray, in the name of the father, and the son and of the holy spirit, AMEN.

Raven crawled back into her bed that night frightened, worn out and only a mere shell of herself and fell asleep. The following day, as she got on the plane leaving her former life behind, she was not sure what tomorrow would hold, but what she was sure of was, whatever it held for her, she would put on her big girl pants and face it alone. Her plan was to achieve the rank of Lieutenant, and once she had accomplished this mission, she would finally, adopt a child and become a single mother, as she was no longer willing to suffer at the hand of others, or accept abuse, just to have a mate.

The plane landed, and Raven found herself in a world she had never seen which comprised of hundreds of young teenagers, while she was now a mature twenty-nine-year-old.

She saw recruits jogging from point A to point B all over the base as she heard a loud and obnoxious voice yell, "Recruits, fall in." This was about to take Raven to a whole new level of self-discipline, and as she would soon learn, she was already a great candidate for discipline.

A few days passed, and Raven was now a recruit. The TI's came around looking for musicians. A Military Training Instructor (aka) Drill Instructor is referred to as a TI. Raven had been a musician all of her life so, the TI's pulled Raven from her regular flight and placed her in the United States Drum and Bugle Corps. Raven had learned how to play every instrument except the guitar throughout her musical career.

Her new assigned musical instrument would now become the steel marching quad drums which, could weigh in at over fifty-five pounds. Raven was up for the challenge even though she only weighed in at 120 pounds soaking wet. The funny thing was, Raven, did not mind as she loved her music, and this was a treat for her.

Each dormitory had a dorm chief. *Dorm Chief's* had the responsibility to make sure that every order was followed and, all standards were met, in the TI's absence. It was said that most dorm chiefs don't make a lot of friends because they are the enforcer of the flight, but this would not be the case for Raven.

When Raven first arrived into her new flight, they had placed a young lady in as dorm chief, but within one week, she was removed because, they believed that she lacked the qualities of a leader, but who would their chosen replacement be?

After the instructors had considered the prospects for Reese's flight. The TI's now knew who they believed possessed the qualities that the military needed to be in charge of this flight, and that was Reese. Yep, you heard it right; Raven Reese was now being placed in the position of dorm chief for the females that belong to the Drum and Bugle Corps. Horatio's words had come to pass. Before Raven left to join, Horatio told Raven that, once she got there, that they would be putting her in charge of things.

Raven Reese was finally getting the last laugh in on all of those that had ridiculed and shunned her during her lifetime by calling her worthless, stupid, weak and dumb.

Now, the same female that had suffered so much at the hands of others was now the same female that the United States Military believed had the right stuff to lead her flight of recruits to the victory of graduation.

Raven could not wait to call home and tell her father, that he was right, which by the way, would be the first time in life Raven said to her father, that he was right about anything. So, this would become a moment to be cherished for both parties.

Weeks passed, and things got harder, but Raven Reese was able to handle it, not only her new responsibilities as a new dorm chief but, her duties as a recruit. As the last few weeks of boot camp were narrowing down, she was called to the office of personnel, where she was informed of a clerical error that had been made regarding her rank.

They said to her that her recruiter should have brought her in as a lieutenant but, they had given her the wrong rank.

They explained to her that they would make the correction as soon as her technical school was over. This had been Raven's dream to become a lieutenant in the first place.

Even though Raven was in this new world of military training now, she continued with the same prayer that she had said before leaving for the service and never forgot to include GOD in her daily prayers.

During this time, Raven had got a few surprises from her flight. They say dorm chiefs simply do not make a lot of friends and in Raven's lifetime she'd had trouble with females that refused to allow her to be a part of their friendship circle, but things had changed now; in the military, she had finally found a place for her personality.

~~~

As the time was coming for lights out, and with all the craziness in the barracks after a full day of exercise and other duties, Raven forgot to prepare her locker, uniform, and boots for inspection. She accidentally fell asleep across her bunk bed, and in the meantime, everyone else was scrambling to get finished with detail duties, that Raven had assigned them. No one woke her since they could see she was dog tired from the day's activities. Everyone went to bed as lights out approached. Everything was tranquil and still until a door swung open and the light went on, and a deep, masculine voice bellowed, "Everybody, get your sorry asses up, and get the hell out of the beds."

Three TI's were standing in the doorway with arms folded and at a parade rest position, a startled flight of females scrambled to get out of bed abruptly. Raven thought she was dreaming and was a little slow to awake, but when she woke and saw the TI's, she popped up into attention. But wait, she also realized that she forgot to prepare for an inspection that night. Raven could not do anything but think to herself, holy crap, I'm so screwed.

You see, the lockers were all closed as that is a requirement for the barracks and safety, so Raven could not see inside her cabinet, but she knew the TI's would check hers if no one else's. After all, she was the dorm chief, and they must set the example. As the TI's made rounds, they snatched lockers open, and pulled out underwear drawers, jerked boots up to check for what the Air Force called a 341.

A 341 is the form used to document discrepancies. Any recruit with common sense knew they never wanted a 341 pulled on them. Raven began to cringe as the TI's came towards her locker because she knew if they opened the locker door, it would be game over for her. As the TI's approached her locker, one stopped right at Raven and placed his TI hat down towards her face as he looked under-eye at her and said, "Recruit, your locker, right?" Raven responded, "Sir, Yes, Sir" and the other TI reached for the locker handle as Raven took a hard swallow. Just as the locker door swung open, Raven's eyes jumped right out of her pretty little head because she was not ready, for what she would see.

What she saw was, her uniforms were hung neatly, her underwear drawer had been folded to perfection and her boots, well, her boots were so shiny, she could have used them as a mirror to put on the red lipstick that she loved so much as a civilian. How could this be, Raven thought to herself as the TI's moved to the next locker.

Raven looked around at her flight, never moving her head, only her eyes while she still stood at attention, and as she did, she started to get winks from each member of her unit. The winks made Raven's heart melt, as she realized her entire flight had stepped up on her behalf and did what all the people in Raven's lifetime had not done for her, which was, they had her back.

These were total strangers that were all thrown together by a decision to join the armed forces, and within a few weeks, they had banded together to protect one of their own and someone who was not just one of their own, but someone that they took orders from.

After the TI's left and everyone had passed inspection, they all rallied around Raven's bed, and she asked, "Who did this for me?" She wanted to thank them for supporting her when she was so tired. Instead of one person stepping forward and saying, "It was me," the entire flight of twenty plus females all said simultaneously, and with an uplifted voice and smiles, "Oh, we did."

Raven had been given the nickname of Purple by her hospital roommate when she was a young girl. It seemed that her TI's and flight resurrected the name again, even though they had no prior knowledge that Raven had received this name as a child. Apparently, she emanated the color of *"Purple"* as her aura for her entire life and, everywhere she went.

So, as the flight went on to tell Raven, "Purple, we knew you were so tired, and you always do special things for us, so we wanted to do something special for you because we think you are one of the coolest dorm chiefs around."

Raven's heart and personality that made everyone push her away in her lifetime, was the same personality that these females found lovable about her. Raven loved her flight of females and would have done anything to help them. Raven saw them all as little sisters that she never had, and this new family meant the world to her.

The day came for graduation, and even though everyone there had family and friends that flew in from miles away to support them on this day, Raven had no one there for her, but she received her graduation ribbon with as much pride as anyone with family there.

To her, she had just done the impossible as many had told her that she was simply too old to be going up against teenagers fresh out of high school. As usual, Raven saw things differently, and what she saw was that she had not gone against teenagers much younger than herself, she had gone with them. This day, Raven gained not only new friends, but a new perspective on her life, and she learned that day, that if God brings you to it, he will for sure carry you through it, as she felt, contrary to popular belief, she had done the impossible, but not alone.

After graduation, Raven took a flight to her next duty station, which was a technical training school in Sawicki, Colorado. Once she arrived, a whole new type of world opened for Raven. One day Raven had gone to class, and once class started, she became ill. As a small girl, she had a fragile immune system and was extremely sickly frequently. Eliza would give Raven cough drops to help her sleep through the nights, but the side effect was cavities, because of the excess sugar. This created dental issues, and this day, when Raven took sick, it was because of a bad tooth. Once she got to class, she began to have a severe toothache. The instructor released her that day to go to the dental clinic, but before it could be repaired, her tooth exploded in her mouth. Classes were held daily, and Raven was put on quarters for three whole days, which caused her to get behind in her studies.

Once Raven was well enough to return to class, the instructors thought she needed individual sessions to catch her up.

They had her go down the hall to a classroom to receive one-on-one instruction. Raven made her way down the hall and, she sat there in her chair; the door opened and in walked a man.

This was not just any man, because this man caught Raven's attention immediately as he walked into the room. He was very tall, with thin lips, and the cutest pointed nose that was placed perfectly between the most gorgeous eyes that Raven had ever seen. His facial features were unlike most men that she had seen. To her, he was beyond handsome. He was downright hot.

As he walked in and smiled, Raven sat mesmerized by a smile that appeared to be so peaceful. The instructor walked over to the table, and pulled up a chair, opened his book and began to teach Raven the lessons that she had fallen behind in. The thing was that, even though this man was teaching Raven, she could not focus on anything that he was saying and, in her mind, all she could hear was his soft and soothing voice and the way it sounded with every word he spoke. For whatever reason Raven could not take her eyes off him, that is until he would look up to see if she was comprehending what he was teaching, and Raven would quickly look down as if she heard every word he had said.

She also noticed as she would look down and he would speak to her, she could see him looking at her as he spoke, and this gave Raven chills down her spine. What was happening to Raven? Why was she so intrigued by this man? Why was he so mystifying to her? Raven tried to pull herself together and do what she was assigned to do, but her mental state had become less than stable as she could not focus for one moment on anything other than him

This class session lasted for one week, and each day, Raven would go through the same scenario as he would catch her looking at him and she would catch him eyeballing her.

At the end of the week, the session was over, yet, Raven could not get this guy off of her mind. In the following days, she would take her breaks and walk the halls, hoping to see him. In the meantime, Raven continued to pray the same prayer every night relentlessly for a mate, and she arose each day with a new lease on life. Another week had passed by, and she started to believe that she would never see the instructor again, and it was now time to move to the on-the-job training phase of the course.

As she made her way over to her allocated building on the first day of OJT, she arrived and gathered with her classmate's. Everyone was about to find out where they would be placed and who they would be assigned to for the remainder of the required training.

As Raven stood chatting with her fellow soldiers, she stepped away to take a break, and that is when it hit her like a ten-ton mac truck. As she stood on the outside deck looking across the base, she realized it was Valentine's day, and everyone seemed to have someone special in their lives except her. Sure, she had numerous men that liked her, for various reasons, but none of them loved her unconditionally, and none of them held any major significance in her life.

She stood there and tried not to let tears trickle down her face as she was in uniform and did not want to appear meek or weak. Raven realized she should pull herself together and make her way back inside because soon instructors and workstations would be assigned, and she did not want to be late. In the military, if you are fifteen minutes early, you are late, so late was not an option.

Raven went inside but quickly realized that her mascara was smudged and went over to the open area kitchen sink to wash her hands and her face.

As she reached into the sink to wash her hand, a man was putting his hands under the running water at the same time without either noticing the other and then they looked up at each other. Well, it was a miracle because the man was the same instructor that she had been walking all over campus looking for. He smiled and struck up a conversation with Raven just as it was time to be assigned to instructors.

Bronze Bloodline of the Phoenix

They started to call out the names of students and the instructors that they were assigned to. As they got to Raven's name, they called out, "Reese, you are assigned to Reid's class." Well, Raven took a step out of line, and as they pointed to the instructor that Raven would be assigned to. She thought she was dreaming because her instructor was none other than Casey Reid. Reid was the instructor that tutored Raven back a few weeks ago, you know, the one she walked the halls looking for and the one that she had just shared a handwashing session with.

For once in Raven's life, she felt as if fate had finally dealt her the right hand as she stepped over to her new instructor. One day Raven was out on the back deck, with another co-worker having a smoke break and Casey showed up to take one. They noticed each other, and Casey asked Raven if, she had Native American in her bloodline? Raven replied back, "Why yes, yes, I do. Do you, because you look like you do?" Casey was quick to answer Raven back with a "That's what they tell me."

Raven stood looking at Casey for a few minutes, and then she realized, she knew. She remembered something that Horatio had told her before she left home to go into the military.

He had said to her, "That she would meet her future husband in the military." Raven thought about the one question she had asked Horatio when he made that statement which was, "Daddy, how would I know, if I met the person? How, would I know it's him?"

She remembered what he said with five little words, which were, "Oh, believe me, your heart will tell you."

Raven snapped back to herself, as she was in a daze, and she looked over at her co-worker and said in a low voice, "That's him, that's the one." Her co-worker thought Raven had lost her mind as she replied, "That's who?" Raven quickly responded, "That's the guy that I am supposed to marry.

But then, her co-worker replied with a sharp and sarcastic voice saying, "Girl, that's who? Fool, you don't even know his name". Raven told her co-worker, "Maybe not, but I know he is the one. My heart tells me so".

Within three days, Raven received a note from Reid, asking her if she would like to go out with him. This note had been handwritten and slipped into Raven's palm, as Reid passed her one day at work. She moved away quietly to the ladies' room to read what he wrote. Raven had no idea where all of this was going, and she did not care, if, Reid was part of the trip.

Raven took Reid up on his date, and they scheduled a romantic evening together at a jazz club. Reid was a vocalist and had a voice made of pure gold. His vocals were so magnificent that everyone called him the "Singing Instructor." As the day came when Raven and Casey were set for a date night, Raven went all out. She went into town and bought the most elegant evening dress she could afford and made sure she had the shoes to match. After all, she was her mother's child, and Eliza would have had it no other way.

She spent over three hours having her hair done, just for the evening. To be able to dress up for the evening was a treat. All females wore their blues in the Air Force, as dress clothing.

Raven spent hours preparing for this date even though she had sworn off men, because of her history of misfortunes, but somehow Casey was different because her heart said he was unique. That night, Raven got dressed and walked out into the lobby to await a cab to take her to where she was to meet Casey. When she walked out all five feet and six and a half inches were framed in a black sequins short evening dress, matching black sequins stilettos and much like her mother, she wore dark stockings that enhanced her long shapely legs. Oh, and let's not forget just to prove that Raven was her mother's child, she wore her signature ruby red lipstick to top everything off.

As the cab driver pulled up to the military base and Raven stepped into the car, she told the driver that she had a curfew and that she must be back on base before twelve o'clock midnight or she would be considered AWOL. Off she went to meet her prince charming at the jazz club.

When the cab pulled up, Raven stepped out nervously as she was not sure what the night would bring, and she hoped Casey would recognize her when he saw her. He always saw her in military clothing, but tonight he would see what was behind the BDU's.

Casey looked different to Raven tonight, and she realized he was even more attractive than she thought. They both quickly moved to a table, and it was as if no one else was in the nightclub except Raven and Casey. They became so entangled with each other, they totally forgot about the time.

They talked and laughed for the longest time before they were abruptly interrupted. Raven and Casey's base was a little more than thirty minutes away. Therefore, Raven would have needed to leave the club at no later than eleven twenty-five that night to have a chance of making it back on time. The abrupt interruption was the nightclub owner informing Raven her cab was now there. Raven and Casey looked at their watches and behold, it was now eleven-forty-five at night. Now, there was a problem.

Raven freaked out and jumped up from her table and ran to the door, and then she remembered, she wanted a kiss, so she ran back to Casey and grabbed a quick one. She bolted to the door and just as she was trying to scramble to get into the cab, her right shoe flew off. She had no time for technicalities, so the driver kept going. The trick was they had to beat the clock and midnight would arrive soon. They raced to base trying to beat the clock and luckily Raven had made some terrific friends in her dorm because they would be the only ones that could save her butt that night.

Bronze Bloodline of the Phoenix

The cab pulled up close to the area that would allow Raven to jet to her dorm before being found out. The problem was that the dorm doors automatically locked just as midnight approached and Raven could not get in.

Well, until a secret admirer on base, saw her panicking trying to get inside and he saved Raven's butt, by sneaking the door open. It was now twelve-fifteen pm and ironically, the one person who had a crush on Raven, who she saw only as a friend, was the one person who saved her career that night.

Raven nor Casey had any way of reaching each other as neither knew where the other lived. Even though they had no idea about each other's whereabouts, fate would play a role in the love affair that was about to take flight. Three days passed and Raven had not heard from Casey, and by now she had felt used, yet once again. She watched the phone, and she became like a zombie. She refused to eat; she did not want to sleep, and all she could now do was cry, as she felt she should never have believed that life could deal her anything good, including love.

During all these weeks at training, she continued to say the same prayer each day; she hoped it would bring something different, but this time, GOD heard his small angel's prayer. Because the phone rang. It was Casey, and he needed to tell Raven why he did not call her over the past three days. He proceeded to say she scared him.

He told her that he had never had these types of feelings before, and he was not sure how to handle them, but he was now confident about them. Raven already knew how she felt; therefore, there was one last thing she needed to do. She immediately got off the phone because she had to make two last calls to tie up any loose ends. She called Flynt and then she called Wyatt and what she said to them would set everything into motion.

She asked both guys, Wyatt and Flynt a question that she knew the answer to, yet she had to hear it from them.

She asked them each if she were to come back to the state, where would that put their relationship? The answer Raven received was just what she needed and wanted to hear which was, "I don't know," and she replied to both, "Yea, well I do know, so just so you know, I won't be coming back and have a great life."

All loose strings had now been tied, and she called Casey back to let him know, she was all his, both heart and soul. Oh, remember the stiletto, the one that flew from Raven's foot at the club that night just before the stroke of midnight. Well, none other than her Prince Charming retrieved and returned that shoe. Not only did he find the shoe, but he had also discovered his princess that the shoe belonged to. Raven now understood that her prince would not be riding a white horse. He would be wearing those Air Force Blues.

Bronze Bloodline of the Phoenix

For once in Raven's life, she felt she was now on the right track and that God had not forgotten or forsaken her, he merely had other plans. She had believed that her prayers for someone who would love her as much as she could love them had finally been heard. Raven thought that Casey might have been slow responding to her after their first date, but he was now full speed ahead, and there would be no turning back for either. The two of them were not sure where all of this would head, but wherever it was, they would be there for each other at all cost. Raven now knew that GOD might not always come when you want him to, but she sure knew one thing, he would always be on time.

Casey and Raven began to spend every waking moment together, and the love between them was undeniable and was becoming relentless, for two of GOD's angels had finally flown right into the wings of the other

Dallas P. Elkheart

Episode XXVI: Ouija? What? I'm Not Alone

Raven's time for training was just about over, and another miracle happened. You see, Raven was scheduled to be deployed as soon as she finished training school to serve in support of Operation Desert Storm. A few days before her training ended, the war ended. This meant she would no longer have to deploy to a war zone. Casey was ecstatic and made some plans.

Casey was stationed at the base in Sawicki Colorado, but once training was over, Raven would have to go back to her original base in Mississippi. This would mean, the two of them would have to be separated, and they might never see each other again. This simply could not happen in their eyes. Casey and Raven by now had fallen deeply in love. Casey had decided that he would request to move to a base close to her to keep them from ever being apart and Raven thought that was one of the most selfless acts that a man could do for a woman. With that said, Raven then made the decision that since she had been in the military far less time than Casey, that she would be the one to request to be moved to his base instead.

Heaven had someone watching over these two carefully. Raven was able to have her request granted, and the two of them would now be together. After Casey heard the news, he had a little surprise for Raven.

Even though Raven did not know it, but he wanted to be

sure she had a roof over her head, and a safe place to close her eyes while in his arms. On March 15, 1991, exactly one month and one day after their eyes met each other, Casey had Raven come over to meet him at his new apartment. When the taxi arrived, Casey met her outside in the parking lot, greeting her with a loving hug and kiss.

He walked Raven to the door, and as he opened the door, Raven was stunned as he said, "Well, what do you think?" Raven stood in the doorway breathless as she looked around at the small one-bedroom apartment, and she said, "Oh my God, I love it!!!"

What came next was a game-changer as Casey told Raven, "Well good, I know you love fireplaces, and since I got this for us, I hoped you would like it." Everything stopped. Raven could not believe what she had just heard. Raven loved fireplaces as she never grew up with one in the south, and she seemed to be mesmerized by them.

She loved watching the colors of blues, golds, reds, and oranges as it burned and would lose herself in the soothing flames. This man, Casey Reid who had only known her all of one month, yet, had been willing to adjust his life and move to be with her. He also had just gone through the trouble of getting a new apartment, not only for him but for them. As Raven stood there embraced with Casey, her heart was overwhelmed with joy, love, and a grateful feeling of belonging for once in her life.

She had finally found a man, that was her soul mate, and they could not wait to start their lives together in their new home.

After about four weeks, Casey had continued his education in leadership school, and Raven had taken a part-time job off base at a corporation. The plan was to help each other become debt-free, so when their new lives began, they could focus strictly on their future and not their past.

Casey had been married previously as well but had separated from his wife a few months before he met Raven, and Raven was still separated from Wyatt. Neither one had filed for divorce as neither one knew what they really wanted at the time. Things had now changed, and they both now understood that they wanted each other, and they knew that they belonged in each other's wings.

~~~

Raven's dreams at night had now turned into full blast visions, and they were becoming more powerful than ever; however, Casey had not learned of Raven's abilities or gifts. Not yet. One morning Raven woke up in a fearful state. She jumped straight up and out of bed and ran into the living room where Casey was up and watching television, but not the news channel.

She said to Casey, "Oh, my God, a plane just exploded, and bodies are everywhere." Casey just looked at her, because he was not sure about what she meant, as he thought perhaps, she had a dream and was informing him about it. That was not it at all. Raven had just seen her very first national catastrophe. She asked Casey to turn the T.V. to the news channel. As he flipped the channels, and within 30 minutes, there it was. An airplane had just exploded with more than 232 people aboard, and there were no survivors. What she had seen was an airplane explosion as it occurred, but before it was known publicly. What she did not know, and perhaps someone should have pre-warned Casey was that her visions were about to become full-blown, and her gift would become unleashed to its maximum capacity, and no one would be able to control it.

One evening, around seven o'clock, Casey and Raven had come in from work, and after supper, they went to a general merchandise store, where they thought it would be cool to get some fun games to play together.

They ran across some old and familiar games that had brought many American family's much joy, such as the game operation, a deck of playing cards, and checkers.

As they walked further down the aisle, they spotted another game, called Ouija. It is supposed to be only a kid's game, at least so Casey and Raven thought…. But boy, did these two get this one wrong.

As they passed the Ouija board, Raven stopped and asked Casey, "Hey, look at this game. What kind of game is this?" Casey replied that he did not know much about it, but told Raven, "It looked like a fun game. Why don't you grab one?"

Raven picked up a box with the game in it, but a strong urge struck her, and she did not want that box, she wanted a different box with the same game in it. Casey wanted to know, "Why, didn't she want the other game? What was wrong with the box she had in her hand".

However, Raven was persistent, that she wanted the other box. They headed to the front cash register and placed everything upon the checkout stand, but something was terribly wrong here.

As a matter of fact, Raven was so insistent about the other box that she told everyone, "Could you wait one minute, please." She grabbed the box on the checkout counter and headed all the way back to the games to return the box she had and get the other box. The question now that faced Casey was, "Why?" Why was it so crucial for Raven to get the other box, and what was the difference? What he did not know, he would soon find out, the hard way.

Casey and Raven made their way home and put everything away, except the Ouija board. Raven flipped the box over to read the back of the box before putting it away. They both noticed that it had a warning on the label that said, "Do not play this game alone." After reading the advice on the box, it gave Casey an issue to be concerned about, so he told Raven, "Babe, let's agree not to play this game unless we are together, OK?" Raven agreed, and they put the game away. A couple of days passed, and, in the afternoons, they would play a different game each evening to pass the time before bed.

One afternoon, they tried out the new game, and Raven pulled out the Ouija board. They both sat down and set the game up and then read the instructions and then began to play. The way one plays this game is, by using a little piece of wood called a planchette.

The planchette is placed on the board, and a person's fingertips are lightly placed on the planchette. Then you ask the board questions. The planchette should move with no effort, and if it does, then something, not someone is the reason it moves. Raven and Casey sat down to play the game, and Raven decided she would be the first one to ask it questions and she had a few she could not wait to ask it.

She began by asking the board about her and Casey, and she asked it if she and Casey would stay together?" The planchette started to move to the yes location and stopped on yes. She asked it again how long they would be together, and it spelled out, "forever."

Raven laughed because she just knew Casey was moving the planchette with his hands and was trying to be funny. She told

Casey, "Stop it. Stop moving the thing." Casey replied to Raven, "I did nothing." "You had to have moved it."

She decided she would ask a question that no one knew because she had not yet told Casey. Raven then asked the board," What was my name at birth, if you're so smart?" The board then, threw Raven for a spin as the words began to spell out slowly, Bella.

Raven moved her hands and jumped back and said to Casey, "Ok, smart ass, that is so not funny." Casey responded, "What are you talking about?" I did not do a thing. And besides, you never told me that. Was it right?" Raven sat their stone-faced as she could not believe how accurate the board was with her name.

She paused for a moment, and then she placed her hands back on the board and told Casey, "Come on, I've got another question." Raven then asked the board, "How many children will Casey, and I have?" The planchette drifted over to the number three and stopped. Raven moved her hands off the board and said, "See, I know it's lying since I cannot have kids."

Casey tested it for himself with a question that he knew he had not yet, told Raven, which was, "What was my mother's maiden name?" The response he received threw him a real curveball when the board responded, "Martin." Casey could not believe it since; he never told Raven his mother's maiden name. It was accurate.

The two of them got a little spooked and called it quits for the night. Anyone that knows anything about Ouija boards should know that you never stop this game, without saying goodbye, but they did not know this, so no goodbyes occurred. This would prove to be their second mistake as the first one was when they purchased the board. The Ouija board is anything but a game as they would soon learn. They did not know it, but the board is used as an oracle to gain information about the future. Several days passed before they tried it again, one afternoon they pulled it out.

This time, Casey had an exam that he would take in a couple of days, and he was curious about the test results. They sat down that afternoon and asked more questions, and the first thing Casey asked was, "What will I make on my exam this week?" The board was quick to respond with numbers this time, and it gave the numbers 96. Casey gave the boards answer, very little thought. As the date came about for Casey's exam, he received his results and could not call Raven quick enough to tell her what he made on his test.

After getting his result, he became concerned about Raven because he was now beginning to believe something was eerie with this game. He phoned Raven, and as she answered the phone, the first thing that came out of her mouth was, "So, how did you do on the test?" Casey hesitated at first, and then he stated, "I passed it. I made a 96."

Both Casey and Raven got quiet, and then Casey told

Raven, "We need to talk, but not at home." Casey was now starting to believe that something could hear their every word during their personal conversation, and this concerned him seriously. Four days passed, and things had become a little creepy at their new apartment. Items were being moved around. Keys would come up gone and then reappear, cups and glasses would be moved.

It had gotten dreadful. At night, they would wake up in the middle of the night, and they could feel something in their room, yet they could see nothing. They could feel a presence standing by their bed upon sleeping or waking.

Casey had been raised in the church and held a spiritual foundation as Raven did, but he was at a deeper understanding of spiritualism than Raven was at this point. Casey decided one night to pull out the board; his intent was to find out, whether it was just a game or were they in over their heads.

As Casey pulled out the board, he also pulled out another piece of ammo, the Bible. He knew how he would determine just what they had on their hands. Casey and Raven wanted to find out what they had come across. Raven asked the board, "Just who are you? "This time the board replied, "CJ." Raven then asked, "Where are you?" The game board replied, "Hell."

This startled both Casey and Raven, and she asked it, "Are you dead," and it replied, "Yes." Raven then asked it, "How did you die?" and the board responded, "car wreck."

Raven, being Raven could not leave well enough alone, so, she hit it with a big question that she wished she would never have asked. She asked the board, "Where did you die?" As if she really wanted or needed to know, but nevertheless, she asked. The board then replied, "Outside in front of the apartment." This stopped Raven right in her seat as she sat still and looked over at Casey.

Now it was Casey's turn, and he kicked things up a notch or two and took things to a whole new level. He started with a question that apparently upset the board when he asked it, "Do you know Michael?" Everything halted, the planchette stopped moving and refused to move. Casey then asked, "You know, your brother, the archangel Michael?" Apparently, this was not what the board wanted to hear, and Casey realized, they no longer had just a game, nor were they any longer playing a game. They had an entity and were dealing with pure evil.

The following day, Casey told Raven not to touch the game unless he was there. That afternoon, after supper was over, they went into their bedroom and sat on the side of the bed. Raven pulled out the game as Casey wanted to find out if it would answer the question this time about Michael the Archangel. Raven opened the board, and as they began to ask it questions, things took a turn for the worse.

The board let it be known that CJ wanted Raven and that it had nothing but contempt for Casey. The fact was Casey was too spiritual for it and found Casey as a rival and only in its way. It knew that Casey would do whatever it took to protect Raven and himself from the grips of evil and it would not stand for that.

As Raven and Casey sat on the side of the bed perplexed at what the board had just spelled out for them, something crazy occurred. Casey was sitting on the same side of the bed where Raven was, and with no warning, he fell backward and into a profound sleep. Raven realized something had happened to Casey, and she tried fruitlessly to wake him. She shook him; she yelled out his name, she even pulled him by his arm, but he would not move. He was like a male version of Snow White placed into an eternal sleep. Raven sat there for a moment as she tried to find a way to get Casey awake. She still had the board and planchette on her lap as she asked this entity where "CJ was right now?" To her surprise, it spelled out, "Near." Raven began to look around as if she thought she could feel someone in the room with her, and it was not Casey.

Raven, then asked the board one final question as she took a chance on her answer. She asked, "What do you mean near? How near?" She was not ready for the answer she received. The answer was, "Very Near." When Raven looked around to her right, she saw Casey, but when she looked to her left, what she saw was mind-blowing.

What she saw was a butt impression forming right beside her on the left side of her bed. The entity was now sitting right by her side. Raven lost it, threw the board and the planchette across the room as she jumped up from the bed in an all-out panic. Right about that time, Casey woke up abruptly, and it was a wrap, they were so done.

Raven and Casey now knew that what they had was a real entity and unseen force, and dangerous. What started out as a game had now become a threat to their souls, and immediate action had to come, and quickly.

The following day Casey had instructed Raven to not discuss anything at home. Each night for the next two days, they would sit in their car to have all conversations about how to handle it. Raven was afraid the entity would try to harm Casey as it wanted Raven by any means necessary. They now needed to seek outside help from a priest or someone that understood what they had accidentally conjured up. They placed a call to Ariel Books. It was a bookstore real enough, but it was not just any bookstore. This bookstore had a specialty in crystals, some jewelry, different oils, herbs, incense, and new age books. The biggest thing that they specialized in was Mediums. They needed a medium because they can identify hidden things the ordinary senses cannot.

As they drove over to the bookstore, Casey and Raven had to figure out how to go about telling them what had happened and

Dallas P Elkheart

what they needed. When they arrived, Raven and Casey got out and walked inside the store.

As they entered, they both stepped inside the front door and stopped, to see which way they should go. Before they knew it, a lady walked out of the backroom and said loud enough for all within the store to hear, "It's you." She repeated it but looked directly at Raven and said, 'You, it was you that opened the door".

She went on to tell Raven that she had the gift and that the board used her gift to enter this space of time. Raven knew she had something but had no clue what it was, and now she knew. Apparently, she had been born with the gift of precognition, which is a gift that GOD gives some and not others, that allows one to perceive an event before or as it occurs. She was also developing the gift of second sight as she could now see things that others could not see. This entity used Raven's power to manifest itself into energy, enough energy to have the strength to move objects and even harm someone. It was now imperative that they stopped this thing before it became even stronger.

Raven and Casey had now done some research at the public library, and what they found out was frightening. They learned of a couple, Ed and Lorain Warren and this couple was also born with a gift. Ed was a renowned demonologist, and Lorine was an actual medium. They both had written documentaries on Ouija Boards and the power that they possess to bring forth demonic spirits.

The entities will usually find someone born with a supernatural gift to access through the Ouija Board. Raven and Casey did not know this when they purchased the game board. They were told by the medium, what they would have to do, to rid themselves of the unwanted guest.

Raven would be the one that would have to send it back to where it came from since she was the one with the gift that the spirit drained and used as his energy to manifest. She would need to perform an exorcism if they were going to ever be able to free themselves of this evil entity.

The medium explained to Casey that they could not just throw the board in the garbage. She said, "It would cling to the next person who found it." They would need holy water and salt. Raven would have to send it back and then burn the board. She warned them that upon burning the board, they might hear screams.

That afternoon they began to perform the exorcism. Casey and Raven prepared the holy water and salt and prayed over it. They also read Psalms 23, while Raven commanded that the demon depart from them. Granted, no screams were ever heard. The following day, the thickness in the air around the apartment was gone, and things seemed to go back to normal gradually. Even at night, Casey and Raven felt no presence in their home or bedroom. Now the question was, "Was it gone for good?"

Dallas P Elkheart

PART VIII: Treading New Ground

Episode XXVII: Two Little Devils

Raven and Casey were now so in love that it was inevitable that they were destined to be together. By now, they had cleared themselves of the misfortune of dealing with the Ouija board and had learned a valuable lesson. They learned before entering new terrain; it would behoove one, to do their homework first and research things in advance. Things had now begun to move fast as if it had been preordained by a higher power for the future of these two.

Even though they met on February 14, 1991, and moved in together by March of 1991, they were now planning for bigger things. They had made the decision to help each other clear up one last hurdle, and that was their previous marriages. Neither one had completed their divorces at this point and had only separated from their spouses. Now it was time to finish the race. Raven had taken on working overtime, and Casey decided that he would first help Raven remove Wyatt from her life, once in for all. After all, Raven saw Wyatt much like a roach, that enters a home, once they're in, they will be holy hell to get rid of, as he was.

There was one more thing that Casey needed for Raven to do, and that was to bury the hatchet between her and her father, and Casey did not mean, between the eyes either. He felt that no matter what had happened between Raven and Horatio, she had no right to keep him out of her life as he was her father and she did not have the authority to judge him.

Casey felt whatever Horatio did in the past, was just that, the past, and that Horatio might be judged one day, but by a higher power, GOD. In Casey's eyes, Raven was not to be that judge, jury, nor conviction crew and that she needed to fix this rift with her father and quickly.

But first, Casey told Raven that he wanted her to call Wyatt. He wanted them to talk so that they could have some closure to things. He was a realist, and he knew that without a conclusion in both their lives, it would be hard for all parties to move ahead without looking back. Raven also wanted Wyatt to know, that she now had a new life and wanted him to hear it from her. Raven called Wyatt up, and the two began to talk. Wyatt wanted to know when Raven was going to stop the madness and come home to him. Raven let him know in no uncertain terms that," It ain't going to happen, captain." She was now the master of her own ship, and the only co-pilot she needed or wanted was God and Casey, and Wyatt's services would no longer be required. End of the story.

Wyatt told Raven that if she thought he was going to pay for the divorce, he wasn't, and if she wanted it, she would have to pay for it." Raven quickly responded, "No problem, consider it done." She then hung up the phone. They then decided that Casey needed to see his ex and put closure behind what once was, so

Raven and Casey agreed that it would be a good idea for him to pay his ex a visit. This was hard for Raven. She was not sure if once they saw each other again, that Casey would have a change of heart and decide that perhaps Raven was not the best choice for him.

But, regardless of the outcome, she remembered what it was like to have someone dominate and control your thought processes as everyone had done to her, her entire life. She would not allow herself to do the same to Casey, and she decided to put on her big girl panties and suck it up. Casey went over to his ex's and stayed for quite some time, and yes, Raven did become worried, but she too was a realist and knew she had to allow things to play out the way she believed GOD had pre-ordained it to be, even if that meant she would lose Casey, forever. After a few hours, Casey's car pulled up, and Raven and her new love were now able to make plans legally for their life together.

By June, Raven's divorce had become final, and Casey's was now in the process of finalization. By October, they were engaged and, marriage plans were now in the works. One small thing though, Horatio did not know about any of this.

Raven had told both Horatio and her best friend Megan about Casey. Megan was stunned because the engagement ring was, yes, you guessed it, a two-carat diamond ring. Megan could not get past this part. She and Raven remembered that a lady had told her of this man, who she was to meet. Yes, it turned out to be Casey.

He did wear creases in everything he wore; he was military and in the military well-groomed is part of the uniform. She had also foretold of the ring, and yes, Raven was now wearing the two-carat ring, yet she was afraid to tell Horatio about it.

Since Raven had been married before, not once but twice and neither one had worked out, she felt as if her father would not approve of her marriage to Casey. Yes, she did tell Horatio about Casey, but not that they had planned to marry. Megan was excited for Raven as she knew all the hell that Raven had been through in her life---well at least, most of it.

As December rolled around the wedding was set to take place in Lake Barnes Nevada. The two had decided to drive there for the wedding and honeymoon and then head down to visit a friend in Boehner, Florida, and from there they would finally head to Mississippi to see Horatio. The couple had already headed out to Lake Barnes and arrived on the 20th because they would be married on December 21, 1991. Oh, for the record, Casey also had not told his mother about the plans to marry. His, much like Raven's was a case of a failed previous marriage, and he just did not know how to break the news to his mother.

Casey thought that since they were about to head out to the wedding, now would be a good time to call his mother and break the news. As he allowed the phone to ring while Raven was in the other room, getting into her wedding gown and veil, his mother answered the phone. Raven heard Casey on the phone with his mom, and she rushed in to yell in the background a hello to her. His mother knew about Raven but did not realize just how serious these two were. Or did she?

As she heard Raven in the background, she told them both, hello and asked the question, "Where you guys at?" Casey hesitated and then answered her and said," Ah, we're in Lake Barnes, Nevada, me and Raven." His mother was a swift lady and being fast on her feet, she stated, "Well, I guess that is a good place to be when you get married." Both Raven and Casey's mouth dropped. They asked her why she would say that, and she replied, "That is, why ya'll there ain't it?" No one said a word as Raven and Casey looked at each other as if they stole something, and Casey finally gave in and replied, "Yes." To the surprise of both, Casey's mother was pleased, and then she welcomed Raven to the family with open arms.

They headed downstairs and out to the limo as everyone in the hotel watched the two of them come down a lengthy set of triple staircases. All eyes marveled, and hotel guest began to clap for the two of them as they waltzed down the stairs. After the wedding was over, Raven and Casey now headed back to the limo as Mr. and Mrs. Reid, and they prepared to head back to the hotel. When Raven went to get inside the limo, the craziest thing happened. Raven's wedding dress was rather full and puffy and had a long train on it, as most southern belles wear, and when she went to raise the bottom of her dress to get inside the limo, she went to sit down in the back. Just when she went to sit down, she forgot about something.

She forgot that the seats in a limo are much farther back than the back seat in a Toyota... When she sat down, Casey was trying to help her into the vehicle as the Limo driver was trying to do, but, Raven, being Raven, simply sat down without looking back. Well, she kept going back and back and backwards until all one could see was her little white stockings and wedding shoes in the air. By the time Raven had stopped falling backward, all you could see was butt on the floor and toes to the ceiling. One might even say when Raven fell for Casey, she really fell hard, and there simply was no more elegant way to put it.

Her glory had been busted, and her shame had been seen by all, and there would just be no way, to ever live that one down.

Three days later, the love birds made their way finally to see Horatio. Raven had not seen Horatio nor the house since she left for the military almost one year earlier. As they drove up to the house, memories flooded Raven's head, and fear set in. She was not sure of how her father would take Casey, as he had never liked any man that Raven had in her life enough to believe that she should be married to them.

Then, there was the house, oh yes, that horrible, wretched house. Raven experienced nothing but terror in the house from the first day she arrived there as a toddler, and she did not believe it would be any better now. Horatio saw their car pull up and came out to greet the two with open arms and a big smile. This was the first time that her father seemed to be glad to really see her with someone. As the two made their way into the house and sat down to chat, Casey needed to use the restroom.

Horatio showed him which way to go to get to the restroom, and as Casey made his way down the hall, Horatio sat down again and looked over at Raven. Raven sat up in her chair as she prepared to receive one of her father's throat cut remarks as usual. But, to her surprise, Horatio looked over at her with a gleam in his eyes and that same old smirk on his mug, as he said to Raven," You done good" and gave her a thumbs up. Could this be possible? Had Raven finally after thirty years, finally received her father's blessings? Did this mean that she believed her father thought that she finally did something right for once in her measly life? Was he now giving her his approval?

It did not matter because this day, for Raven Gabriella Reese Reid, she had done the impossible: she had received a long-awaited smile from her hardcore father, Horatio Reese. She was on cloud nine as her new husband Casey made his way back to his seat.

These two misfits finally found a place in this world, and it was together, and nothing else mattered to Raven now, because, in her eyes, God had answered not one, but two prayers.

Once the trip was over, Raven and Casey went back home, which was over 20 hours away. By the time they made it back, they had made another decision. They had decided to move to a larger apartment because they needed more space now. After all, a family of three or four will never be comfortable in a one-bedroom studio, or maybe a family of five.

Casey and Raven had moved quickly on their meeting, moving in together, engagement and marriage, and now was not the time to drag their feet with starting their own family. Casey new Raven could not bear children as he knew about her past medical problems. Casey, on the other hand, had never had children of his own either, even though he had been married previously.

They both desperately wanted to share a child between them, yet Casey refused to put Raven in harm's way, by having her subject herself to medical interventions, surgeries, or IVF. So, the decision was made, they would adopt.

Three months later, they began the adoption process just like Horatio and Eliza once did, except there was a slight difference. Casey and Raven loved each other and had discussed how they would raise their children, and everyone was on the same page in Casey's house, unlike Horatio and Eliza's situation they both wanted a child.

Episode XXVIII: Friends to The End

After several months of intense scrutiny involving financial responsibilities, personal and professional reference checks, FBI background checks, in-home visits, and home studies, they finally qualified to become parents. Casey and Raven were all set now, except they would have to wait until a newborn was available. Raven often wondered what it would have been like for her and Casey to have at least one child together. She almost hated the fact that her life left her unable to give birth to their own baby.

She always knew that she and Casey would have had a beautiful baby that looked like Casey. Raven believed it would also have her hair of waves and curls and both of their personalities. Although the adoption process was now in motion, it was not without incident. Things were now about to become strange and exciting at the same time, at least for Raven.

A few hours before receiving a surprise phone call while at work, Raven began to have abdominal pains. They rushed her over to the medical clinic at her job, and the on-call doctor told her that, "he could not find a thing wrong and wasn't sure why she was having abdominal pains." She laid on the exam table for about an hour until she began to feel better and then went back to her desk to work. About ten minutes after arriving back to her work area, the phone rang. It was the agency, and they had good news. They were calling to inform Raven that, a baby boy had just been born, and he was available for adoption.

Apparently, Raven had just had false labor pains, and some might even call them sympathy pains. Raven hung up and immediately called Casey, and he was overjoyed as well. Raven spent the rest of the afternoon wondering what the baby looked like. The following three days were agonizing for both as they awaited the day to pick up their new baby. The day came, and they headed over to the foster home to bring home their little bundle of joy.

They arrived at the house and walked to the door to ring the bell and inform the foster parent they had arrived. The door opened, and there stood a female, to greet them both. In her arms was this baby that was simply beautiful and everything Raven thought that she and Casey would have produced if they had naturally had a baby. Well, someone above must have heard Raven's order and this day, she would receive one baby to love with a side order of curly wavy hair, that had a cup full of Casey's looks and a teaspoon of a little personality that would mimic them both.

As the foster parent walked away to lead them to a seat, Raven whispered to Casey, "Oh my god, he is beautiful, and I wish that were the one we were getting." By the time the two had made it to their seat, Casey sat down first, and Raven followed suit. The foster parent walked up to the couple and said," Mr. and Mrs. Reid, here is your son." Yes, you heard right, that adorable, tiny baby with the wavy hair that held curly locks on the ends, that favored Casey like a miniature version of him was their newborn son. They had already picked out a name, and this little tyke's name would become Casey Conner Reid II.

Raven could not believe how her life was changing with every breath she drew. She was starting to think her footsteps where now being led in a new direction, and things were finally coming together as she was now thirty years old.

She was currently living in another dimension as far as she could see. This was the first time in her entire life that she had been given something that had eluded her every time it was near the palm of her hands, a man that loved her and one that she loved, happiness, contentment and now a newborn baby. Raven had begun to live her dream, and she started to feel human for once in her life.

After about eight months, they thought it would be a great idea to extend the family. After all, little Conner as they called him was now almost nine months old, and they thought he should have a playmate. Nowadays, Raven had become a stay home mom. Casey believed that Raven should only focus on the family and not have to be burdened down with a job and children. Raven loved the idea as she would never have to hear that her child took his first steps today or he cut his first tooth today as she would be there for every moment and event her new son would experience, and she loved it.

About two months later, they were blessed with a baby girl that they named, Star Anansi Reid, but then, the government made the decision to close numerous military bases due to realignment and that they would have to relocate. Their base happened to be one of those bases.

You see, Casey was an Instructor, and they would need to find a military station, where he could continue his career field. After thinking long and hard, they made the decision to relocate to Sal Quebec, Texas. But another heartache was headed their way, as they found out that the adoption agency where they got their baby girl from had not prepared the paperwork correctly; therefore, they could not take her out of the state. Not to move, was not an option, as Raven and Casey were still military, even though Raven had now come out of the service due to a medical issue that would plague her for years to come. The steel drums that she carried when she played during active duty had created a spinal injury due to the excessive weight and stress to the spine. She did not know that this type of injury would prove to become an enemy that she would never defeat, later down the road. The family had to make some tough decisions, and one of them would be that they had to learn to let go.

They could not take Star with them upon departing their state, and they were forced to move forward without her, all due to a social worker's error. This was devastating for them all, especially little Connor.

Casey, Raven, and baby Connor made the long move to Sal Quebec, Texas, over eighteen hours away. They were now minus one family member, yet this would not stop the Reid family from extending their family later.

Horatio, the proud grandfather, loved being a part of Raven's experience as a new mother, and he seemed to adore Casey. Horatio and Casey built a strong and close relationship that would prove to be Horatio's best one in life.

Raven would sit back as Casey and Horatio would talk on the phone for long periods, as she smiled. This did Raven's heart good as she could see that now she knew why Horatio told her she did well because Casey was a wonderful husband and a doting father.

After moving to Sal Quebec, Texas, Casey and Raven bought a sizeable four-bedroom home for their family as they still wanted to extend the family unit. They both settled in, and Casey began his job at his new base. Raven was still a stay-home mom and would spend a couple of days a week chatting with Megan. Megan and Raven were always as thick as thieves. During the time that Raven was married Megan was not. When Raven had left Wyatt, Megan got married. Now, Raven was married, and Megan had now become divorced. Casey loved Megan because Raven adored her. Casey had the type of personality, that when anyone met him, they loved him. He had a soft-spoken nature, carried a spiritual aura about him, and had a heart of gold, therefore who could dislike a man like Casey? Casey had spoken to Raven about Megan and wondered if there would be any way they could help her get through the tough times, as Megan was trying to start over.

Casey thought that maybe it would be a good idea for them to extend themselves to Megan and help her. After debating about it, Raven thought it would be a great idea. When Megan and Raven were young girls in school together, they used to dream of living close by each other and one-day having children close to the same age, and they even joked about the day their kids would grow up and marry each other.

So, after significant consideration, Casey and Raven called Megan and asked her to come out to where they were so she could make a fresh start. Casey had decided he could help Megan get a job on the base where he worked, and Raven had connections to help Megan get a lovely apartment and perhaps meet some wonderful people.

Raven wanted nothing more than to help Megan set up a whole new life right there together, and she hoped one day Megan would find Mr. Right, settle down, and they could live out their dreams as best friends raising their families together. Raven even started looking for an apartment or house for Megan.

Bronze Bloodline of the Phoenix

Everything was set, and Megan had agreed to come out to Sal Quebec, Texas and start her life over. Horatio, on the other hand, was having a bit of a problem with this decision, as he believed that having Megan out might not be such a good idea. Raven and Casey could not see what Horatio saw, but then again, when had Raven ever seen eye to eye with her father? Casey also had a friend that had been displaced due to the base closure. So, he had likewise extended their home to his best friend. He hoped to help him get a new start as well since they both worked together on the base that had previously closed. The irony of this situation was that Casey's best friend, who was named Sandy, had first set his eyes on Raven and had wanted her for himself and had made his intentions known to Raven. This was before Raven had laid eyes on Casey and before he knew Casey liked her, so nothing ever came from that, and it would not prove to be the problem. However, there would be a more significant issue that would arise.

Once Megan came out, Sandy showed up some six days later, and everything was running smoothly, at least in the short term, that is.

After about one month, Raven took Megan to help get some things set up for her. Sandy had already landed a position on the base and was working steadily. Megan, on the other hand, seemed to not be interested in finding work, and Casey had become a sole provider for her as well as his wife and child. Little Conner was now eighteen months old, and Sandy adored his godchild.

Another month went by, and Casey had noticed that the only thing Raven seemed to be doing was housekeeping behind Megan. Megan would not help Raven with the housework. Sandy was pulling his fair share of the housework as was Casey, but Megan seemed to not really care much for cooking, cleaning, or any type of housework, at all. Megan still had not even left the house, not one time to seek a job, nor housing not even to meet new friends. Megan and Sandy had struck up a relationship, and Megan would tend to make comments about Raven's ring that Casey had given her recently which was a four-carat diamond ring that Megan simply thought was out of this world.

Megan would hint to Sandy that she was looking to get a ring, just like Raven's and Sandy would blow her off and say," Well, that's good, and I hope you get it." The fact was, she was making remarks to him to hopefully get a marriage proposal out of him. But Sandy did not want any part in it. Megan thought Raven's ring was out of this world, and Sandy thought Megan, was out of her damn mind., In his eyes, the only ring Megan would get was around her collar.

After the third month, and Megan still not having looked for a job, Casey called a family meeting with Megan, Sandy, Raven, and himself. He proceeded to ask Sandy and Megan," what was their long-term plans." Casey wanted to know what everyone planned to do as he was now ready to have his little family all to himself and hopefully get a chance to go over and visit with both friends, at their place.

There was another reason Casey called the family meeting as well. He had started to notice Megan was now wearing sweatpants around the house, but not just any sweatpants, these had the crotch out, and everyone could see her unmentionable's when she wore them. Raven was not the jealous type of person, and it never dawned on her to ask Megan about the sweatpants. Casey was starting to get somewhat perturbed with Megan's choice of sportswear in his home and especially around his little son and wife. He felt as if Megan was beginning to disrespect Raven and his son and being the type of man Casey was, that was a no go as far as he was concerned.

At the meeting he asked Megan, "Meg, I noticed that you are coming in very late at night and since all of us work, and my son's bedroom where he sleeps is near the front of the house, I would like to ask you if you could come in a little bit earlier when you go out." You see, Megan was getting out of the house, but she was not job hunting, and she would come in at around three o'clock in the morning.

Both Casey and Sandy would have to be up and ready to leave for work at approximately five o'clock in the morning. This prompted Casey to mention it to Megan in hopes that she would try to be just a little bit more understanding. He also told Megan, "I also noticed your sweatpants, and I would like to ask if you could please be a little more respectful of my wife, son and myself and put something else on around us."

Well, this hit a raw spot with Megan. As a matter of fact, Megan became more rebellious towards Casey and Raven, but Raven just blew it off and did not mention it to Megan. One day the guys both Casey and Sandy were out on the back patio, and they had decided on a barbecue for everyone's supper, Casey thought the girls would like that.

Raven saw Megan in the hallway, and she stopped as she was passing Megan's room and asked Megan, "Meg, what's wrong? It seems like you have changed over the years, but why? What happened to you?"

Apparently, this set Megan in a stinky mood. The main reason that Raven had asked Megan the question was that, everyone had noticed that her entire personality appeared to be different. She spoke and acted differently, and she seemed she might be on some sort of medication. Casey and Raven thought she might have taken to drugs. After all, Raven and Megan had lived apart for nearly five years, and Raven was seeing someone that she no longer knew.

The moment Raven asked the question, Megan sprang up in Raven's face and said, "Am I going to have to pop someone up in here"? Well, all Raven could see was red. Raven was no longer that shy, abused and used little girl, that was afraid to speak up for herself. In fact, Raven had now become a no-nonsense kind of girl that was no longer allowing people to walk all over her. Therefore, if it was World War III that Megan wanted, then it was war, she was about to get.

Without warning, Raven, herself sprang up from the bed where she was sitting and got right back in Megan's face and told her, "You don't talk to me like that in my own home. I don't know who you think you're talking to, but I am about to show you."

The guys overheard the commotion, and they jumped to action and quickly ran inside the house. Megan and Raven were squared off in the hallway, and Raven was just about to knock the holy hell out of Megan when Casey and Sandy grabbed her and dragged her out of the door. For the next week, Raven tried to avoid Megan as she felt Megan had gone too far. Raven was not having it and would not stand idly by and allow a person she had tried to do nothing but help, threaten her in her own home. To make matters worse, Raven had got wind of something Megan had begun to do. Megan was now telling Raven's friends and neighbors that she, in fact, was the real Mrs. Reid and that baby Connor was her child, and not Raven's.

That was it because when Casey got wind of it as well, he then began to realize this was not a healthy friendship. As a matter of fact, it was becoming dangerous for his family. One day Megan told Casey that she had a gun and was going to have to pop her some people. Well for Casey it was game over.

That was it, Megan was no longer welcome in his home with talk like that. That same evening, Megan left for the evening, and no one knew where, nor with whom.

Casey and Raven got on the phone and called a shelter to see how to go about helping someone find a place to stay. You see, Casey was a kind man, and even though Megan had threatened his family, he was not about to put Megan out in the streets so far away from her home.

That evening Casey packed all of Megan's things neatly and sat them by the door. Raven had been so upset after her and Megan's fight that she was no longer coming out of her room for fear they would lock horns again.

That night when Megan walked in at three o'clock in the morning again, Casey was sitting there waiting for her. Raven could overhear the conversation as Casey told Megan," Hi, come on in and don't get too comfortable because you're not staying." He went on to say to Megan that, he and Raven had found a place for her to live". He gave her the paper with the address and phone number on it, as he knew she was hundreds of miles away from her old home where she used to live." Megan was not a happy camper, and she replied to Casey," I don't need ya'll to find me shit." As Megan

Bronze Bloodline of the Phoenix

grabbed her pre-packed bags, Casey walked Megan to the door, and as she left, she gave him a hateful and disgusting look. Casey slightly smiled at Megan and said, "I hope and pray you find what it is, that you are seeking." Just like that, it was all over. Twenty-five years of friendship was gone down the drain, in the blink of an eye. One might even say, they were friends to the very end.

Episode XXIX: Double Shadows

With every dark night comes a bright and brand-new day, and now, with Raven and Megan's end of an era comes a new beginning. Casey and Raven moved on, but before Megan moved on, she had one more trick up her sleeve. Megan wanted to take revenge on Casey and Raven because she never believed she had done anything wrong. In Megan's eyes, how was it wrong to take her best friends' identity, seduce her husband or even, take away her best friend's only child? There was nothing immoral about that, not at all, right? Megan also believed that Horatio should know that Raven and Casey only brought her there to give birth to Casey's baby. Yep, that's right, Megan went back to their old hometown and paid Horatio a visit and told him that, Raven and Casey had her to come out only to birth a child for Casey. When Horatio called Raven, he was furious that Raven would not listen to him and brought trouble into their home by having a divorced and jealous young lady come to live with her and her husband.

Raven did not see it that way, but this time, she agreed with her father and told Horatio, "Daddy, you're right, Megan has changed a lot since I once knew her." Horatio surprised Raven by saying, "Naw, baby; you got it wrong, Megan ain't changed. You have."

It did Raven's heart good to hear her father finally tell her that he thought she had changed. He went on to say to her, "You settled, you got a man, and ya'll got a baby and a house.

She still thinks you're single and running the streets, and I'm glad you know better. Casey, on the other hand, was devastated because much like Raven, he had grown to see Megan as a little sister. It pained Casey to think that after all these years that Raven and Meg had been friends, it was now over.

As time passed, and they got their home back, it was time to think about the future again. Here is where things get weird. They had decided on adopting more children, and they wanted another little boy. Raven had always had a dream of having six children. She wanted five sons, one year apart and then she wanted to wait two years and have one final little girl. So, this one would be son number two. They had previously chosen a name from the bible for him and gave him the middle name of Casey. The name picked was, Abraham Casey Reid III. All they needed now was the baby.

One day they got a call from the agency. The agency wanted to give them all the information about their new little arrival that would come to his new mommy and daddy. Raven wanted to know the child's original name and told the agency that they had already picked out a name for him.

As Raven disclosed the name, the social worker burst out and laughed so hard, that you could hear the tears coming from her as she rolled in laughter.

Raven wanted to know, "Just what was so funny? "The social worker responded, "OK, get this; that name you gave me, is the same name the child already has." Raven was flabbergasted, as she could not understand how that could be. Casey and Raven were excited to extend the family one more time with the pitter-patter of little feet.

At the end of six months, Casey and Raven decided once more, and now, they were about to have three pitter-patters of small feet running through the house as they welcomed their one and only baby girl, Koko Kalilani Reid.

Putting a twist on things, God showed how he plays such a part in one's life as he did with baby Abraham.

The social worker and Raven had an instant replay as Raven disclosed the name that she and Casey had chosen for their new daughter. Once again, the social worker revealed that Koko was already their daughter's name. What are the chances? No one could make things happen that weird. Right?

Now it was complete, Raven and Casey now were the proud parents of three children, and Raven could not have been happier. But wait, Raven started to remember that years earlier, the board game that they played backed in Sawicki Colorado, indicated, that they would have three children.

Raven never believed that until now. She also remembered that the old lady that told her of her husband and about the ring was the same old lady that said to Raven, she and her husband would have three children. Raven never really contributed all the apparent coincidences to soothsayers, because in her heart she thought that her prayers had been answered. Raven always believed that GOD and Casey were her rock and her sanity, and nothing would shake that faith in either. As time passed, Casey, Raven, and the kids were happy, and they always filled their home was songs, dance, music, and prayer.

Horatio was pleased as he was now the grandfather of Raven's children. Even though his biological daughter Margaret had children of her own, he held a special place in his heart, just for Raven. In Horatio's eyes, Raven may have grown up, but he still viewed her as his baby girl.

Casey had mixed feelings; he was not aware of it, but he was about to come to a crossroads in his life. The thing is, it would catch Raven and the children in his whirlwind. Casey was having questions about life. No, not just life, but about his life, and his purpose on this earth. He was becoming confused and not sure of what direction to take his family in. He had read the Bible a lot and tried very hard to understand his feelings at this point in his life. In the meantime, Raven was headed in a new direction because now; she had become an entrepreneur and had just opened her business.

She had wanted to work as the children were growing and beginning to start school. Casey and Raven never wanted to use babysitter's, and Raven came up with the idea, that if she worked for herself, she could still have and raise a family while bringing home a little extra bread to go with the butter that Casey was already bringing in from his job.

She knew she had the skills and background required, and, she had already run a business when she was only eighteen years old. So, she knew it equipped her to open a corporation. She began to work full time. She saw clients daily, sometimes working from seven o'clock in the morning into the late hours of the night. Many times, she would not be finished with clients' work until one o'clock in the morning, yet she still tried to make time for the children and Casey.

Casey had become a civilian as he did not want to be deployed and away from his Raven and children. So, after twelve long years of military service, he called it quits. He told Raven that he could not serve two masters, GOD, and work and that if he tried, he would give more to one, than the other and for him, that would not do. The biggest thing was he was no longer willing to put himself in a situation where he might be required to take another's life.

Dallas P. Elkheart

Episode XXX: Christine's Legacy

During all this time, Horatio had gotten older and had told Raven, that he would like for her to find her birth mother. He was afraid he would pass away one day, and Raven might be alone. Horatio knew she had Casey, yet he felt as if he would like to know at least, that she had one parent around for them to be able to seek guidance and support from. Raven did not want to find her birth mother as she thought she would dishonor Eliza and Horatio by doing so. After all, they took her when no one else wanted her, and she felt as if the birth mother did not desire even to see her now. She had made it through life just fine without her and felt a bit of contempt for her. Raven thought that she had thrown her away as if she was a bag full of old goods.

In time, Raven wanted to appease Horatio, and she began her search for her biological mother. She located someone who was believed to be her, yet no proof had been given to confirm or deny that the woman she found was in fact, Christine Masson. She formed a long-distance relationship with the woman believed to be Christine yet; Raven could not understand why she could not find the same feelings in her heart for her as she had for Eliza. Raven never really felt as if this new birth mother deserved to be called MOM. Raven had learned that she was the oldest of approximately forty children. She also learned this birth mother, that she believed to be Christine had given birth to three other children.

The thing that did not sit well with Raven was that Christine kept all three of those children, just not her and that she had taken the name Bella Masson and gave it to the next child that she had.

This made Raven angry, and therefore, it made it difficult to feel an attachment to the lady, because to her, the thought that this woman not only discarded her like trash but, had the gall, to think so little of her that she not only gave her away but, also her name. To Raven this added insult to injury. Raven remained in touch with the lady called Christine true enough, but the relationship to Raven was dead, much like her Eliza.

As time passed by, Casey had now started to have dreams, and one dream was about one of his children. This dream haunted Casey, and he could not understand the meaning of it. Casey would soon see that sometimes gifts are given to many, yet few understand their powers. The Reid family was happy, but the children had to see doctors regularly, at least one to two times a week. Casey and Raven did not just adopt all three children and become a typical family; instead, all their children were born with severe health issues. Casey and Raven knew just what they had to face together as a family, yet neither parent minded doing so. Casey was, after all the oldest of five children and was already somewhat like a father figure to them when his mother left him in charge of the younger children. Raven had always wanted to be a mother and had felt that life had stripped her of the chance to do so on more than one occasion.

To Raven, being a mother was easy. Since nursing and medical training had once been her thing, she felt as if she had everything that she needed to be a good mother and she knew in her heart Casey would be the best father ever.

The rearing of these children would be especially challenging to Raven and Casey. The children had different needs and issues because of several combined complications. One of them was that each one's biological mother had severe drug and alcohol addictions before and during pregnancy. Another was that the birth mothers used flawed judgment and promiscuity in their encounters.

The third problem was that they received no prenatal care during their gestation period. All these things contributed to the children being born with developmental and health issues.

After a few months, Raven had gotten used to the children's needs and schedules, but she now needed more challenges. She was used to doing more than one thing at the same time, and she knew she would soon need to get back to work. She did not want to have to leave her children with a daycare provider.

Casey was a blessing to Raven since his fatherly skills kicked in. Often, he would work all night and come home and take the children off Raven's hands. During the day, Raven would work in one area and run between her babies and her clients, since she had opened her business from home. Whenever one of the children needed to meet a medical appointment or needed medical care, she would work up until it was time for their appointments, grab the children, run them to the doctor's office, come back home, and go back to work.

Casey and Raven worked day and nights, and the family still enjoyed each other, and the time they would spend with the children. Her oldest, Conner, was now in pre-kinder and her second oldest was about to start pre-kinder the following school year. The boys were both only one-year and seven days apart. Conner was now five years old; Abraham was four, and the baby girl Koko was only one year old.

~~~

Is it possible that one knows their own fate in advance? Are premonitions real? Well, some things in life, might leave one questioning this or perhaps answering it. One afternoon Casey, Raven, Conner, Abraham, and little Koko were spending some fun time in the family room. Unexpectedly, Abraham made an unusual comment to his siblings.

Abraham said abruptly, "I got another house I'm goin to." Conner responded, "Abe, you talkin' crazy. This yo house. You ain't got no other place. This home". Abraham came back with, "Nope, I got a big house somewhere else, I'm gonna live in.? Now, one might have to ask themselves, "Who would take children's play to heart?" Well, once you hear the situation with Abraham, this might leave a person asking the question, is it possible to know one's own fate, even before it occurs?

As a result, of Conner being in school, Raven had met one of Conner's schoolmate's parents. They all seemed to hit it off, as did all the children. They would spend their weekends visiting each other and allowing the kids to play together as the adults would watch movies or have family outings.

One afternoon the families had gotten together, and the children were all in the bedroom playing and watching cartoons together. The adults were in the next room, talking and laughing while playing cards.

Out of nowhere, little Conner came running into the room, screaming, "Mommy, Mommy, Mommy, Ryan hit Abraham in the head, and he fell on the floor."

All the adults jumped to their feet to check on the kids and see what had occurred. Ryan was the friends' youngest child, who was Conner's age and classmate.

Raven ran in front of the others to see what the problem was. Raven made her way to Abraham and grabbed him up off the floor and brought him back to the room where all the adults were. Everyone tried to determine just what injury Abraham had sustained, but there were no physical marks or bruises to be seen.

Raven, having been in the medical field, knew that she and Casey needed to keep a close eye on Abraham. They needed to see if he showed any signs of an injury, so they kept him awake all night so they could observe him. They wanted to be sure that he had not sustained an injury to the head and allowing him to sleep, might make him fall into a coma.

Raven and Casey took the children home, and Abraham seemed totally fine. He wanted to play some more, but Casey insisted that he remained seated and still for the rest of the night. Several days passed and everything looked normal, except that Raven had noticed something about Abraham.

What she had noticed was that Abraham had developed an insatiable appetite and thirst. She spoke with Casey about it, and they were concerned. The concern came not from the event that occurred the previous week but from other issues. All the children required medication on a daily and sometimes hourly basis. For Abraham, it had been determined that he had two things going on, which were, his body appeared to be larger than most four-year-old's'.

His chest cavity was oversized, and his feet were two times the size of a four-year-old. This meant that he was more massive in stature and size than little Conner even though Conner was the oldest. The second problem was that Abraham had been diagnosed with "Tourette Syndrome." These issues create a repetitive and stereotyped accommodated symptom. This disorder usually comes about between the ages of three and nine years old, and Abraham had just turned four. The doctors had issued Abraham some heavy medications to assist him and his parents with the condition, therefore this was a concern for both Casey and Raven.

One morning, Raven had gotten up, got dressed, and was preparing to take little Conner to school as she waited for Casey to get off work. He was working on the night shift and would come in around seven-thirty each morning.

That morning, when Raven greeted Casey as he walked through the door from work, Casey told Raven, "Go ahead to work, I got the kids." Raven usually would have to drop Conner off at school, then come back and get her office opened to do business for the day. Casey headed back to their bedroom to change clothes, and Raven checked on the other children to make sure everyone left was asleep as Casey was going to take a quick nap himself.

As Raven walked past the bathroom, she noticed Abraham was not in his room. In fact, he was in the bathroom and was standing by the toilet. She asked him, "Abraham, what's wrong? What are you doing up?" But Abraham replied, "Mommy, I don't feel so good." Raven became concerned and told Abraham, 'Baby kneel down by the potty, so you don't fall and hurt yourself."

Raven thought that Abraham might become dizzy and tumble into the corner of the cabinet or hit his head on the porcelain potty. She immediately ran down the hall to grab Casey. She said in a panicky voice, "Case, something is wrong with Abraham." Casey asked Raven, "What's going on?" Raven stepped back and looked into the bathroom, and Abraham was now lying on the floor.

Raven, fell to her knees and said, "Abraham, baby, Abraham." At this point, Abraham only looked up at his mother as he now lay in the fetal position. She knew it was now time to call 911. She grabbed Abraham up in her arms and ran to her room, screaming, "Baby call 911, NOW".

It stunned Casey as Raven charged into their room with their son in her arms. Raven quickly pulled the covers back and placed little Abraham in the bed. She grabbed all the medical equipment that she still had from when she was in nursing school and began to check her son's vital signs. Casey was on the phone with 911 as his voice shook and tried to tell the dispatch operators what the medical emergency was. Raven, on the other hand, realized her son's eyes had now become dilated, and his temperature had plummeted to 70 degrees. Raven knew her son was in trouble. Raven screamed to the operator to get someone there and fast.

As the operator tried to keep Casey calm on the phone until a medical unit could respond, Casey told Raven to take a winter hat and place it on Abraham's head to keep him warm, since body heat is lost from the top of one's head. Raven realized things were moving far to slow, and her son was falling into a coma. She lost patience with the operator on the line and told them, "Tell the ambulance, I will meet them in my front yard with my son.

She grabbed Abraham up in her arms, and Casey followed with the cordless phone as Raven screamed, "Somebody help, help, please." As she got to the door with little Abraham, his small body became rigid and stiff as a board. She now knew time was running out for her son and soon. She turned sideways to get her son through the door as his tiny body was now going into convulsions. Soon as Raven hit the front porch, her scream for help could be heard ringing through their neighborhood. One neighbor heard her, and he met her in the yard as he took the young child from Raven's arms and placed him on the ground.

    Abraham was now fighting for his life, and Casey and Raven were as helpless as lambs. Raven kneeled on the ground as two firefighters were just arriving.

    They were there, but Abraham needed far more equipment then they had on them. One firefighter stated to the other one, "Where the hell is that ambulance?"

    Raven's heart sank as she heard the other firefighter say under his breath, "They are 14.53 minutes away." Raven knew this was not good. Casey was now attempting to gather all the children and give them to the neighbors to get the oldest Conner on to school and little Koko over to another neighbor hoping to spare the children from this horrible scene.

As the ambulance finally pulled up, they could not stabilize baby Abraham for at least another five minutes. Raven crawled in the back of the ambulance as they tried desperately to save her son's life. Casey, in the meantime, was grabbing the family car to follow the ambulance with his young son's life hanging by a thread.

The ambulance pulled off, with sirens blaring, and then Raven heard them say something that she would never, ever forget.

The driver called in ahead of arrival and said to the hospital, "We have a code 3 in route". Raven could no longer try to pretend that things might get better, because her medical background told her that, this meant that, her baby boy was coming in on the doorstep of death. If they said, code 4, that meant DOA or (Dead on Arrival) and code 3 meant, on deaths doorstep.

As the ambulance pulled up, and they unloaded her young child, rushing him inside, both Casey and Raven had to give information for the intake of their child as the hospital hurried to keep little Abraham alive.

By the time the hospital had gotten all the medical and insurance information for the Reese's, they were told they could go up to ICU to see their son. As they got on the elevator, they held on to each other for comfort, but this day, there would be none. The elevator opened, and Casey and Raven walked down the hall towards their son as Raven heard the intercom say, "*CODE BLUE. CODE BLUE, ICU.*"

At that moment, Raven could feel it, and she knew, that was her son. During this time, a social worker appeared, and told the Reese's that she had been called in and needed to speak with them because anytime a child under the age of twelve years old is admitted with this type of condition, they must talk with the parents. Raven told the social worker, with tears in her eyes, "Dammit, not now, my son's life is hanging by a thread. You're going to have to do this later, but not now. Our son needs us." Raven broke out into a trot which then became a full run as she bolted down the hall to ICU. The moment Raven rounded the corner, they stopped her dead in her tracks.

They had her son, laid out straight, with one nurse holding a defibrillator over him, and an entire medical team surrounding her son, trying to bring her baby back to life. Casey was almost to the end of the hall when Raven shot back down the hall passed him screaming her head off.

She ran down the hall and threw herself into the wall screaming, "NO, NO, NO, NO, NO, GOD NO." Casey realized what was happening and ran towards Raven.

As they both stood embraced in each other's arms, in tears and feeling overly helpless at the end of a hallway with nothing but pain in their hearts, they realized that not even their love for each other could make this one right.

They were able to bring Abraham back, and they placed him on a ventilator. The doctors came to speak with Casey and Raven and to find out what caused all of this. He asked them if, "Abraham had sustained a hit to his head?" At the time, Raven and Casey's minds were fuzzy from all the drama that was occurring around them. They could not remember the hit to the temple of the head from two weeks prior. All that came to their minds were, about a few days before this day, Abraham fell out of the top bunk bed, but Raven nor Casey could remember him sustaining a hit to his head from it.

After speaking with the doctor's, the nurses then came to get Casey and Raven and take them down the hall and around the corner. What the two of them did not know was, they were now being taken to a chaplain. Typically, hospital chaplains are brought in when there is a fatal outcome about to occur. They did not prepare Raven and Casey for a fatal consequence to their situation, and this day would not go as planned.

The family was later approached again by the doctors, and what they were told, sealed the fate for the entire family that afternoon. The doctors explained that Abraham's brain had now swollen two times the size of a child's healthy brain and that his body organs had shut down. They went on to say that the following morning at eight o'clock they would perform one final test to see if Abraham's brain was still receiving signals and if not, they would pull the plug from life support.

They told Raven and Casey that, if they had anyone who might like to say goodbye to little Abraham, now would be a good time to contact them."

But wait, "What the hell just happened here?" Raven's mind could not even perceive how this all happened, and Casey was even more confused. They were still entitled to military benefits, and this meant, they did not have much say about the matter. In return, this also meant that the military hospital would have all the say-so about pulling the plug on little Abraham's life support. Raven and Casey could not hold back tears or questions. In the back of Raven's mind, she thought to herself," Hell has found me again." The two parents went home for the night as they still had to care for five-year-old Conner and one-year-old Koko, plus the family pets.

Not knowing what to do, Raven called Karne, her so-called biological birth sister, the one she'd found when looking for her birth mother. Karne came to Raven's aide.

Karne came up with the idea that Raven would live to regret. Karne sent for Raven's birth mother as she felt Raven needed a mother figure in the picture at this point.

Raven was not ready for this and did not think it was a good idea, but Karne set things into motion without Raven knowing it. The following morning, the doctors called Raven and Casey early before daylight. They needed to tell them about the results. Casey and Raven headed back over to the hospital because the results were not good.

The results were that little four-year-old Abraham would never wake up again as he was now clinically declared brain dead. As Raven and Casey arrived at the hospital and headed to the children's ICU, about one half of the way down the hall, a woman walked towards Raven. Raven was so devastated and could not believe that yesterday morning everything was normal, and by yesterday afternoon, their entire world had changed. As this woman approached Raven, and as Raven looked up, she was getting closer, but she was not alone. Could this be? Would this be? The woman reached Raven, and as Raven reached her, they both stopped right in their tracks. Karne was with the woman as they all stood in the middle of the hospital halls. It was her; Christine Masson had finally appeared. So, this day, not only was Raven saying goodbye to her middle son, she was now saying hello to the woman who thought so little of her as a newborn and had cast her to the side, just like trash in a bin.

Bronze Bloodline of the Phoenix

Raven and Christine had no time for hellos as everyone had to be in little Abraham's room one final time to say goodbye. Casey, Raven, young Connor, baby Koko, and Christine all walked into young Abraham's room one last time. The doctors had decided that no brain function would ever be restored to four-year-old Abraham. Therefore, they were about to pull the plug of life from him. They asked Raven and Casey if they would like to donate Abraham's organs to help other children, but Raven quickly said, "NO, if his organs were not good enough to sustain his life, I will not impose this same fate to another child or their family. So, NO."

Raven sat on the bed and held little Abraham in her arms as she said out loud, "God, please allow me to take his place, please." This miracle was not to occur as GOD had made the final decision. Raven told Abraham as she held him one last time, "You came into this world alone, but I will be dammed if you leave that way."

As Casey, helped five-year-old Conner to say goodbye to his little brother and allowed baby Koko to kiss Abraham goodbye one final time, Raven held on tightly to young Abraham. Her husband, Casey, stood solemnly by, holding on to what was left of his family in his arms, then they pulled the plug from the wall. At that very moment, four-year-old Abraham Casey Reid III's, life was no more. The light had just been dimmed, and breath had just been exhaled out for one last time, as a child of barely four years old, met the face of GOD.

Dallas P Elkheart

PART VII: The Sparrow Watches Me

Episode XXXI: Haunting Memories

Casey, Raven and newly found and self-proclaimed birth mother Christine Masson, all wept as they stood up and prepared to go back home. The Reid's would now leave as a family of four and not five. Raven stood there with tear-filled eyes, and a broken heart as she now knew fate would never allow her to escape its grips of disaster.

The family went back home, trying to understand what had just happened to their family in a matter of hours. How did they go from a happy and thriving family of five to a broken family of four, just like that? Casey and Raven had become spiritually inclined by now as their family spent many hours reading and learning the words written in the Bible, while trying to instill the words that they knew they needed to live by, into their children. Raven had decided that she knew better than to put a question mark, behind GOD's period. When God has had the last word, that is the end of the conversation.

As the next couple of days passed, and the family spent every hour making funeral arrangements for their son, Christine, asked if she could take the two remaining children overnight, allowing Raven and Casey to grieve in private. Little Conner only being five and baby girl Koko being one year of age, did not understand where their brother was and had a tough time comprehending that brother Abraham would never come home again.

Two days before the services for young Abraham, the school where young Conner attended pre-kinder, was getting bizarre reports coming in from other students.

What was being reported was that children playing in the playground at school were saying to teachers, other staff members and their parents at home, that they were now not only seeing young Abraham but playing with him in the schoolyard. Some of the children also experienced the same thing in their yards at their homes. How could this be? How could a deceased child be playing with anyone, in a schoolyard or otherwise? What were all the children experiencing? These were some of the unanswered questions that Raven, and others would now have.

The night before the funeral services, there was a service held for the viewing of little Abraham's body by neighbors, playmates, and their families. That afternoon, the funeral home sent a family car to pick up Raven, Casey, the children and young Conner's best friend, Ryan. Ryan was the friend that hit Abraham in the head at the family outing and knocked him off the bed. Raven and Casey tried not to treat Ryan any differently because he was only a child. He did not know that any of this could have contributed to this outcome. Even though it was never proven that Ryan's strike to Abraham's head started this chain reaction, in

Raven's heart, she just knew it was, but refused to ever accuse the child or his parents of such an act.

She felt that doing so, would not matter because to her, her son was still just as dead, and no accusations thrown out could turn back the hands of time, not even assumptions.

As they arrived and went in, the family made their way down the aisle and stood blankly looking into the tiny coffin with their son's small body lying as still as the dark night. It was a nightmare to the entire family. Raven felt as if her whole life had brought her and her family to this one moment in time, and nothing would or could ever be the same again. After the viewing services were over, Casey and Raven took their family and headed back to the family car. The car pulled off; Raven stared out of the window while the dark night engulfed the homes, they passed by traveling back to their house. All the children were able to sit in the back seat with Casey and Raven, to include Ryan. Ryan sat by the window and out of nowhere, Ryan pointed out of the window.

Raven looked to see what Ryan was pointing at but could only see the black dark because they were now traveling on an old country road heading back to the city section where they all lived. Ryan stated, "Look, there's Abraham. See? There he is. There's Abraham."

Raven jerked herself around to see what Ryan saw, but for once, she saw nothing. As the family entered the home, Raven walked into the main living room and saw something startling.

She had three photos, one of each child, sitting on a coffee table in the front living room. They were individual photos of them as toddlers. She had the two boy's photos flanking the baby girl's picture that sat in the very middle. When Raven walked in, she noticed that the images were turned around facing backward, that is all except Abraham's. She thought to herself how odd that was. Raven had cleaned the living room the day before but thought perhaps she was disoriented and placed them the wrong way.

The following day, the family loaded and headed to the cemetery to say goodbye to Abraham, and as they arrived, Raven's newly found biological sister Karne, met Raven as she stepped out of the family car. She told her, Raven, "we need to talk." Raven was not in the mood for idle chat, as she was about to bury her child, and her attitude was anything but chatterbox that day.

Karne told her, "No, Raven, I have a message for you from Abraham." This caught Raven's attention as she thought that Karne had pulled one hell of a stunt and at out of all places, her son's funeral. Raven stopped to see what Karne had to say, because, Raven was about to let her have it, both barrels and a piece of her mind. Karne told Raven, "Abraham, told me to tell you, the reason everyone has seen him and not you, were that, he knows you're not ready yet.

He knows you're not strong enough to talk to him. He said that when the day comes, and it will soon, he will come to you." Raven was speechless as she could not understand, why Karne would pull such shenanigans now, of all times".

Once the services were over, everyone headed back over to Casey and Raven's home to spend time together as they all grieved over the loss of their child. Raven put little Conner and Koko down for naps as they still did not understand what had really happened. The rest of the family and friends gathered around the table. Raven stepped outside with Christine Masson, to share a cup of coffee together as they chatted.

When Raven walked out on the front porch, Christine seemed shaken by something, and Raven asked her, "What's wrong." Christine went on to tell Raven that, while she stood there on the porch, she saw Abraham standing on the porch. She went on to tell Raven what he was wearing, and Raven stopped and said, "Wait a minute." Raven ran inside the house and found an old picture that was in her and Casey's bedroom in the top dresser drawer.

She had taken this photo of Abraham on Conner's first day of school about three weeks prior. In the photo, he was wearing the exact items of clothing that Christine described. Raven showed the photo to Christine and Christine gasped. When she saw the picture, she said, "That's what he had on. Oh, my GOD. He wore that same shirt and pants in the same pose".

Raven did not know how to take this piece of information, nor what to do with it. After everyone was all gathered around the table about one hour later that afternoon, five-year-old Conner woke up from his nap. He staggered out of his room to the kitchen where all the teenagers and adults were and what he said, changed many lives that day and the way they would all view life later.

Five-year-old Conner, walked to the kitchen table, with a wild, but peaceful look upon his face. He blurted out, "Mommy, Mommy, I just saw Abe, Mommy. Some man brought him to see me, Mommy. There was another man with them too. That other man said that was his father and that they wanted to let Abe, say goodbye to me. They said he had to leave before I got back from school, so he never said bye, Mommy." But then, the most amazing part was when little Conner stuck out his chest and smiled as he said to Raven, "And Mommy Abe got wings, Mommy, Abe got some wings.".

Well, that did it. There was not one dry eye in the entire room of almost fifteen people. Everyone stopped and could not believe what they had all just heard coming out of the mouth of a babe. How did this little boy, know about any of this? After all, he had barely started to learn his ABCs", let alone, understanding something this complex.

Had he just seen his brother? Had there in fact, been two men that brought Abraham to see him? Was he dreaming or how did he see any of it? Did Abraham really have wings, and if so, how did he get them and who gave them to him?

Were the two men from life's creation? Was it, in fact, Jesus and his father that escorted Abraham to see his brother one last time, since he died while his brother was at school? These questions would remain in everyone's heads for the rest of their lives. That is everyone, except Raven and Casey.

The two were spiritual enough to understand what had just happened and with everything else that had occurred, from school to other things, they knew that what little five-year-old Conner had seen was in fact, the face of Jesus, God, and his little brother. End of the story. This would not be the last incidence of miraculous things to occur as the next year, would be full of questionable events.

Karne, Raven's biological sister, had been right, Raven's time was coming. Raven had not been ready before, but now Abraham believed she was. One night about one month after Abraham's death, and as Raven slept, she began to have a dream. The dream was unlike any that she had ever had. This seemed as real as it gets. Abraham stood in her dream as a four-year-old, and he spoke to Raven, He told her, "Mommy, don't be sad, I am all right." Raven tried to tell her son, how sorry she was and that she should not have waited for the ambulance to get there, that she should have used her car to make it to the hospital with him.

She wanted to tell him that she tried her best, to do everything in her power to fix things wrong with him, but she just did not have enough time with him to fix them.

Abraham said to Raven, "No, Mommy, you weren't' supposed to fix it. This was the way GOD wanted it." Tears streamed down Raven's face, and she could feel her heartbreaking in this dream, as she reached for her son, and he told her, "No, Mommy, I have to go now." Raven began to beg him to stay and not to leave, but he began to fade out as he kept saying, "I have to go now, Mommy, I love you, I love you." Raven woke up and sat straight up in her bed as she looked over to the side of her bed because that was where this conversation had taken place. She now believed that the home her son mentioned three months ago, had now, come to pass.

In her dreams, she was lying in her bed, and he was standing right beside her talking to her. The weird thing was that she could still smell the fresh flowers from his funeral services as she woke up and sat in bed. Now the question would always remain,

"Was it a dream, or was he there?" This was one question that would haunt Raven for years to come, but never get answered.

Many strange events began to take place after that night. Things would occur almost daily, enough to make Raven want to move from the home. Pictures would mysteriously turn themselves around, and Abraham's photo would be the only one not turned around. Doors began to open and shut all on their own, leaving the family sitting with mouths opened and in awe of it all. Sometimes the family would forget and leave the iron turned on, and right in front of their eyes, it would mysteriously shut itself off.

Doors that should be locked at night, but accidentally left unlocked, would lock themselves right in front of the family's eyes. On one occasion, Raven and Casey took the children to buy a keyboard. Raven missed being able to play the piano like she used to do as a child. They brought the keyboard home in a box and sat it on the floor

The keyboard was still in the box, and both Raven and Casey thought that perhaps someone had left batteries in the console which caused it to accidentally play. When Raven opened the box and pulled out the keyboard, to everyone's surprise, there were no batteries, because it did not work on batteries. The fact was, it was purely electronics, and it required being plugged into an electrical outlet even to create one sound. That evening, the family sat in the family room where everyone hung out; the keyboard began to play. It played a five-note tune… mind you, before Abraham died, there were precisely five family members.

~~~

Raven had now started to have visions not only during her sleep but when she was awake. She had now developed more than one gift. She found that she had, Claircognizance (intrinsic knowledge), Aura reading (detecting energy fields that are around, places, people or things), Clairvoyance (receiving people, objects, locations, and physical events) along with Precognition (ability to see or perceive future events).

Raven believed that all these gifts were given to her by GOD as he did with Joseph in the Bible.

Her gifts were now even occurring at the company that she owned. She was able to tap into her clients and friends' lives and foresee life-threatening events, health issues, family issues, and even those that had unseen forces around them. She loved the gift, but sometimes felt it was a curse because it was so powerful now, she rarely got a full night's sleep anymore, and her mind was never at rest. She would pick up on things about her children, and Casey, even Casey's family. She once described it as television that never turns off and the channel is on 24-hours a day. For Raven, it felt like a full movie would show, and other times just commercials on every channel. She was even picking up on events of Karnes life and family, her biological sister. Raven had become a full-time human, walking antenna and a television set that picked up on everyone's channel.

There was an incident where Casey and Raven had been invited to a co-worker's get together. One of Casey's coworkers was having a barbeque and asked him to come over and bring his wife with him.

The night before they were scheduled to go to the event, the craziest thing occurred. As Raven went to sleep that night, her body did something that it had never done before. It seemed as if Raven's spirit left her own body and traveled that night. She found herself over to Casey's friend's home as she could see people she had never met before. Raven found herself in the house, and she was walking around each room. She could also hear conversations and see things that she should not be seeing. She also had never been to their home.

The following day as they made their way over to the barbeque, Raven did not want anyone to know about her gift. She certainly did not want them to know she had already been to their home, well mainly the way she got there at least. As they walked into the house, she saw the same people that had been there the night her spirit had traveled there. Casey and Raven took a seat, and the evening was going fine, that is until the doorbell rang. Raven already knew who it was as this had already occurred the previous night in her travels. She made the mistake of saying who was at the door. Luckily for Raven, no one caught it, when she said the name of the person who was ringing the doorbell.

An hour passed, and Raven now needed to use the restroom, and here is where the problem began. She asked the lady of the house if she could use her bathroom. The lady told her, "Sure, no problem." The lady of the house stood up to escort Raven to the restroom, but Raven forgot that she and Casey wanted to make sure these people did not know about Raven's abilities. She forgot to pretend she had never been there before and she told the lady, "No, that's OK, I know my way around. Your bathroom is down the hallway to the end of the hall on the left-hand side, before you reach the bedroom at the end."

This took the lady by surprise, and she told Raven, "Yea, but how did you know that?"

Raven just chalked it up to a good guess, because she was not about to tell this total stranger how she knew the layout of her home. The woman then said to Raven, "If you need more," but before the woman could finish her sentence, Raven blurted out, "Yes, I know, the tissue is under the cabinet of the sink on the left side behind the soap." The lady's mouth dropped as Raven realized, she had talked too much. Raven quickly covered it up by saying, "Ha-Ha, another good guess" and promptly left down the hall to the bathroom before the lady grew suspicious.

After Raven came back from the bathroom; she made her way into the kitchen. All the men were watching a music video, and the ladies had gathered in the kitchen around the kitchen sink. One lady at the event said to another lady that, "Her daughter was pregnant," but Raven could not keep her big mouth shut and said, "She is four months pregnant, by Steve." Oops, Raven had just spilled the beans, and the lady that had the pregnant daughter said, "Oh, you heard about it too." Raven smirked and played it off as if she had. The fact was, Raven had heard the entire conversation the night before when her spirit exited her body and traveled.

Once the event was over, Raven was curious about how she was able to travel in her sleep. She knew nothing about how it could be done, nor had she ever wanted to do it. Raven was, however, wanting to know more about it and if it was dangerous to do. As she researched it, she found out some disturbing news. She found that if one does this, it would be a good chance that when their spirit returned to re-enter their body, something could already have taken the empty vessel. There could be a possibility that one may never get back into their own body.

This scared the pants off Raven. Each night after that, she would psych herself out, telling herself at night before bed, "I will not leave my, body, I will not leave my body." She would say it over and over before going to sleep in hopes to trick her mind so that this could never occur again.

Dallas P. Elkheart

Episode XXXII: Teardrops Frozen in Time

Horatio had a terrible time accepting the death of his grandson. Each time he spoke with Raven, he would say, "Lord, I wish I knew what happened to my grandbaby. He posed to bury me, I ain't pose to bury him." The fact was Horatio never got past Abraham's death. It seemed as if a piece of himself died when his grandson did, and it was as if, he could not move past this incident. Soon Horatio's health began to take a toll on him along with his age, and he could no longer live alone.

Raven and Casey had a lovely four-bedroom home and had spoken to Horatio about moving to Texas with them, but Horatio always had jokes, and he stated, "Naw, ya'll got too many dam kids for me" and laughed about it. Casey and Raven both seriously thought that it was now time to bring him to live the rest of his life out with family that could take care of him. Besides, Raven and Horatio had finally developed a close relationship after everything that had happened. Maybe it was because Horatio had softened up some as an elderly man. Perhaps it was the fact that Raven had matured and had learned how to just agree with her father on everything. Or just maybe it had something to do with the fact that Horatio had now been diagnosed with Alzheimer's' and Dementia. Both diseases are devastating on a family, not so much on the person who has it, but on the family that must watch someone they love, forget how much they are loved. The only good thing that would come from it is, when someone has Alzheimer's, they tend to forget what they were mad about, and who they are angry at. This disease is like a tape recorder, once it's full, someone, somewhere, must unwind it and it rewinds itself backward until one day, it is all erased and empty. Either way one looked at it, Casey and Horatio were as tight as a father and son could be, and Raven could not be happier about it.

Horatio moved into a veterans nursing home, against Raven's wishes, but she went along with it. She thought this was her father's life, and it was his right to choose where he wanted to be. Raven and Casey would often take the children and make the long flight down to visit him every chance they could. It was hard on the couple as they now both had full-time jobs and with the kid's school now back in session; it was difficult, but they worked it out.

Horatio and Raven were talking regularly. He always called Raven and would want to chat with Casey first. This made Raven happy as she now believed her two big guys were close, and this enhanced Raven and Horatio's relationship. Casey had been the only man that Raven had known that her father approved of and thought the world of.

One day, Raven received a phone call from the home where Horatio was now living. They told Raven that, "Your father, has developed a life-threatening problem." Raven asked them, "What happened?" The home went on to tell her that, "Your father had a nurse clip his toenails, and she accidentally snipped it too close and that it got infected." Usually, this would not have been a problem for most, but Horatio was a diabetic, and now this was a problem.

They said to her, the infection is spreading fast and that she needed to come down to see him."

This threw up many red flags from Raven, after all, she still carried her medical training with her, and she knew that would not end well for anybody and especially her father.

She immediately hung up the phone and called Casey. Casey told Raven, "Get me two airline tickets. I am going down there and bringing Papa Horatio back here to Texas with us." Raven did what Casey asked her to do.

Casey left work telling his supervisors, "My father-in-law was in bad shape," and that he was leaving town because he had to go and bring him back here with him and Raven. Casey took the next flight out headed to Horatio's rescue. Once he arrived in Mississippi, he took Horatio and loaded him up and headed back home on the airlines. But there was a severe problem, Horatio's foot now had developed gangrene in a matter of hours before Casey could get there. Casey called Raven before taking off from Mississippi and told her what he found, and Raven told Casey, "Just get him home. I will call and get things set into place for a medical team to receive him and treat him as soon as you arrive".

Bronze Bloodline of the Phoenix

By the time Casey had reached Texas, papa Horatio's memory was fading in and out, and both Casey and Raven realized his Alzheimer and Dementia had kicked in at almost 60% because of the injury he sustained. Raven met them at the airport and, she already had a medical team waiting for Horatio at the hospital. Once Raven saw how bad her father was; she pushed the pedal to the metal to get Horatio to the hospital. After they were there, the doctor examined Horatio and what he found was gangrene had now moved from his toe through his entire foot, and to save Horatio's life, they would need to amputate his foot. It devastated Raven and Casey; yet, they knew this had to occur to save him, so they permitted the doctor to do so.

The following morning, the doctors met with Casey and Raven, once again and disclosed another finding to them. He found that morning that the infection was still moving further up, and they needed to do an emergency surgical procedure to remove the leg up to his mid-thigh.

Here was Horatio now well into his eighty's and that day, several things changed. Because of such a traumatic occurrence of gangrene, the removal of his foot and part of his leg and then the following day another traumatic surgery, Horatio was now an amputee, and his Alzheimer's and dementia had moved to 80%.

Raven, Casey and the two children cared for Horatio daily at this point. He needed them, and they made sure they were there.

Casey loved Horatio, and they would spend endless hours playing one of Horatio's favorite games each day, which was checkers. Horatio would cheat Casey. Casey would let him, and then he would say, 'Papa Horatio, If I did not know better, I might think you cheatin'", and Horatio would say to him, "Foot, Y, sho I am" and they both would just laugh.

Casey loved to hear Horatio tell him each time it was time to set up the checker game to, "Ring it up." He would do that as he took his hand folded together with his fingers interlocked and use his thumbs to circle each other while looking all under eyed at Casey and smirking as if he was scheming.

Every day after work and school, the family would meet up at home, eat quickly, and head over to see about Horatio. Each day Raven, Casey and the children would watch Horatio lose a little more of his memory. Raven feared that one day he would no longer remember her or her family. Casey and Raven would enjoy putting Papa Horatio in his wheelchair and taking him for a spin around the hospital. Casey would set him in it, and Horatio would lean over, and act as if he was pulling the crank on a lawnmower. Casey would always ask him, "Papa Horatio, what you doing?" and Horatio would respond, "I'm trying to crank this thang up." Everyone would fall out laughing at Papa Horatio.

One day the doctors spoke to Casey and Raven and told them, "Horatio's body was tired and that the funny thing was, they could no longer find a pulse, heartbeat or respiration on him, and they could not understand how he was still alive; usually this would be considered clinically dead, but something strange was happening with Horatio." He went on to say, "That he believed that Raven was the reason that Horatio was hanging on, and he believed he needed to hear both Casey and Raven tell him that it was ok to leave and rest."

Raven and Casey stood there just looking at each other, and then Raven told Casey, "That could not be correct; you cannot live without a pulse, blood pressure, or respiration that is findable. Could you?"

The following day, Raven brought her own medical equipment and checked for all the same things herself, but once she had finished, she looked at Casey and said, "Casey, I need to speak with you privately for a moment." Raven stepped outside the door with Casey and said," You ain't even going to believe this one. They are right. There was no blood pressure that I could find in either arm, no heart rate that I could detect, and I saw him sitting there, but you could not see his respiration at all. His chest was not rising nor falling. What the hell is going on?"

Could the doctors be right? Is it possible for a body to be physically dead, yet in some miraculous way, the body still functioned? Again, these questions could only be answered based on one's belief system, but Raven and Casey believed in God genuinely. They felt that contrary to most belief systems, man has no control over his very own footsteps, nor his next breath.

Therefore, he could not do the impossible, but God's powers were above all others, and they knew he COULD do the impossible. To them, nothing else followed.

So, Casey and Raven made a hard decision which was, to free Horatio. To free him, they felt they needed to give him and themselves closure. Casey walked inside the hospital room and sat on the bed by Horatio.

By now, Horatio had gone into a blank stare as the memories of all his yesterdays had now totally faded, and he could no longer speak, not even blink.

While holding Horatio's hand, Casey told him, "Papa Horatio, you will never have to worry about Raven or your grandchildren as long as there is breath in my body. I will make sure they are loved and taken care of. This, I promise you. I know you're tired and need to rest, just know you can rest at ease."

Even though Horatio had a blank stare upon the wall in one area for a couple of days, once Casey told him this, it was as if he heard and understood every word. For once, he moved the blank stare from the wall and slowly looked over at Casey, though he never blinked. It was as if Horatio wanted Casey to know, thank you for telling me this, son. He then moved his eyes back to the spot that he had left on the wall and lost himself back into his world.

Raven then called her half-sister Margie, the doctor's said, "she needed to catch a flight and get there fast because daddy was on his way to cross over." Margaret's response was less than stellar as she responded to Raven with, "Call me when it's over." Raven just hung up the phone with no future response as she could not believe what this woman had just said about her own father.

If anyone should have said that, perhaps it should have been Raven since she was the one to suffer all the insults, physical abuse, and his wrath, not Margaret. To Raven, none of this mattered as she had found a strong bond with her father throughout the last few years, and she was thankful for that.

Raven stood still and looked at her father and remembered something that had happened a few days before he could no longer speak.

The doctors wanted to see what the extent of his memory was. One doctor pointed at Raven and said, "Mr. Reese, do you happen to know who she is?" Even though Horatio no longer had memory, somehow and somewhere a memory triggered, and he looked over at Raven and said this, "Sho I do, I wouldn't take nothing in the world for that stinker there." Horatio used to call Raven a nickname, and he always referred to her as his "Stinker."

Tears welled up into Raven's eyes because he knew who she was and that she had meant something to him, even though he could not remember who Eliza, his wife was who had passed on, nor who Margaret, his own biological daughter was anymore. He remembered his Raven.

He surprisingly remembered two more things, Casey, his son-in-law that he had grown so close to and his grandchildren, all three of them. Raven tried to make peace by telling her father that she knew he was tired and needed to go. She told him just how much she loved him, but it was hard. Not hard to tell him she loved him, but hard to not be selfish and ask him to stay.

That night, they left the hospital for the last time and, at the same hour and on the same date, that his grandson passed away, just one year later, Horatio "Big Fellow" Reese, drew his final breath.

The phone rang, and Raven simply did not want to answer it, but she did. The hospital told her that her Father Horatio had just passed away. Raven responded, "Thank you for calling" and hung up.

Her heart died again for the man that was once upon a time a cruel and inhuman man to her, yet through the years, had once again stolen her heart, much as he had when she was a little girl, and she now mourned him so deeply. Raven asked Casey should they go up to the hospital, and Casey replied, "Baby, go up there for what?

You and your dad were able to get some closure, and now he is at peace. Raven Gabriella Reese had learned that she was now, no one's little girl anymore.

The day before the funeral services for Horatio, Margaret and her husband flew out for the services. Casey and Margaret's husband went over to the funeral home to see Horatio as his services would be a closed coffin. As Casey walked over to Horatio's casket, he stood there looking at him and told him how much he was going to miss him, but then something strange occurred.

While Casey stood there alone soberly paying his respects to Horatio, he saw something that made him rethink death and the possibility of there being something after death over in his head. As he stood there, he said that it seemed as if Horatio made a movement. Casey had always been a skeptic, even with everything he had experienced, but this day, things changed. He came home and told Raven, "I need to speak to you privately." Margaret and her husband were still there and would stay for another three days. They needed privacy for this conversation.

Raven took Casey into the privacy of their bedroom and said, "What's wrong Case, you look like you just saw a ghost.", Casey then replied, "I'm not sure what I just saw."

He began to explain to Raven what occurred at the funeral home. He told Raven that it looked as if, "Papa Horatio, did the "Ring it Up" thing as he laid there."

Casey told Raven that, he thought he saw his folded hands with fingers in a locked position, move his thumbs in a circle as if to say, "Ring it up." Raven had enough previous experiences of her own and knew that Casey would never blow something like this out of proportion, so Raven stepped away and made a call.

The call she made was to the funeral home, as it had been the same one that took care of her son, just one year previously, on the same date. She asked the funeral home director if perhaps they allowed her husband to see her father before they embalmed him? Raven thought maybe, just maybe Casey experienced an involuntary muscle movement after death called, "Rigor Mortis," which is considered the third stage of death. The director told Raven that they had not allowed him to see her father until they had already embalmed him and that they could not explain what he experienced. Either way, Casey had been shaken to his very core, and there was still no other explanation except, perhaps "Papa Horatio" needed to get the last word in after all.

There was one final twist to this whole thing though. Horatio used to have a favorite spiritual song called "Eye on the Sparrow." He used to tell Raven as a little girl that when a person died, they do not ascend for three days.

Those three days are used to go back over the earth and pick up all the things like, your nails and hair that you left on earth so that there are no traces of you left along the way of your journey. Right after Horatio's death, the next three days would make Raven question all of this...

The first day, Raven was cleaning the house, and someone knocked on her door. She went to the door, but no one was there. She thought maybe she missed the person and went back to cleaning. The second day, the knock occurred again, harder and stronger, but she was ready this time. She stood by the door and waited for the knock to reoccur several times, to make sure there was someone there. She planned to quickly jerk the door open as to not miss the person knocking. But, as she yanked the door open, no one was there again. She stepped outside on the porch and looked for someone, anyone that was in the area, but she saw no one, not even a car parked near her home.

This spooked Raven, because both times, she was home alone. On the third day, it was a sunny and beautiful day, and she was in the back bedroom, with her back to the window, cleaning the bathroom with the window open.

As she worked, she began to hear a knock, but not on the door this time. This time it was on the window. She was afraid even to turn around as it still had left her spooked from the previous days. She decided to turn around anyway as the knocking continued. She raised up, and although she was afraid to turn around and more fearful of what she might see, she turned.

To her surprise, there was a tiny sparrow, flying mid-air and staring at her. Raven had always loved birds of all types and often heard both Eliza and Horatio speak of sparrows and the connection with GOD. Raven stepped over to the window as the little sparrow was in mid-air, like a hummingbird, but slower. Raven looked closely at the little bird, because somehow, the sparrow's eyes, seemed strange.

They looked human and as if she had seen those eyes somewhere before. Raven and the little sparrow stood eye to eye for a few seconds. Then, after a few seconds, just as quickly as it occurred and without warning, the little sparrow seemed to take one final look at Raven, as if it wanted to say something to her and then, it simply flew away. The knocking never occurred again, and she never saw that little sparrow again. Maybe Horatio had been right all along since that sparrow appeared for exactly three whole days and on day three it was as if he ascended back into the heavens.

Episode XXXIII: Nobody Listened

Things transformed after losing Papa Horatio. The family really missed being able to take care of him. They enjoyed giving him the hugs and kisses that he so needed and deserved as an elderly man. Raven knew that throughout Horatio's childhood, he did not receive a lot of hugs and kisses. Therefore, it was hard for him to know how to give it during Raven's childhood. The entire Reid family tried so hard to make it up to him before he left the world and it was apparent that Horatio "Big Fellow" Reese had left his mark on the family forever.

As time moved on, Raven, Casey and the children, tried to pick up the pieces of their lives and move forward by filling each day with a lot of laughter, family time, and games together. Casey and Raven traveled and tried to show the children the different cultures and traditions in other parts of the world on each family trip. In the meantime, Raven's company thrived, and she seemed to love her new career. Casey and the children would end their day by coming up to the office with Raven and working the evenings together as a family to help Raven. By now Raven's business had become so large they had moved it from home to a large office building a little less than five minutes away from home. Everyone looked forward to assisting her with closing the office at night. This allowed the family to have their private home time after hours. Raven had also finally gotten her long hours narrowed down to a science and was able to allocate working and office hours. She also had staff working for her now, which lightened the load off her.

Although Raven had a routine at the office, she continued to have visions that were overwhelming her. She had them numerous times a day and by now 365 days a year. There was one strange vision that sent Raven, her family, and Raven's clients into a spiral.

One night around October 1, 2002, Raven began to see horrific images. She had them nightly about a gunman. This gunman had not been heard about yet, as neither the media nor the public would know about the gruesome things he would do, but Raven knew. She began to see a mortuary.

On that night, she could see it, but she could not see where it was or a name on the outside of the building as she could only see the doors. She walked inside of it and saw eight bodies lying on eight different tables. She made her way around the room, pulling the white sheets back, and she could see women, men, and a child. She did not seem to know any of the people, yet she could tell they were shot violently. Raven could see a hearse pulled up, with an opened door on the backside of the morgue. She walked over to it and crawled into the back of the hearse where there was a coffin. Inside this coffin, Raven could see a man. This man she thought at first was Casey because he had some of Casey's facial features, but upon a closer look, she realized it was not Casey, but in fact, the gunman that would be identified some 24 days later in October of 2002 as, John Allen Muhammad, the D.C. sniper.

For over twenty nights, Raven would be tortured with haunting dreams and each day she, Casey, her children, staff and clients would turn on the T.V. and see her previous night's dream become someone else's public daytime reality and nightmare.

Raven could see all the small details of the killer. She could see the type of gun he was going to use, the size and type of bullets used in the weapon and the locations where each victim would be shot. It got so bad that Raven's clients would tell her that she needed to contact the FBI, but her family felt that that would be a terrible idea. Why? One might ask if she knew these things in advance and she knew the FBI could not find the killer and *she* could, why wouldn't she contact them?

Well, the answer is a lot easier than one might think. The reason Casey and Raven's family felt that it was not a good idea was this, "Who would believe her? How many people would ever think that a young lady that no one knew could see any of this, let alone all of it? "Some of Raven's clients had known her for years, and they knew how accurate her gift was. Raven's secretary, Rene, felt that she should contact the FBI and tell them about her gift and inform them of his next location before he killed another person. Casey and the children, on the other hand, thought that the FBI would think she had some dealings with the killer and that was how she knew all of this and would never believe she could pre-see it. So, this became a dilemma for Raven, and it took a toll on her. She could no longer sleep nor eat as she contemplated the idea of contacting someone, but who?

As more and more assassinations occurred over a twenty-four-day timeframe, the police and FBI had sought a vehicle out, and they now had a description of the gunman, or so they thought they did. They were incorrect, and Raven had already seen the gunman, and she knew what vehicle he was using, and it was not what the police nor the FBI were after. They thought the gunman was of one race, but Raven knew better. After all, she had seen him and stood within fifteen inches from his face, and she had noticed every detail about this man. The car they were seeking was a white van, but Raven knew that this too was incorrect. She had seen the actual vehicle color in her premonition. She even saw how he used the back of the car's keyhole and a sniper rifle to take out his victims.

This affected Raven mentally and physically so much that she was becoming weak. It was as if the vision was draining her of her energy. One thing that she began to learn was that, if she had just one connection to a location where a disaster would occur, then she was given the gift of precognitive vision about it.

Her link to this incident was clear. Casey's family still lived in the area, and they raised him in the locality where this all occurred. Raven began to go back over all the things she had precognitively seen in her lifetime, and yes, there appeared to be a pattern. There was always that one connection, and it did not matter how the link occurred. It could be either that, she knew someone from the location, or she had crossed their paths at least once, or they were related to someone around the area or, she had stopped by or merely passed through the location herself.

The night that the police and the FBI caught the killer, Raven knew it before they did. As she slept, Casey was watching the news about the killer, and Raven woke up, well somewhat, and said to Casey that, "Tonight, they will catch him and then it will be over." Raven then went back into a deep sleep. Raven Reid was right because, within the hour, a news flash came across the screen with breaking news that in fact, The DC Sniper had been caught and they described everything that Raven had seen in the news report.

That is correct, Raven Gabriella Reese Reid, had just pre witnessed, firsthand for over twenty plus nights, the gruesome killer's path of destruction and methods of doing so. The sad part was that she could only tell the surrounding people each day about it before it occurred. After it was over, it would be almost three years before she would have something so wild happen to her and her family. However, don't think, not for one minute, that life was finished with Raven Reid's gifts, and neither was God.

During the next few months, she traveled back to her old hometown. On this trip, Raven and Casey learned the visions she used to see as a child had finally happened. The visions that she had years ago, of the town that she grew up around had, in fact, now been torn down. The new architectural buildings that she saw had finally been built.

Another incident happened sometime later, within the year where she had a client that had become very close to her, and Raven eventually hired this client as part-time staff. Her name was Candy. On the days Rene needed to be out, Candy would work her shifts, and some days they worked together.

An average workday for Raven was now around seven o'clock in the mornings until eight o'clock at night. Raven had become good at what she did. She was now seeing as many as twenty to thirty clients each day. When Candy was not working for Raven, she had a regular job elsewhere, that she would go to. Every day on her way to her other job, she would drive by Raven's office and blow her horn, waving at Raven and Rene on her ride to her other job. One day during Raven's lunchtime, she caught a disturbing vision as she stood outside her office door taking a break with Rene. Raven looked over at a car in the parking lot, and she saw something in the back of an empty vehicle. Raven knew the car was unoccupied because it was sitting in the parking lot as she came in to work that morning. She had parked her own vehicle diagonally across from it. As she looked at the car, she could not make out just what it was, so she walked over a little closer to get a better view.

What she saw, caused her mouth to drop wide open. As she peeked into the back seat, she saw this thing, that appeared to be wearing a full black robe with a hood, no visible face, and it had some sort of object in its hand that looked like a "*Sickle;*" the object is known in many mythologies as a tool carried by the "*Grim Reaper.*"

Raven had not seen this ever before, and she stepped a little closer and as she did, this thing in the back seat, jerked its head up as if it had seen her. Raven jumped back and just as quickly as she saw it, it faded out, and she could no longer see anything or anyone in the back seat of the empty car.

Raven told Rene what she had seen. Rene said to her that, "in her culture, that was the sign of death coming your way."

Raven thought that was what it meant, but she had experienced seeing it that day for the first time. Was Raven having a precognitive vision again of something and if so what? Should she be worried about her family or even herself at this point? She would soon learn that her attachment to people could allow her to see things she really did not want to see or experience.

The following day, Raven and Rene came to work, and after they opened the office and was ready for business, the office phone rang. It was another client that was best friends with Candy. Candy had been going through a divorce, and apparently, it turned nasty, because during this phone called the client wanted to speak to Raven. Rene put the call over to Raven's phone and what she heard, floored both ladies.

The client was calling to tell Raven and Rene that, Candy had been assassinated on her way to work that morning. As Candy made her way out of her driveway, someone had been watching her.

She had an entry gate that she had to use to come out of in or der to access her home, and as she exited the gate, it required her to get out and lock it back. Once she was out of her car, someone surprised her from behind, forced her to her knees, placed a gun to the back of her head, and pulled the trigger. They found her car door locked; the engine running and her purse sitting on the front seat.

Just like that, Raven had seen the pre-death of a close friend, and employee which left both Raven and Rene in a pool of tears and thousands of unanswered questions. The police never found who did it.

~~~

Raven's visions were now bringing about a ton of health issues. She had seen her life and her trials on her face, as she would peer into the mirror. She could see time passing as her hair started to get a bit of gray, but she had decided that no matter how gray her hair became, or how old her body was getting, God granted her all of it and she would wear it with pride. Casey was still experiencing a change, spiritually, and it was becoming more profound. He felt that he was not sure which direction he should go, and Raven always told him, not to fight it, and allow God to do his work. She always felt as if one day Casey would become a minister or a man of God and each day, Casey would lead his family closer and closer to it as they would read and try to gain a clearer understanding of the Bible.

Raven loved computers and had worked with them for now over twenty years. She used her knowledge of computers to help Casey get a better understanding of what they read. She had bought software that she thought would be interesting. It was called "Bible Codes." Apparently, a collaboration between religious and non-religious leaders developed this software, and they wanted to disprove the bible, so they developed software that could literally decode it. It sounded interesting enough, and Raven purchased it for her and Casey to investigate.

On a Saturday evening, Raven and Casey started to use the software, and as they began to find things, it drew Conner and Koko's interest. The things that the family began to discover made them strengthen their faith, while it also made them wonder about all the things that they all thought they knew. Raven's parents Horatio and Eliza used to tell her about the book of life, yet, they never explained what they thought it meant.

It has been said, that on judgment day, every man wants God to find his name to be in the book of life, and they prayed theirs would be there. Well, this day, Raven, Casey, and the children would come closer to learning just what that meant. Raven was using the old testament when they ran the software, and she was trying it out the way the instructions told her to. She found numerous things that were encoded in the words and pages. She found Princess Diana, President John Kennedy, Napoleon and others with how they died and in most cases the year. The software results are gathered and retrieved by using equal distance letter sequencing.

As Raven found these things, it surged the family's interest, and she decided to try her name and see what was there. She was not ready for what she found.

Her name pulled up in it, and it was found in Genesis and not just her name but her full name. Then she tried Casey's name, and it showed up. It was crisscrossed with Raven's name. Then she added all three children's names and their names crisscrossed Raven and Casey's names. This frightened them all as they thought something might not be right. How could this be? Raven then tried her parents' names, and Eliza's name crisscrossed Horatio, but wildly enough, Raven's name crisscrossed her parent's names. This was a bit overwhelming for everyone.

They learned that day that apparently, things in their lives had already been pre-written to be, by a higher power. We just do not know it in advance.

Casey and his family learned that even the address in which they lived was already listed. It coincided with their names. Numbers associated with them also were meticulously placed around their names like phone numbers, social security numbers, and so forth. It all started to make sense and, that was why none of their previous relationships or marriages worked, and that was why their children already had the names they had chosen. That day; it showed the Reid family a lesson that no school nor university could or, would teach. The Reid family had a one-on-one God-taught lesson about their lives. After that day, Casey and Raven decided, not to use the Bible to find out anything more. Their intent from that moment on was to try and live right and do the right things. That way, their names stayed in the "Book of Life" which appears to be the Bible.

Many other unexplained things were about to hit the Reid's. It would leave the entire family reeling in the very spot where they stood.

Dallas P Elkheart

PART X: Each One, Teach One

Episode XXXIV: That Light

In 2005, a lot of strange things would occur for the Reid family, that many never have or will ever experience, even in a lifetime. Raven was not the only one born with a gift or blessings. She was about to see things that should be impossible to experience, yet, the man she married named Casey, would bring on new visions that some would one day consider, questionable.

Raven and Casey were like a hand in glove. Casey was the hand, and Raven was the glove, and the closeness that these two shared was simply undeniable. They were so close that, if Casey hit his knee at work, Raven's leg would swell up and bruise right in the same location as his injury. Casey, on the other hand, would feel Raven's sicknesses or pains from different medical procedures she would have. Doctors had also noticed that Raven and Casey had the same vision, which by medical standards was considered impossible, yet that was the case. The doctors would sometimes set the charts side-by-side and believing they had made some mistake would retest them, to be sure they were correct. Raven and Casey would get the biggest kick out of defying medical theories.

These two love birds would soon find out just why they had so much in common to include gifts from God. Raven and Casey always used sign language as a form of communication, especially since Casey had become hearing impaired because of being in the military. Raven had become friends with some people from her hometown, who were deaf and speechless, so sign language had become one of her second languages, so to speak of.

She and Casey would use the "I Love You" in sign language, most of the time. The way to sign it would be to hold up one's thumb and then the index finger while putting up the pinkie finger. Now, while keeping your ring finger along with one's middle finger down, hold the handout with the palm facing away and move it back and forth slightly.

One day, Raven was spending time with young Conner in the family room, and Casey was washing the dishes. Their kitchen and family room had a large open pass-through window between them, so while in the kitchen everyone was still somewhat together and viewable.

This day, as Casey was washing dishes, Raven and Conner were watching television in the family room as young Conner sat by his mother's feet on the floor. Raven and Casey had just signed to each other the "I Love You" and smiled at each other as Casey dropped his head back down to finish washing up the dishes. Raven looked down at Conner, but, as she looked back up at Casey, she noticed something odd. A small lighted area was forming right in the top middle part of Casey's head. Raven sat there for a minute, thinking perhaps it was only the light from the kitchen shining on his head. As she continued to watch it, the light built up to be brighter and began to take shape.

This light was taking the form of a cross, right smack dab in the top middle part of Casey's head. Raven was shocked, and she took her hand and began to poke Conner while whispering Conner's name, so, not to alert Casey. Conner looked up at his mother, and Raven said, "Conner, look up at your dad. Tell me if you see anything". Raven thought this was her gift showing her something, but to her surprise, young Conner said, "Wow, moms, look!

There is a cross on the top of dad's head." Raven quickly told Conner, "Slowly, ease up and go get the camera, but do it quietly." Raven wanted to snap a photo of this occurrence as she knew no-one would ever believe her about this.

Conner did just what his mother told him to, and Casey never moved his head from the position, since he was still washing dishes. Conner came back to the room and handed his mother the camera, but just as she focused the camera on the cross on Casey's head, it began to fade out, and before she could take a shot of the image, it was gone. Casey raised his head, and with a surprised look on his face, he smiled and said," "Hey, why is everyone staring at me? What did I do? Did someone get a greasy cup that I just washed or what?" Raven tried to explain to Casey what they had just seen, but Casey was not buying it as he only attributed it to the light that was on, in the kitchen. Conner tried to tell his father that they had seen this cross and that he and his mother both saw it. Raven told Casey she was trying to snap a picture to show people, and that was when young Conner said, "Mom's, you were not supposed to take a photo, it was only meant for our family to see this." Raven just sat back in her seat while rubbing young Conner's back as she said, "Yea, son, I guess you're right." Raven never said it, but she believed that Casey's journey of searching for answers in the Bible and his confusion about what his purpose in life was, had been answered because she felt on this day, God had just anointed Casey.

Koko had missed the entire thing as she now came strolling in from her bedroom, but Raven and Conner knew what they had seen, and they understood it well. Life would never pass the Reid's by, without the entire family becoming a witness to many mystical things and miraculous miracles.

~~~

On August 2005, one of the worst catastrophic disasters happened in the United States. This was because of a hurricane called "*Katrina*." The family's favorite thing to do was to gather in the family room. Labor Day rolled around, and school was out for a holiday. Casey and Raven were off work that day. As "Katrina" struck on August 29, everyone in the United States stayed close to the television listening to the news to see if everyone could get out of the way of the hurricane's wrath as it barreled onshore.

Raven was a little concerned since her half-sister Margaret had a daughter that had recently got married and had just built a home in the area of the hurricane's path. Raven had called her half-sister's friend, Anna, to find out if her niece had been evacuated safely before the storm hit land. As they were talking on the phone, Casey was reading the Bible and doing some studies of it.

Conner played with his toys, and Koko was coloring in a book over by the large glass patio window which was about five feet wide. The sun was shining, and it was a beautiful day where they lived, so they had the patio door and all the windows in the family room open to enjoy some fresh air.

While on the phone with Anna, Raven was chatting and looking over at the children when suddenly, something appeared to be happening. As she talked, she began to see a figure forming at the patio screen door.

She could see something almost like a mist gather in one location right at the screen. Raven and Anna continued the conversation, yet Raven seemed to space out during the chat. Anna asked Raven if, she was alright since she had developed diabetes, which caused her to space out periodically. Anna thought perhaps Raven's levels were off. Raven responded to Anna and told her, she was fine, but it looked as if someone was at the patio window.

Anna told Raven to see who it was, but Raven told her she was already in the family room and looking directly at the patio screen. As the image began to form, Raven also began to see an outline now creating itself, in the form of a person. At least that is what she thought she was seeing. Anna asked Raven who it was. Raven said nothing and remained silent. She could see a face now forming along with hair, and as it took shape, she started to see the shape of the eyes, lips, and nose as well.

Raven told Anna again, "Girl, I do think it's someone at my patio door," and Anna again asked, "Well, who is it?" Raven started telling Anna what she was now seeing. She began to describe the hair; it was almost as if it was somewhat wooly, shoulder-length with some curling to it. The eyes, she said, were practically almond shaped with a not so pointed nose and thin lips. But then, the defined shape of something started to form on the head, and Raven stopped talking all together.

Anna said to Raven, "Girl, get up and go to the door," but Raven responded, "Oh my lord." Raven was now seeing something forming around the top of the head that looked like thorns. Raven began to tell Anna what she was seeing, but before she could finish her sentence, Anna said," Dear God, I know who it is, Lord have mercy." At that moment, Raven could also see who it was, and with her mouth wide open, she began to hit Casey's leg to get his attention. Then she whispered under her breath, but loud enough for them to hear, "Conner, Koko, Case, lookup." The image that could now see standing at the patio door looked to be around six-foot and two inches tall. It appeared to be a man with woolly hair that was shoulder length. He had almond-shaped eyes, thin-lips, and a somewhat pointed nose. The image wore two distinct items, one was a burlap like robe, and the other was thorns around the crown of the head.

Anna yelled over the phone, "Girl, that is Jesus." Yes, as the entire family looked up, this was who they believed was standing at the back-patio screen door and peering into the room where Raven's family sat. Just as it appeared, the moment that everyone saw the figure and acknowledge who it was, the image began to dissipate in the same order that it began to appear and in a matter of seconds, the figure was no more.

Raven and her entire family had just witnessed a sight, that many will never see, and that was, they had all just become a witness to the image of "Jesus" as Casey was studying the Bible and going through a transition of some type in his life.

The following days, Raven noticed that no one in the family was mentioning what they had all witnessed a few days back, and this bothered her tremendously. She knew she had not hallucinated about what she saw that day, because they all saw it. So, to her, why was everyone acting like nothing had happened. Finally, one day at the supper table, Raven posed the question, "Why is everyone acting, as if nothing happened to this family the other day? We just saw Jesus standing at our back door, and we ALL saw him. SO, what's up with that?"

Young Conner, now all the age of twelve years old, but quite wise looked up from his plate, paused as he was chewing his food and said to his mother, "Moms, when you get a chance to see Jesus on your porch, there just ain't nothing left to say." Raven sat back in her chair and looked around at her family and then glanced back at young Conner and said, "You're right. What is there to say?" From that day forward, no one spoke of the profound sight they had all witnessed, as they now knew that for whatever reasons, Jesus had made his presence known only to them. They would all carry this with them for as long as they lived. They met the man that many said was a fairy tale, some say never existed, and others say, he wasn't real. The Reid family says otherwise; they know what they saw, and they now know he is real. Besides, Raven and her family thought, they would rather live their lives believing there is a GOD, and die and find out there isn't one, than to live their lives believing there is no GOD and die and find out there is. So, to them, there was just nothing left to say about that.

Episode XXXV: Taking A Higher Road

Life seemed to settle down somewhat for Raven and her family. The children were now in high school, and Raven's business was running smoothly and thriving. There was one thing though; Raven now needed an even more significant challenge in her life. She could not help but think about her education and how she wished she could have finished. Raven wanted to finish her college degree and believed that this time, things could be different. She was now much older and more stable in life. All the drama in her life was somewhat over, and Casey had given her more stability in her life than she had ever had. Ok, well kind of. Koko was still pretty wild and, giving everyone problems to include the school, but short of that, life was good, and Casey and Raven were as close as close could be. Connor was also in high school, and now he had a part-time job on the weekends. Raven thought that was a good idea since Connor was a child that needed challenges in his life as much as his mother did, and after all, he was his mother's son.

Raven and Casey discussed it, and they decided for Raven to go back to school and finish what she once started. Raven needed to get her transcript from her old *Alma Mater* at the university so, that she could pick up where she left off. But this is where Raven realized something. A hefty balance had accrued when she and Wyatt got married and left the university. The problem was she did not know she had to withdraw, so the fees continued to rack up.

Casey and Raven decided it was time to pay the piper if she intended to complete her mission.

Raven contacted them and requested her balance and was given a balance of close to three-thousand dollars. Raven told the school that it would not be a problem. After taking care of an old ghost that followed her, she received her records. There was one last thing though, Raven wanted Casey to go with her, and that they do it as a team. Casey was reluctant to do so as he believed his college education as an instructor was good enough for him. Casey could never deny Raven anything, and this would be no different. Soon Casey gave in and agreed, and they both began their new degrees in Business Forensics. In 2007, Casey and Raven began to take full load classes at the university to accomplish a four-year degree in less than three years. They would do this at the same time as Casey worked a full-time job and Raven ran a corporation. Not to mention, they both took care of a house that was comprised of two hormone-filled teenagers and family pets. Somehow, Raven had spilled her love of multitasking onto her family, but this would prove to be a good thing for all parties.

In the meantime, other things were also transpiring around Raven. Raven's old secretary Rene had retired, and Raven missed seeing her. Rene had a granddaughter, and Raven had Koko; they had raised them playing together in the business office since they were small girls. Raven and Koko decided one day to pay Rene and her granddaughter a visit.

When Raven and Koko, first arrived at Rene's, Rene began to tell Raven about an issue she had been dealing with at their home. Raven sent the girls to go and spend some time in the other room, which would give Raven and Rene private time to speak about the issue.

As Raven listened to Rene; Raven began to understand that Rene had something in her home that was not welcomed and had not been invited. Rene wanted Raven to see if she could pick up on what it was.

Raven realized she needed to walk through Rene's home to see if she could pick up on anything. While walking through the house, Rene's oldest son was there and asked Raven to check his room. Raven walked through his room, and when she got to the bathroom in his bedroom, she stopped. She looked down at the floor in the bathroom and asked him, "Who was the man that died in here?" Rene's son said, "Wow, you picked that up. Yea, some guy died there before we got the house. We did not know him, but they told my mother about it." Raven told Rene's son to go and get a Bible for her, and as soon as the son came back with it, Raven opened it up and told him which page to keep it opened to. She went on to say, "You need to keep it open and each day read aloud a passage from it. Never close it. Leave it open over here by the bathroom. I can tell that this fellow is not a nice spirit at all and could be dangerous".

Rene came walking down the hall about that same time with her little dog in her arms. She wanted to check and see how things were coming along. Rene also had a gift that she was born with, except her gift made unclean things follow her home from places she went to. Rene told Raven that she had something similar to the "Grim Reaper" follow her and had decided he liked her house, and he had no intention of leaving it. Rene had tried everything she could think of to remove him, but it refused to go. Sometimes it would make itself known to her or her family negatively by moving and knocking things off, and he would sometimes form into a shadow person.

As Rene walked into the area where Raven and Rene's son was, something weird happened. Rene came into the doorway of the bedroom. She was talking to everyone when without warning, an unseen force threw Rene backward into a closet door. Whatever caused it, began to beat Rene's head into the door and seemed to have her pinned up on the closet door, while she was still holding her little dog. At the moment, this all happened, Raven and Rene's son screamed, and this alerted the girls. The girls ran to the door, and all they could see was Rene up against the closet door with her head hitting it as hard as it could. By now, Rene's eyes had rolled upward in her head, and all one could see was the white of her eyes.

Raven, not knowing what to do, sprang into action by grabbing Rene's head with her hand and trying to soften the blows that occurred each time her head would hit the closet door. Raven was horrified as she had experienced nothing like this in her entire life, but she knew something evil had taken hold of Rene and was now possessing her body.

Raven screamed to Rene's granddaughter, "Get my daughter out of here. Get her outside to safety. "Raven then told Rene's son, to get the Bible fast, and bring it here. Raven did not know what to do, so she did what she felt should be done. She began to pray aloud as she marked Rene with the cross of, The father, The Son and the Holy Spirit". As Raven prayed louder and louder; Rene's head began banging against the door harder and harder. Rene's son was dumbfounded, and he had shoved himself into the corner across the room, afraid to move or say a word. Raven became so unsure of what she was doing, she called upon Jesus Christ.

She said in a loud voice, "Jesus, I need you right now, I cannot do this alone. I don't know what I need to say; I need you more than ever, Jesus, help me help her".

It was as if he heard her prayer because what happened next was unexplainable. Suddenly, Raven began to speak as if Christ himself was coming through her and speaking to the demonic force before her. Raven seemed to take command of the very thing inside of Rene. Every time Raven would say some words out loud, she would make the sign of the cross on Rene's forehead, throat, chest or either arm and say, "In the name of the Father, the Son, and the

Holy Spirit, Demon I command you back through the gates of hell, for you hold no power here. Raven continued doing this for at least twenty minutes.

The harder Raven would pray and command the demon to leave, the less it would take Rene's head and beat it into the closet door. As Rene's body began to slow down, hitting the door, she was still holding her little dog when she suddenly stopped, and her body went to a standstill. Raven was still holding Rene's head in her hands. Rene's eyes started to unroll and return to normal. Rene was drenched in pure sweat and holy water. The sweat came from the horrendous experience Rene had just been through. The water came from Raven because, during this event, she had asked for Rene's son to get her some water and took it and created holy water as part of this ritual. Raven did not realize at first that she had performed an exorcism.

Rene's eyes rolled down, and she looked at Raven and then her son, asking them both, "What happened?" Rene had no clue what they were all looking at her for, nor why Raven was holding the back of her head still. Raven was not sure if it was Rene speaking yet, so she asked her a question that she knew the demon could not get right. Raven and Casey had given Rene a beautiful Bible as a present a while back to hopefully help her understand some things she had asked Raven and Casey about. Raven then asked Rene, "Rene, is that you in there?", Rene replied" Yea, it's me," Raven asked, "Rene, you all right?", Rene replied, "I think so." Raven then said, "What is written in the Bible for you?" Rene hesitated and then stated, "God be with you."

At that moment Raven knew Rene had been released from the grips of the demonic force that had taken over her body, because before giving her the bible Raven and Casey had written that in it. Raven was still in shock as she never believed in a million years, that she would be placed into a situation that would require her strength, faith, and knowledge of God to perform such an action. As Raven went to leave the house that day with Koko, she turned around at the exit door of Rene's house and grabbed her daughter. Raven blessed her with the sign of the cross and a loud prayer. Raven did not want whatever it was to follow or attach itself to her child. Rene hugged and thanked Raven.

One could immediately tell there was a different persona at Rene's house now. The air seemed lighter, and it was no longer gloomy in there. It was as if the sun now shined in Rene's house.

~~~

Casey and Raven were close to graduation from the university, and Conner was about to graduate from high school. Raven and Casey had spent the last three years, doing their homework together in the afternoons and, would do their work assignments with the kids each day after work. It was all about to pay off.

By September 2010, three years after Casey and Raven started at the university; they would fly to their graduation some seven hundred miles away and walk the stage with over six-hundred other university students. The most significant part of this was that they both walked the stage as husband and wife, achieving another one of their life challenges. The coolest thing was that they did it as a family.

Conner also graduated and ended up as a recruit for the United States Armed Forces. Young Conner had made it against all the odds he had to fight as an infant. He would now be joining the ranks in which his mother, father, grandfather, grandmother, and his great grandfather had been a part of.

PART XI: Blurred Bloodline, Sure Destiny

Episode XXXVI: No Classroom is Required

Koko was a horse of another color that people always spoke about. She was getting into trouble almost daily with her parents and at school. Koko came home from school one day and told Raven and Casey that nothing they had to say to her was more important than what she had to say.

Koko had caused so many problems with stealing her parent's money, wallets, credit cards, and clothing. She had taken on a part-time job. She had lost many of her part-time jobs previously because she was stealing from her employers. Casey and Raven had spent the last seventeen years, running in behind Koko to doctors and courts and the family had become burnt out with her and the issues. One day Koko left home about six weeks before graduation and never returned, as she had told Raven and Casey previously, that they had nothing else that they could offer her. It would be a few years before they would hear from or about her again. They listened to rumors about her whereabouts, but nothing substantial. The police, refused to look for her as they had warned her almost ten years back that they would no longer use their resources to continue to look for her, only to retrieve her, bring her home and have her to run off again with different people.

You see there was a bit of history there with Koko that made the past seventeen years a living hell for everyone within the Reid home to include Conner. Raven and Casey had noticed items missing from home, and they did not understand why. They had always tried to give all their children everything they needed and a lot of what they wanted, but it was never enough for Koko. She always seemed to want and need more. Koko told Raven and Casey that she wished they were poor because she had always wanted to be poor and live like she was poor. One should always watch what they wish for because they just might get it. Well somehow, Raven and Casey did not quite see eye to eye with Koko on that note, but then again, one could be sure that a man with very little would have a different take on that subject as well.

The schools also began to have trouble from Koko. She had become a thief and a compulsive liar who had become a big problem with them. The biggest question anyone had with Koko was about her attitude because she had lots of it. And then there was her mouth. Oh yes, that mouth of Koko's. It had become such an issue that one day Raven, received a phone call from the school, which then obligated Raven to call Casey at work. This required Casey and Raven to leave work and come to the school. What the fuss was all about was that Koko had decided she would no longer listen to an adult and had cursed out one of her teachers at school. This set Raven and Casey on fire as they had experienced a hefty dose of her mouth at home and were still trying to deal with it there.

It ended up being so bad that the school had her arrested. They asked Raven and Casey if they would like to bail Koko out and take her home. Both Casey and Raven quickly replied, "NOPE, she's all yours." That was because, throughout Koko's life, she had been more than a hand full. She would continuously run away from home, and the police would often find her in areas of known child molesters and newly released convicts. They would remove her and bring her home, and within three weeks as soon as Casey or Raven would not agree with the lifestyle she wanted, she would bolt again.

Finally, on the last time, three policemen returned her home but gave Koko, a stern and fair warning. They told her that they were no longer prepared to pull the entire police force off the streets to come and find her after she would pull her shenanigans with her parents.

On one Occasion, Koko had stripped off all her clothes except a small hair bow and a pair of shoes. This happened outside Casey and Raven's home when she was in kindergarten. A neighbor found her standing on the street corner. To this date, no one knew what that was all about. A neighbor saw her and grabbed her before the nearest child molester could and, brought her naked behind right back to the house. When Casey and Raven first adopted Koko, she would lie in her baby crib and growl as she bit into her pillow, but no doctors could find the reasoning behind that issue.

As Koko got older, she got worse. She would torture her older brother and call him stupid and dumb, which hurt Conner significantly. So, one day, Koko decided she no longer wanted to live with the Reid's and left. Raven and Casey realized that Koko was of age, and they could not force their love upon their daughter, and they allowed the sleeping dog just to lay. Doctors had tried to resolve Koko's issues throughout the past seventeen years. Casey and Raven had spent years at the psychiatrists, trying to get Koko help, but the diagnosis was grim.

Casey and Raven found the nest empty, and they did not mind, as Raven went seeking even more education, so she went back to school once again, so she could become a teacher. Casey had achieved a significant promotion at his job. Raven and Casey were now free to focus on themselves, as the children were now adults and doing their own thing.

Throughout Raven's life, she knew she was different, but the most important thing that had Raven thinking was when she would look in the mirror. She never saw one culture in her features; she saw many and could not figure out who she was and what made her tick. She knew she liked things that some cultures did not like, and she was interested in things others were not involved in, so the question continued to plague her, "Who am I?" Raven remembered a movie she once watched called, *Alex Haley's Queen*. This movie stemmed from the series Roots and seeing the original grandmother who was of mixed heritage; she remembered she felt just like the grandmother who said in the film, "I don't fit anywhere." This was Raven, and she only fit in Casey's world but fit nowhere else. Raven would not rest until she learned who she was.

Dallas P Elkheart

Episode XXXVII: Who Do You Think You Are?

After completing her teaching certification, Raven taught school. She started in elementary, then middle school, but tried her best to stay away from high school. Her daughter Koko had put a bitter taste in her mouth for teenagers, so Raven could never picture herself teaching anything above eighth graders. Well, that is until a position came open that fit her to the tee. With the degree Raven had received, she was qualified to teach 28 different courses. A teaching position came open where she would be able to be creative, use her degree to its fullest, and teach everything she had done throughout her business career. Raven reluctantly applied and got the position, but then her entire world changed.

Raven was able to create classes according to the way students learned, and this was right up her alley. She was now teaching computer technology, law, accounting, debate, and all the beautiful things that she was good at to include poetry. The wildest thing was, Raven, was teaching high school grades nine through twelve, and this ended up being just what Raven needed. She became extremely close to her students as they were with her. Each day Raven would come home and talk about her classes and students most of the evening while Casey would tell her, "Wow, I'm jealous. You seem to be so happy with the kids, and I have never seen you this happy." Yes, Ravens' students became her life along with Casey. Casey would become fond of Raven's students as well. To Raven, it was as if she was a mother to more than one-hundred and twenty children.

In the meantime, Raven was having some health issues, and the doctor had run several blood tests. One day the phone rang, and it was Raven's doctor. He needed to speak with her because her blood work had come back, showing something. Raven panicked at first as the doctors told Raven that, she had a blood disorder called 'Thalassemia' which causes the body to make an inadequate amount of hemoglobin resulting in anemia. The doctor told Raven that the blood disorder does not come from the United States and that one or both parents would have to have it for it to be passed down to her." He also said that this blood disorder comes from the Mediterranean area overseas and that it was hereditary, meaning everyone in her bloodline would have it and pass it on from generation to the next generation.

Now the doctor had their attention, because more than ever now, Raven needed to know who she was and where she came from. So, Raven was about to find out, just what particles were floating in her pool (gene-pool that is). Raven was about to request a DNA test finally to determine just who she was.

Raven did the DNA test with a mouth swab, and off it went to the lab. She knew what she saw in the mirror each day, but is what one sees really who one is? These answers would blow man's theory of classifying another based on the color of one's skin, right out of the water. Raven waited almost three months.

One day Raven received an email, telling her that her test results were ready for review. Upon opening her result, her mouth hit the floor. For the past fifty years, Raven Gabriella Reese Reid had never known much about herself, only what her parents told her. She also only knew the things people would say to her like, "you look Native American," "you look Egyptian," "you look Middle Eastern," "you look like you're from India." Well, this day, there would be no more guessing nor wondering. This day Raven would have her results, and everything would become apparent.

Raven found out that her father's bloodline was from Europe. Her DNA showed that her bloodline was from Britain, Ireland, Portugal, Spain, and the Balkans. Her mother's line was from Egypt, Ethiopia, Morocco, the Philippines, India, Asia, and Native American. The funny thing was that a nice portion of Neanderthal was in her bloodline. Many had thought this culture was extinct, as she did, but it is not. The Neanderthal was out of Eurasia. She found that she was related to a few famous people that she had heard about but had never met. Her bloodline was infused with a couple of millionaires, a renowned author, and a renowned musician, all from her father's side. But her mother's side told a different story, as she learned that she was a descendant of *Pharaoh Ramesses III of Egypt.*

Bronze Bloodline of the Phoenix

This was one of the most shocking revelations ever to Raven, and now she understood just where her courage to fight and survive came from. She learned why she was not like everyone else, because, her bloodline, was more than just a bloodline. It was much like the metal, bronze. It expands when it hardens, bends but does not break, does not produce sparks when struck, and has low friction when placed with other metals. Raven Reid was much like bronze; a mixed metal that was commonly used, but very flexible in life. Therefore, she had lived a life that might have made others succumb to the weight on her shoulders, yet; she fought to rebuild her life and allow God to guide her footsteps.

The results were so shocking that Casey wanted to learn about who he was, and his results were just as surprising. He also carried similar bloodline traits to Raven's except that; he had more bloodline from Australia and the Indigenous people of the Oceania tribe. It was also determined that he too, was a descendant of, *Pharaoh Ramesses III of Egypt*. Strangely enough, DNA testing never linked Casey or Raven to each other as blood relatives.

The results were surprising as now both Casey and Raven understood more about themselves and each other. Soon, they realized that they both had blood disorders.

Casey had a G6PD blood disorder that also came from the Mediterranean as well. Soon they realized why they had to adopt because if they had given natural birth to children shared between them, it would have ended up as a disaster each time for the couple. Raven and Casey now knew God had not made a mistake, and that everything had happened as it was pre-ordained to be.

~~~

After learning of their heritage, they both had a new take on life and had considered a different path. Raven closed her business down after 16 years to focus strictly on teaching, and Casey was thinking about what to do after he retired, which was only around the corner. Casey had thought of going back into education as he could see how much Raven enjoyed it. But, was that really what he wanted to do?

One day Casey told Raven that he wanted to spend the day at the park and discuss where to go from here. Raven thought it was a fantastic idea as the only responsibilities they now had besides their jobs were the family pets. The two of them headed off to spend the day at the park.

Even though Casey and Raven frequented the location, they parked in a new parking lot. Both got out of the car and began to walk, and they saw a track with plenty of shade trees on it and thought this would make an excellent five-mile walk. As they began to talk, they were having a very soulful and spiritual conversation about God and Satan.

They saw a woman sitting under a tree in a lawn chair. She almost looked out of place as no one else was under this tree but her, nor around it. She looked peaceful and relaxed all stretched out, but as they passed her, they had taken all of six steps, then they both did a double take. As they did, the woman was no longer there, nor was her chair. They looked around to see where she had gone, but there was no one near the area, and there were no traces that the woman had ever been sitting or lying on a lawn chair. Raven and Casey were dumbstruck because they just walked a couple of steps passed the area before looking back and over at her.

They continued to walk, and now, this was the conversation. It was geared more towards what happened to the woman that they saw under the tree. Raven then posed the question to Casey, "Do you believe that God lets you know if evil is around you, and if so, how would you know?" As they rounded the walking track, Raven noticed a man that seemed to appear out of nowhere. He was on the other side of the track, and he too was under the shade trees and looked to be watching them as they were walking past. He was standing up by a picnic table.

He was tall and wearing a striped sweater which would typically not be strange, but what was weird was that it was almost one hundred degrees outside and dead in the middle of summertime. Raven asked Casey, "Do you see that man? He looks strange."

He looked like someone from the movie "Nightmare on Elm Street, and he was wearing a sweater similar to the one that the character Freddie Kruger wore in the movie." This creeped Raven out, and Casey told Raven, "Yea, I see him." Raven and Casey made their way around the track, and on their second round of walking, the man was still there, but this time was different.

This time the man saw Raven and Casey, just as they were approaching the area where he was, and by the time, they got ready to pass him Raven told Casey, "Let's just pretend we don't see him and hurry by." Well, the couple thought they had skated by the man when he got from under the tree to them in a matter of a nanosecond. It was as if he teleported from point A to point B. Once he appeared, he stopped Raven and Casey, and with a strange voice, as his head twisted sideways almost at a 90-degree angle, he blurted out and abruptly in a deep barrel amplified sounding voice saying, "Do you believe in, Jesus? He reached his hand out with two items like business cards as if he expected them to take them, with no questions asked. Casey responded quickly, "The Christ? Yes, I do." This was not the answer the man appeared to want to hear and shoved the card in both Raven and Casey's hand and then shot away, just as quickly as he had got there.

It was not what the man said, but how he said it. It was a voice that sent chills up Raven and Casey's spine. He seemed almost demonic like even in his appearance. As Raven and Casey walked away, holding the cards, it seemed as if it was creating some type of burning sensation in their hands. They realized something was not right and incredibly eerie about it all. They quickly made their way to the closest garbage can and disposed of them. Funny thing, as soon as the items hit the garbage cans, the burning sensation stopped immediately. It spooked the couple, and they could not understand the strangeness of both incidents and why they had all occurred within a matter of thirty minutes of each other. It was as if one was an angel they saw and the other a demon. But what had they seen? Who had they seen? What was the significance of either encounter?

Raven and Casey decided they'd had enough for the day and headed home. They had been to this park tons of times and never had an experience like this. After they arrived home, they got a cup of coffee and headed to their back porch to discuss the events that had occurred that day and try to make some sense out of it all. As they were sitting on their back porch having the discussion, the evening had one more trick up its sleeve. They saw a man walking past the house on the sidewalk. The man also had the same type of sweater as the man in the park.

The difference was that, as he walked past their house, he turned his head at the same 90-degree angle as the man from the park as he was walking; he looked them straight in the eyes from afar. How can one walk straight ahead, turn one's head at a 90-degree angle and, not trip and fall at all, while never missing a beat?

This man kept his head turned to the right the entire walk as he passed them.

Raven was curious as to who it was since they knew he did not live in their neighborhood. So, she got up from her chair to see where he was headed. He had just passed the home, and there was a bush that blocked him for one second. As Raven stood up when the man began to move past the one bush, she noticed there was no one passing the bush, nor had anyone stopped.

As a matter of fact, there was no one there at all. Now the question was, "What the hell did Raven, and Casey just see?" How could it have disappeared into thin air? Neither issue would ever get answered, and neither Casey nor Raven ever had that experience again after that.

A year passed, and Casey would now retire in a few months, but some decisions had to be made. The school was nearing the end for the school year, and Raven also needed to decide. One day, Casey made a statement to her. He said, "Baby, you know, I am not sure, how long I will have on this earth, because of my lung issue, but I do know this, whatever time I have left, I would like to spend every minute with you."

The doctors had diagnosed Casey a couple of years back with "Asthma and COPD." COPD is a progressive and nonreversible lung disease. Raven had almost lost Casey on a couple of occasions, so this was always an underlying issue as Casey never knew when his lungs would give out on him, and she would lose him forever.

She adored Casey as he did her, and they both agreed to spend whatever time they had left on earth together, every waking moment of it. But how could they do this? Once again, the couple would face a decision that could separate them, much like when they first met more than twenty-seven years ago. Could they now still do what is required not to be separated, or would they have no choice at this point in their lives?

Episode XXXVIII: Letting Go

Decisions had to be made and soon. Casey had enjoyed traveling when he was young and in the military. Raven had always wanted to go abroad. Even though the two of them frequently roamed in and out of their country, she wanted to see more. Raven no longer had parents living, because they had been gone for years.

There were no brothers or sisters that she knew of since no blood test was ever performed on Christine Masson; therefore, no DNA had provided any proof of existing family. Casey and Raven's two children were the only family left that she had by now. A few of Horatio's and Eliza's family members were alive but lived in different parts of the world. Casey still had his family, but they were all thousands of miles away.

Raven came home from work one day and rethought her life through and all the hardships that life had thrown at her. She felt blessed to have been given a man like Casey and even her children. She thought about their old age and how they would only have each other to rely on, but then again, that is truly all they ever had anyway, (was) each other.

Both Casey and Raven's health had gone downhill with age. Raven still had her visions, yet not as strong as they once were. She always felt that she had both gifts that God had given her. She had her visions, and she had her Casey, so these were the two things that she was happy with.

Casey and Raven began to dream of where in the world, they could go and live out their days, in peace. They both had decided that Raven would resign from teaching as Casey retired from work. Raven was concerned that they might not be able to survive on one income because, throughout their marriage, they had enjoyed a certain lifestyle.

By now Raven and Casey had decided that they would not let money be their guiding factor and interfere with being together, so Raven submitted her resignation, and Casey put in for his retirement after thirty-three years with the government, and now, things were set into motion. Through the following months, Raven and Casey explored every part of the world, looking for the perfect place to live. They used a spreadsheet, and since they both had been in forensics, they used statistics, to determine as to where they would go to live out their lives together. After meticulously analyzing all the options on the spreadsheet, they had decided.

He had a hard decision to make, but he knew that he and Raven needed peace in their lives, and they both decided to move to Europe. This would mean, leaving all friends and family behind to include Conner and his new little family and Koko. Raven and Casey began the process for themselves and the family pets.

As time got closer, they knew that the hard part would be letting go of the home, family, and friends that they spent so many happy years around and start over.

In October 2018, Casey and Raven Reid took the plunge. They had moved to a country where they had never been, never visited, did not know anyone, could not speak the language and never dreamed of going to. They had purchased a home there over the internet and could not wait to transition. This was a scary time for both as they knew once the airplane lifted off the ground, they would leave the land in which they both were raised, played, married, reared their children and began to grow old together.

After arriving and driving to their new home in Europe, Casey was trying to get the luggage out of the car at around two o'clock in the morning, so Raven took her new keys and went to open the door.

They had never physically seen the home, in person, but the realtor had performed a walk-through with live video for them to get a feel for the home. When Raven had first seen the home back in the states from online, she told Casey, something was wrong with the house and that she could pick up something on the home. Raven for the first time in her life, blew it off as nerves, and maybe she should not have. This house came fully furnished, with the same four bedrooms that they had been used too, but this house had one other surprise for them.

Raven opened the door, and her mouth dropped. The house looked like something out of a turn of the century horror movie. It was damp, smelly, and very uninviting. Casey made his way into the new home, they looked at each other and thought, "Wow, what the hell?". It was too late now they had paid cash for the home, but it was less than they expected. Ok, they had just learned a valuable lesson, never purchase something like a house, without first seeing it in person.

Well, too late. This was now home. All Raven could think to herself was, "What in Sam's hell, were we thinking?" Her nerves had kicked in, and their overruled doubts and their return to sanity had both come too late, so there they were. The two of them were so tired they did not bother to look the house over. They could only make it to the kitchen, and after a cup of coffee and two swift kicks in the butt for making the purchase, they fell asleep at the kitchen table.

The following day, the pets arrived, and it was daylight. They could finally see what they had purchased. It mortified them as the home was nothing like they expected, but this was the type of house commonly found, and that one would expect to see when living in Europe. This home was more for someone who had an acquired taste for old architectural buildings from the 11th-century timeframe. Every part of the world has different styles, of homes and, different lifestyles. Raven and Casey both, decided perhaps they could renovate the house and make it a beautiful home, anyway. Well, that is before they found out, they were not alone.

Raven had a feeling about the house before they had ever purchased it but blew it off. The feeling got even worse after she arrived at it. She always told Casey, she felt as if someone else was there. One early morning Raven was in the downstairs bathroom brushing her hair. She heard a low sound but thought it was Casey watching television in the kitchen. Raven went back to brushing her hair when suddenly, she began to hear something that sounded like a low moan. This set Raven's mind into motion, so she stepped out of the bathroom and asked Casey if he had said anything, and he responded, "No, I didn't say anything." Raven told Casey she thought she had heard him. He said to Raven that maybe it was the television since he was watching a cartoon that Saturday morning. She went back to the bathroom, and just as she picked up her hairbrush, the sound came again except for this time, it sounded as if it was closer than before and louder. It was a deep, low moaning sound as if someone or something was now being tortured. Raven ran out of the bathroom and brought Casey back with her this time. She whispered to Casey, "Baby, can you hear it?" as she pointed towards a back door. "You hear that, right?"

Casey stood still and tried to listen and just as he thought that perhaps Raven had spooked herself, he heard it. Casey was a logical man, and even though he had experienced some strange things with Raven, he was still not sure of what he was hearing. As they both listened, the sound was now louder. It sounded as if it was coming out of some of the old unused rooms at the back of the home. It was a sound that mimicked a human and an animal combined, in great pain and had been suffering for a very long time.

Bronze Bloodline of the Phoenix

Casey no longer doubted Raven from this point on. He had heard the same thing she had. Casey now knew their house came with more than furniture; it had something else there. During the next few weeks, it was difficult to sleep there as every morning at the same time; the moans would begin and last for about fifteen minutes. Even when sleeping there, they spent most of the night with one eye opened, just in case. Casey and Raven no longer felt safe there. Each night, they would sleep sitting up at the kitchen table, prepared to make a quick get-a-way, if they needed to.

One day Raven and Casey began to ask around, and they found out that the town in which they had purchased the home was an old town from back during the 11th century. The actual house they bought was over one-hundred-plus years old. Casey and Raven had made up their minds. They made the decision to sell their house and move to a more modern home with less history.

The new house they found had less history and was more in the line of their needs at this point. As they drove over to view the home, Raven remained skeptical as she knew if there were spirits there or around it, she would pick up on it. As they pulled up to the new home, the realtor opened the gates, and it was as if someone had opened the gates to heaven. There stood a beautiful home with all the amendments that anyone would need. But would this be, the house for them? Would Raven walk in and detect a spirit as in the past? Would this home make both Casey and Raven happy?

Dallas P Elkheart

Episode XXXIX: Reanimation of a Soul

After Raven and Casey made a move to the new house; They met some of the neighbors, and upon meeting them, both Raven and Casey knew this was it. This home sat at the top of a mountain though, and Raven was not sure that she could conquer her fear of heights enough to drive through mountains, to go to and from home daily.

Raven did eventually begin to overcome her fear of the mountain top more and more, and soon began to see it as not just a way to conquer her abundant worries, but to conquer all the obstacles, she had come up against in life. Raven Reid had finally learned to become much like a "Phoenix." "No matter how many times life tried to do away with her, she survived it. She had learned to rise from the ashes of her painful and misguided existence. She gained a love for herself developing the endurance and flexibility of 'Bronze". Raven had used her tenacity, which she pulled from all the mixtures of her bloodline to thrive and survive. With her wings now well-groomed she was able to soar to the top of the mountains to live out her life with someone that did love her, just as much as she loved him. Casey Reid and God were by her side, and this made Raven become more than reinvented as a human being. She had become a reanimated soul. Many days would pass, and Raven and Casey were enjoying the home they now had. It was a large four-bedroom home with a downstairs patio and a huge upstairs one. The upper terrace was beautiful and opened. Casey and Raven would sit in their swing set, holding hands as they overlooked the mountaintop where they lived. They would spend endless hours, looking down into the valley, realizing how God had given them this home together in life.

They felt they were blessed to have met each other, to have spent their lives together and to have experienced being parents, even though they lost one child along the way. Raven would often think of Eliza and Horatio as she would sit evenings watching the sunset over the mountain tops while wishing she could share such a glorious sight with them. Casey and Raven's life is still being written since they are now close to sixty years old. They always enjoy the sunsets over the mountains, and they make sure they are up and, on the patio, watching the sun as it rises in its many colors of the rainbow. They often think through their lives and wonder what tomorrow will bring. As for the people in Raven's past. well, Raven found out that Wyatt Adams had been killed a couple of years back in an auto accident. Noah Evans passed away suddenly, in his sleep in 2019. Flynt Barnes passed away a few years back with a heart attack at a young age, Eric Anderfal went on to marry, and they had one pre-school aged child. Toby Johnston, oh yes, Mr. Johnston. Well, word had it, that some years back, he had moved to Raven's old town back in Texas. Koko now had a business of her own. Connor had since married and was now in college. Margaret was still living and doing well. Jasmine Graham and Raven were still best friends and often spoke, even though they had not seen each other now in more than thirty years. As far as Megan, well, she had moved on in life and has one child who is an adult now. The word on the streets was that her health had begun to fail some, yet, she was still doing well. Sandy was heard from once over the years after the event, but since that time, he was never heard from again by the Reid's.

Christine Masson passed away some years back, but not without Raven knowing it. They had diagnosed Christine with cancer, and she was no longer willing to do the therapy. Raven had experienced Christine's passing.

She had taken a nap, and while she slept, she found herself underneath a beautiful tree. Raven stood up and began to walk away from the tree but stopped to look back. When she looked back; she could see herself lying on the ground underneath that tree. Raven tried to figure out how was it possible to be standing there but, see herself lying down at the same time. She began to walk forward; she could feel something happening inside her. It felt peaceful, more peaceful than anything she had ever experienced. A man stood far in front of her, and Raven thought that this man was someone she knew and knew well. Raven walked towards him. Part of her soul wanted to stay where she was, and the other part felt so much peace, that she continued walking towards the man. This man had on a white robe and stood about six-foot and two inches tall. He had a head full of wooly, yet curly hair and he held his arms out to her.

Bronze Bloodline of the Phoenix

As Raven got to him; she heard him say, "Go back. It is not your time. You must go back". Raven did not want to go back for she felt so much love and peace with this man, but she turned around and went back to where she came from. When she reached her still yet cold body, lying on the ground, she stepped back into herself. Just when she took a giant gasp to breathe, her phone rang. It was Karne, Christine's middle daughter. She told Raven that Christine had just taken her last breath and Raven said, "Yes, I know. I took it with her". Karne knew that Raven had the gift and that Raven meant she had just experienced Christine's passing through her own body. The young man that Christine had conceived Raven through, Kevin, had also passed away a few years back. The fact is, almost everyone that had brought harm or hurt to Raven had already gone to meet their Creator. Raven's message is a simple one; she wants the world to know, no matter who you are, if you damaged her heart or harmed her, she forgives you. She also desires that anyone in the world who may have been impacted negatively, by her decisions during her lifetime to please forgive her.

Many people may never find out, just who they are, or what makes them tick. Others may never find a soulmate that binds them to another, but there is one thing known, and that is, everyone will make decisions in their life that will impact someone else's life, whether they realize it or not. One should always ask themselves first, "Will my decision affect another's life positively or negatively."

One may find, that their choices have left scars upon another's soul, that may or may not ever be healed.

Raven and Casey honestly believe with all their hearts, that had just one element of either's life been changed to include the people they had met in their lives, they would have never met, and this story would have a different ending. Back in 2011, Casey and Raven renewed their 20-year vows and chose a Cinderella wedding theme. After all, that was how they met. Casey and Raven had now been married for more than 28 years and even though no one knows what tomorrow will bring, Casey and Raven Reid, know they will live for each moment together as if it is their last. Often, Raven and Casey stand on their balcony patio holding each other. With her head laid upon his chest, listening to the beat of his heart, they look out over the majestic mountains and down into the lush green valleys. All they can say at that point is, "WOW! What a wonderful life we have been given."

"Everyone has a story, though it may not be told yet."

Quote by D.P. Elkheart

About the Author

Dallas P. Elkheart is an author, former business owner, and teacher. She has a total of over 40 years of working in the public sector. She earned a Bachelor of Science degree and was a Cum Laude graduate from Franklin University, Columbus, Ohio.

She won a scholastic literary award for her writing and has a background in public and academic speaking. Throughout her business and teaching career, she provided an educational environment to teach others how to be more open-minded, prepare for victories and failures, and about the consequences of making bad decisions. More importantly, she has been able to show others how to function with dignity, restraint, and professionalism.

Her work was showcased through television and newspapers for her expertise and style of teaching.

At the time this book was written, she was 57 years old. She is from the United States and has now retired and resides in Europe with her husband of 28 years. She wrote this book based on her own experiences in life in hopes to share some of her failures, trials, and victories. Her intent is, to help others to understand that, anyone can become a victim, but it will take the determination of a "Phoenix," which rises from the ashes of its own enemies and pulls strength from one's ancestors' bloodline, to become victorious.

www.ingramcontent.com/pod-product-compliance
Lightning Source LLC
Chambersburg PA
CBHW020350080526
44584CB00014B/959